MADDEST TEMPTATION

A DARK MAFIA ROMANCE

TEMPTATION
BOOK 1

FERNANDA GRAZIANO

Copyright © 2024 by Fe Graziano

All rights reserved.

No part of this publication may be reproduced, distributed, or transmitted in any form or by any means, including photocopy, recording, or other electronic or mechanical methods, without the prior written permission of the publisher, except as permitted by U.S. copyright law. For permission requests, contact authorfernandagraziano@outlook.com

The story, all names, characters, and incidents portrayed in this production are fictitious. No identification with actual persons (living or dead), places, buildings and products is intended or should be inferred.

Paperback ISBN: 979-8-89316-104-5

Ebook ISBN: 979-8-89316-105-2

Hardback ISBN: 979-8-89316-106-9

*To the girl who had big dreams, thank you for not giving up on them.
She's living them now.*

CONTENTS

Playlist	vii
Content Warnings	ix
Prologue	1
1. Francesca	5
2. Francesca	12
3. Francesca	23
4. Cassio	36
5. Francesca	48
6. Cassio	57
7. Francesca	67
8. Francesca	74
9. Cassio	82
10. Francesca	90
11. Francesca	107
12. Cassio	115
13. Francesca	126
14. Francesca	132
15. Cassio	141
16. Francesca	147
17. Francesca	154
18. Cassio	162
19. Francesca	170
20. Cassio	183
21. Cassio	192
22. Francesca	198
23. Francesca	209
24. Francesca	219
25. Cassio	226
26. Cassio	232
27. Cassio	242
28. Francesca	251
29. Francesca	258
30. Francesca	263
31. Francesca	270

32. Cassio	275
33. Francesca	281
34. Cassio	286
35. Francesca	292
36. Cassio	299
37. Before you go	309
Acknowledgments	311
About the Author	313

PLAYLIST

Cold – Maroon 5
She's an Actor - Austin Giorgio
Dangerous Hands - Austin Giorgio
Power Over Me – Dermot Kennedy
Wildest Dream - Taylor Swift
Dangerous Woman - Ariana Grande
Francesca – Hozier
Addicted to You – Avicii
Everything I Ever Wanted - Billie Eilish
Fever- Michel Bublé
Take Me to Church – Hozier
I Feel Like I'm Drowning - Two Feet
Till Forever Falls Apart – Ashe
Work Song – Hozier
I Want It - Two Feet
Lost! - Coldplay

CONTENT WARNINGS

Please be aware that this book contains graphic scenes that are meant for a mature audience. While these scenes were written to create a more vivid, in-depth story, they may be triggering to some readers. Please read with that in mind, your mental health matters.

Trigger Warnings: Sexual assault (mention in past), Death of loved ones. Description of violence, Alcohol abuse, drug abuse, blood, emotional abuse (mention in past), torture and violence.

PROLOGUE

I buried my husband on a Friday, the sky was blue, and the sun was shining, its warmth wrapping around me like a second skin. It was a perfect day.

Paolo was finally gone.

I watched the crowd around me, those who had come to the cemetery to pay their respects for my late husband. Three of his mistresses were present, all of them shedding crocodile tears. They wouldn't miss him; they would only miss what he had provided for them. The money, the gifts, and the status.

I looked away.

I wouldn't spare Paolo a single tear, he didn't deserve them. My husband–late husband–wasn't worthy of my sorrow. Once, I had tried loving him, I had been young and naive, desperate for his attention. Our marriage had been arranged when I was fifteen and he, forty-five. I was nineteen when I married him.

Paolo had wanted a young, trophy wife by his side, a new toy he could play with and put aside when he grew tired. I learned pretty quickly to hate him, as well as the abuse, the bruises, the humiliation and worst of all, his refusal to give me what I wanted most, a family.

He took away the one thing I wanted, the one thing I had

dreamed of since I was a child. I always wanted to be a mother, but he stole my dream and broke it into a million different pieces.

Now he was dead.

Pure autumn air filled my lungs, and I sighed with relief, something I hadn't done so in four years. No more pain, no more fear, no more Paolo. For one year I could be free.

I had a year before my father decided to marry me off again–as it was custom in the Outfit all widows had a year of mourning. Knowing Donato Manci, my father was going to marry me off as soon as he could.

A widow, especially a childless one, was a pariah in our midst. Which was ironic given that our husbands were all Made Men. *Mafiosi*. Mobsters who put their lives on the line every day.

I looked at Marie, then at Antoine, her brother, my best friends. They had remained with me through thick and thin. "We should go." I said.

"You don't want to stay until they lower him?" Marie asked.

I shook my head. I wanted to be as far away from him as possible. "Let's go eat something, I'm famished."

"What about the wake?" She insisted.

I shrugged. "I don't really care."

"Great, because I know just a place we could go." Antoine wrapped his arm around mine and led me away, I followed him without glancing back.

Once we reached the cozy restaurant I sat and ordered a vodka tonic. Marie eyed me with concern. "Frankie," she warned me when I gulped it down like water.

"I'm fine." I said, then called the waitress so I could order another drink.

That drink vanished in seconds, too. When I was about to order a third, Antoine stopped me. "I'm fine." I snapped.

"Francesca," Antoine placed a hand over mine on the table.

I took a deep, annoyed sigh. "I really am fine, Paolo is gone, he can't hurt me anymore. I am finally free." *Until your mourning period is over,* I reminded myself but quickly pushed that away. "Can we talk about something else?"

The siblings didn't look like they believed me, but they thankfully accepted my suggestion. "Is everything set for our move?"

"You know you guys don't have to uproot everything and move with me, right?"

"We know." Antoine smiled and looked at his sister. "We want to, Indianapolis has grown boring, and without you here we have no reason to stay," he added, causing my heart to beat painfully against my chest.

Of course, they had, it's where Marie and Antoine had lived since, they moved from France ten years ago. It was their home, and they were only moving so they could be with me. "Don't make me ruin my makeup." I dabbed my napkin under my eyes.

Antoine laughed and shoved me playfully. "I just don't understand why you don't want to move in with us."

I sighed deeply. This again? "You know why."

"Because you want your freedom," Marie stated provokingly.

"Because I can," I corrected her. "This is the first time I get to choose." And although I was terrified of being alone right now, I needed that. I needed to learn who I was, and I could only do that on my own.

At some point throughout my marriage, I had lost myself, and I had no idea who I was, but I knew one thing, if I moved in with Marie and Antoine, I was never going to find out. As terrifying as it sounded, I needed to be alone.

"Plus, we'll all be in the same city, if I need you, all I have to do is visit you." I reminded her.

"I can't wait to move to Chicago," Antoine exclaimed.

I wished I could share his excitement. Moving back to Chicago was the last thing I wanted or needed, but I was no longer welcomed in Indianapolis. Without Paolo tethering me here, there was no reason to remain, and with him gone, our so-called friends had all turned their backs on me. So had his family.

Moving back to the city I was born in and where my family lived, made sense. Even if it seemed like a bad idea. I couldn't put it into words yet, but this move... it frightened me.

It was like revisiting the past, and that was the last thing I wished to do, I still had open wounds that refused to heal, even four years later they still festered. I feared that with this move they would grow worse. But there was no point in staying.

"Yeah," I agreed, lacking excitement.

In two days, I would be back to the city where I had my heart broken, where all my hopes and dreams were destroyed.

So yeah, I was *so* excited to go back.

1

FRANCESCA

I stared at my phone looking at my mother's number flashing on the screen. She had been calling for the past three weeks. We were supposed to have had coffee a few days ago, but I had been too tired to go out. Now, I didn't have the courage to answer, nor did I have any excuses to refuse this encounter.

I covered my eyes as the white screen blinded me, depriving me of much-needed sleep. All I wanted to do was crawl back into the darkness that had cradled me gently and lovingly.

Why did she want to talk to me? It wasn't like we had talked much in the past four years since I was married. I slapped the covers with both hands and groaned loudly, scaring Reginald, my five-month-old gray whippet, who had been sleeping beside me.

My mother wasn't going to stop calling unless I answered her, and this time around I was actually curious enough to know what she had to say.

"Francesca," came Mamma's loud, smoker's voice.

"Mamma." I pinched my temple as a headache started to bloom. I shouldn't have drunk all that wine last night.

Where were my pills?

"*Che maleducata* you have become, making me call you over and over again." I threw the covers aside and left my bed. *Where are those damn pills?* I searched through the mess in my room, but the orange bottle was nowhere to be found. "It has been weeks, Francesca— "

I put Mamma on speaker and continued my search as my mother rambled about how I was useless and how I couldn't pick up the phone. It went on and on for an eternity and I tuned her out.

"Are you listening to me?"

"Yes, Mamma." I stopped rummaging through the mess and gave her my attention. "You were saying how I'm such a bad daughter."

"Oh, don't be such a victim, Francesca," said Mamma, who had just attacked me with her sharp words.

"Mamma, I am busy." I pinched my nose, attempting to stave off the massive headache approaching. "I have stuff to do." Like sleeping and staying locked in my apartment, reliving my traumatic past, while in the meantime, fighting a massive hangover, and probably drinking more wine to chase it off.

"Fifteen minutes, Francesca. I won't take no for an answer. I would come to your house, but you haven't given me your address, which is absurd. You should have come back home."

"Mamma, we talked about this." I sighed. That place hadn't been home for years now. Ever since the day Donato sold me into marriage to a man I hated. I wasn't going to step foot in that place ever again. "Meet me at Magnolia's." I caved.

When Mamma wanted something, she got it, she was stubborn that way. If I did not concede, she was going to make my life hell, and I wasn't sure how many of her calls I could avoid.

I ended the call and thought about changing my clothes. Mamma would kill me if she saw me dressed in leggings and an oversized turtleneck sweatshirt. But I wasn't in the mood to dress up. Dressing up meant I gave a damn, and right now, all I wanted to do was curl up in a ball and watch my cooking shows for the rest of the day.

Instead, I threw on a wool dress that reached my knees—which happened to be the most modest piece I owned—put on some boots, and tried to tame my waves, which had been a messy bedhead for days. The fight resulted in a bun that barely held my hair.

Mamma would be displeased with my lack of presentability, but then again, why did I care? People were bound to judge me whether I wore a gown or walked around with a watermelon as a hat.

As always, Mamma was late, but it gave me some time to order a doughnut in peace without being told I was going to grow fat. I devoured my pastry; it was the first thing I had eaten since yesterday's Jasmine tea.

A family of four sat beside me, and normally, I wouldn't have paid attention, but I was so bored that I studied them for a while. The father, a tall dark-skinned man, stood to order while the mother, a beautiful dark-skinned woman with gorgeous, braided hair, sat down with her toddler and a baby in her arms.

The little boy sat on the chair, looking awfully small for it, but incredibly cute. His red, kid's glasses made his brown eyes look large and filled with amazement as he shared some story with his mother, who, in turn, paid him attention as if her life depended on it.

As the father came back, he kissed his wife and then the sleeping baby in her arms. He settled himself on the chair near his son, and the four of them enjoyed their afternoon.

A tidal wave of sadness threatened to pull me under at that moment. It was so strong and violent that I had to look away to keep myself from being drowned by it. I had always dreamed of this. Of having a family of my own.

I wanted a family that would love me unconditionally. I wanted the kind of love that consumed every cell in my body and made me a hostage. A love that could withstand the storms and the seasons. But that hadn't been what God had in store for me. He had other plans, and although it was hard to accept and understand, I was trying my best to accept life as it was.

Eventually, my mother walked in through the door; she was

dressed impeccably in a gray tweed skirt suit, heels, and jewelry adorning her ears, neck, and wrists. It always struck me hard when I looked at her, it was like looking at an older version of me. We had the same blonde hair, the same dark blue eyes, same full lips, although mine still bore the ability to smile. Same thick brown brows, although Mamma preferred her's thin.

She took the seat beside mine and inspected me from head to toe as she always did. Judging. "You look terrible."

"Hi, Mother," I greeted impatiently, standing to kiss her cheek.

"What is that?" She looked at Reginald who had woken up and was inspecting Mamma as she did him. While he was a pure-hearted soul and wagged his tail in earnest happiness, Mamma raised a well-trimmed brow and inspected him as though he were an alien.

"My baby," I answered, patting his head and offering Reggie a motherly smile.

"You got a dog." Her disapproval was palpable.

"Am I not allowed?"

"You should've gotten yourself knocked up, then you would have real babies to take care of."

"Pleasant as always." I had thought Mamma would have changed, but she was still the same bitter person that she had always been. Stupid me for thinking the time we spent apart would have softened her heart.

I couldn't blame her; if I had been married to Donato Manci, I would be bitter, too. My marriage to Paolo had almost left me so.

"It's the truth." Mamma sipped on her coffee I had ordered for her.

"If you say so, Mamma." I shrugged. Arguing with Domenica Manci was as tiresome as unpacking all those boxes in my apartment.

"How's Marco?" I asked.

It had been four years since I had seen my baby brother, and I missed him terribly. Donato hadn't allowed him to see me. Marco had always been my favorite person. I was ten years older than him, but even as a child, he understood me better than anyone else.

"Working with your father. They've been very busy lately."

"He's just a kid," I complained.

"He has responsibilities. Marco is a man now. He's ready to swear the *Omerta,* even Cassio says so."

I choked on my coffee, the liquid burning my throat. My brother a Made Man? Marco was just a boy. My little boy. The one I had raised. *He's thirteen.* Too young.

"Jesus, Francesca, you look like you have seen a ghost."

Mamma wasn't wrong. I felt like I had seen one. An icy shiver raced down my back and pebbled my skin. It wasn't the first time I had heard that damning name but hearing it from Mamma's lips with all that familiarity, brought back memories of my past.

A past I was still desperately trying to forget. Four years wasn't enough to erase what had happened. It had been four years since Cassio Moretti tore my heart from my chest and stepped all over it, breaking it into a million pieces.

I hated that name.

"How are you?" The nature of her question surprised me, mainly because it wasn't like her to ask those things.

"I'm tired, Mother. It has been a tiring couple of months."

"Well then, it's best we get this over with."

Mother sat straight and took something from her purse. It was a manila envelope which she proceeded to shove toward me.

"What is that?" My hands were damp, so I wiped them on my dress.

"Open it." Mamma's vague response added to my unease.

"What, are you FBI or some shit like that, why the suspense?" I chuckled nervously trying to diminish the tension.

I reached for the manila envelope and opened it, picked up the black-and-white picture, and stared at it for a while trying my hardest to identify what it was. "Is someone pregnant?" It was the only response I could come up with.

"It's a liver, Francesca." Mamma snapped the picture from my fingers.

"Forgive me, I'm not graduated in Grey's Anatomy." Even though I'd watched a total of sixteen seasons until now.

"I have cancer."

There was a long silence that followed. Mamma took the picture and shoved it inside the envelope and put it back into her purse, as though it had never been there to start with.

I waited for the other shoe to drop, for my mother to tell me this was a joke, but Mamma never joked. She had always gone straight for the kill, never sugar-coating things. I took one long look at *her*. Yes, she was skinny, but then she always had been. She was paler and a bit crestfallen, but she had been so ever since my older brother Savio died. But cancer, no, I couldn't believe it.

"How long have you known?"

"Three months." She answered, and I sucked in a deep breath.

"Does father know?" I questioned.

"Yes." She said simply.

"Does Marco?"

"No, and it will remain that way. Your father does not wish for anyone else to know, he didn't want me to tell you –

"Why not?" I raised my voice slightly, shoving my nails into the palm of my hand to keep the anger at bay.

"Mind your tone, Francesca." She looked around embarrassed.

"Why are you telling me then? How have you been treating it? Have you been talking with your doctor? How far along? Is there a cure or some experiments?"

"Francesca, you are rambling. Take a deep breath."

Suddenly, I was a little girl all over again seeking my mother's comfort, but I wasn't little anymore, I was a grown adult. There was no one to hold my hand and lead me through the darkness.

Guilt dug its claws into me, and it was painful. I pushed my nails into the palm of my hands—harder this time—and focused on that pain instead of the one growing in my chest. Mamma had been seeking my help, and I had ignored her. What kind of person did that? What a shitty daughter I was. It didn't matter how estranged we were, I'd be there for her through it all.

"What do you need?" I sounded braver in my head, but the truth was, I was scared shitless of something happening to my mother.

"I have a doctor's appointment next week –"

"So, it's early stages?" My hopes got up. Stupid of me to do so because soon after, Mamma crushed it.

"I'm starting chemo. I'm at stage IV and he thinks, for now, chemo might work," she answered like she was testing the words herself like she was now realizing the gravity of her diagnosis.

"Might?"

"It's pretty advanced, Francesca." Mamma sounded annoyed, but I realized it was just years of learning how to hide her feelings.

Mamma was scared.

My hands were clammy, and fire raced through my body. The wool dress I wore suddenly felt too suffocating. I dug my nails deeper into my palms trying to keep my emotions at bay.

Mamma had lived through so much; she has survived an abusive, cheating, husband. She survived being humiliated. She survived the loss of her son. She was going to survive this, too.

"I'll be there." I took my mother's hand and gave it one hard squeeze.

When I arrived back at my apartment, I sat staring at the walls until they began to move, closing in on me. I was shaking all over. This couldn't be happening. Hadn't God ruined my life enough times already? What else could he take from me?

I headed to my room, opened my safe, and removed the last remaining Ziplock I had left. I'd made a promise three months ago to Marie and myself to never use drugs again, but my world was breaking, I was falling to my knees and there was no one to help me to my feet. I needed an escape. To run away.

I needed bliss.

2

FRANCESCA

Happiness could be found at the end of a rolled dollar bill, and freedom at the bottom of a hard liquor bottle. I welcomed the numbness in my body. I loved this feeling of floating through time and space. Nothing seemed to matter anymore. Nothing could stop me. I was invincible.

The neon lights flashed around me; my body swayed to the electronic music. Sweat beaded at my breasts and raced down my back, but even still, I didn't care. Tonight was about forgetting. Silencing the voices in my head was my biggest priority.

I stopped at the bar to refill my glass; the cute bartender smiled at me as he refilled it with vodka. I took one large sip and sighed as the cold liquid raced down my throat. Mixing alcohol with drugs in this state was probably not a good idea, but I didn't particularly care, as long as it made me forget. Tomorrow, I'd regret it, but tonight, I wanted to feel alive.

"Where were you?" Antoine grabbed me by the arm. "Shit, what did you do, Frankie?"

"Nothing," I pulled away, but he didn't let go. His grip wasn't hurting but it was solid and strong. "I wanted to have fun."

"You promised me, Francesca." He reminded me.

"It was just a line," I explained trying to make him worry less. I hated that look on him, especially when it was directed at me. "I promise I'm fine."

A flash of a neon pink light passed through us, and I closed my eyes as my head spun. "I'm taking you home." Antoine decided and began to pull me away from the dance floor, but I refused to move.

"I'm not a child." I said petulantly.

"No, *chérie,* but you are acting like one."

I rolled my eyes and pulled my hair from the back of my neck hoping it would soothe me. I was burning with the heat of a thousand furnaces. My entire body blazed, even my blood was boiling.

From the corner of my eye, I watched a beautiful man staring at us, the neon lights cast a glow over him, making my insides twist. Except his eyes were solely on Antoine and instantly my cheeks burned. *Of course, the beautiful man was interested in someone else.* I hadn't come here for flirting or *that* kind of fun, but it was good to feel wanted at times.

"Your friend is waiting for you."

Antoine looked toward the beautiful man, then back at me, like he was caught in a dilemma. "I'm taking you home," he said with finality.

"I can take care of myself," I snapped, having the impression he had only come tonight so he could babysit me. I understood he was worried about my well-being, but I didn't care. I wanted the bliss, the numbness. The silence.

He opened his mouth to argue, but I shook my head. "I'm a big girl, I can handle it, go have some fun." I placed my hands over his shoulders and shook him. "That gorgeous man wants your attention, don't keep him waiting."

Antoine's lips turned upwards, and he tried to hide the glimmer in his eyes. I was keeping him from doing what he truly wanted to do. "Go." I turned him toward the man and shoved him through the crowd.

"Text me when get home," he shouted over the music, and I laughed.

When Antoine was gone, I stared at my glass of vodka and drank it halfway. Sometimes, I wished to be as carefree as Antoine or as lively as Marie. It was a terrible thing, but I was jealous of them, of their lives, and their dreams. Pushing those thoughts aside, I went in search of something else to keep me numb.

Two hours later, my tired legs led me out of the club, I could barely walk straight, my eyes were trying to focus on what was before me. Before I realized where I was going, a car honked loudly, skidding to a stop millimeters from me. My heart jumped to my throat and my hands flew to my stomach as if I could keep the contents in there. By some miracle it did.

A man stepped out of the car shouting and gesticulating like a maniac. My ears buzzed; my pulse raced. It was hard to understand what he was saying as my head fought to process that I had almost been run over.

"Are you crazy!" he shouted hysterically.

"What is going on here?"

"This woman came out of nowhere, officer, the light was green, and she simply walked into the street."

"Is this right, miss?" I turned slowly.

Officer? Officer!

Like a bucket of cold water, I stared at the man in blue standing beside me closer than he should have. He kept on approaching until he stopped inches from my face. I was not in the right frame of mind to have a conversation with a man of the law. Not now and not ever.

Instinct kicked in, and I bolted. To be fair, I blamed it on the heels, and the fact that the last time I ran, I was probably a six-year-old. I didn't make it that far; in fact, I didn't even make it to the corner of the street–which was inches away. Arms wrapped around me, pulling me back, and I hit the officer's chest, hard. Like a cornered animal, I fought him knowing that if he managed to question me, he would realize I'd broken dozens of laws.

Paolo made it a rule, I could do whatever I damned well pleased as long as I kept away from the police. He would look the other way as long as I didn't call attention to myself—as long as I didn't get in trouble.

That rule echoed in my head as I kicked the officer and tried to run away again. It was probably the stupidest thing I'd ever done in my life. It was obvious he was larger and stronger than me. The fight was over before it even began. He restrained and cuffed me in seconds. When he shoved me inside the police car, I heard his partner laughing.

"We got ourselves a spitfire over there."

"She fucking kicked me," the officer who'd grabbed me complained. "My shin is bleeding."

I tried to position myself better in the car, my hands and arms were starting to ache, a hundred tiny needles prickled my skin. It was uncomfortable as hell. The car smelled of sweat and leather, but something else caused my stomach to spin. It was strong and pungent. My head spun as they drove me away.

The cool air in the precinct hit my blazing skin, and I breathed in greedily. I stumbled on my heels as the officer who'd grabbed me— the one I apparently hurt—led me toward the front desk. His words barely registered in my mind as he spoke. My head was spinning so fast it felt like a carousel.

Spinning and spinning and spinning.

"You know there is no need for handcuffs, right?"

The officer glanced at me but kept on walking as he escorted me toward the cell. His meaty hand still wrapped around my arm.

"I won't take my chances with you," he grumbled; apparently, he was still pissed that I hurt him. *What a crybaby.*

"It was a mistake," I agreed. "I shouldn't have run; I know that now."

He chuckled dryly. "Darling, that is the least of your problems." He offered with a smile. "You should be more concerned about the charges I'm pressing and the amount of coke you had on you."

"It was one kick," I complained.

He shrugged. "Should have thought that through." *Jesus, what an asshole.* I was sure I barely nicked him. There was no need for pressing charges, he knew it, I knew it.

When we stopped at the cell, his eyes lingered over my body, more specifically at the swell of my breasts. God hadn't given me the ability to make sane decisions, but he had given me a pair of breasts and an ass to match. Apparently, he thought that was more important than my self-preservation.

Thanks, God.

Done with his leering, he unlocked the cell door and pushed me inside. He asked for my hands and remove my cuffs. I rubbed my wrists trying to get the blood flow back to them, and as I did so, I inspected the place.

My eyes landed on a woman who shared the cell with me. She looked my age, somewhere around her mid-twenties. Foundation—two shades darker than her skin tone—caked her face and dark mascara ran down her cheeks. She might have been pretty, but the makeup and the jaded look in her eyes robbed her of that. The fishnet pantyhose she wore was ripped at the knees, and one of her black heels was broken.

"Kimberly." My cellmate greeted me like we were sitting down for coffee instead of being locked in a jail cell.

"Frankie," I offered back, surprised by how relaxed and bored my voice sounded.

"I like your shoes," Kimberly said as she sat up straighter against the wall.

"Thanks," I smiled lightly. "They are Jimmy Choo's." I stared at the ground, or better yet at my lovely sparkly pumps.

It had been one of the many gifts I'd received from my late husband. A bribe. A way to apologize for bringing yet another mistress into our home. Paolo couldn't help himself, and eventually, I grew complacent—which was my fault. I let him shower me with gifts, and sadly, I even grew to enjoy them.

"Why you here, Princess?" The way Kimberly said princess sounded like an accusation.

"You first." I glanced at the corridor watching the two men that stood guard by the door, who were entertained by their conversation.

"I bet daddy will be here any minute," Kimberly accused me again. What was it with this girl? "So, what happened, *Princess?*"

Facing her, I decided whether or not to grace her with an answer, sighing, I offered her the truth. "Trust me, daddy doesn't give a shit." The last time I had talked to him we'd had a heated conversation which ended with him calling me a whore and slapping me so hard I saw stars.

Of course, none of that had been a surprise. My father enjoyed using his fists more than he did using his words, and when he did speak...let's just say it would have been best if you kept your mouth shut.

Kimberly ran her fingers through her messy black hair and slouched against the wall, her legs falling apart and flashing me a view of what lay beneath her dress. "I stabbed my ex with a broken glass bottle."

"Cool." I turned to face the guards again. The metal bars were cold against my fingers as I grabbed them to keep myself steady as my head began to spin. "I'm here for assaulting an officer and having coke on me." *And in you.*

Kimberly was silent for a while and then she began to laugh, it was throaty like she had been smoking for a lifetime. I turned to face her surprised with her reaction. "You," she laughed. "Look at you."

I furrowed my brows wondering what that was supposed to mean. Yeah, I got that a lot. One look at me and people already decided what kind of person I was. A spoiled little princess. A trophy wife. Arm candy. A gold digger. They all judged the book by its cover and never stuck long enough to realize the book was actually fun to read.

"How long have you been in here?" I decided to change the conversation.

"Three hours."

My eyes widened. "Shouldn't you have been bailed out or something?"

"I have no one to bail me out," she explained. "Plus, I was found guilty so... dunno." She shrugged like it wasn't important. Her reaction or lack thereof, left me wondering if this was her first time in here.

"Shit, that's bad," I thought out loud.

That's when it hit me, I wasn't so different from her. Thinking about it now, I had no idea who would bail me out. I couldn't call Marie, not even if my life depended on it. I had promised her I had stopped using, she was going to be so disappointed if she knew I had broken it.

Antoine was also out of the question; he was busy right now, and I didn't want my friends cleaning up my mess—again. I wanted more than just that; I wanted them to see me beyond the broken pieces.

My nails found the soft skin of my palms and I squeezed them hard, trying to focus on the pain instead of how erratic my heart was beating or how I couldn't seem to pull enough air into my lungs.

The officer who brought me in had asked me a few questions and had taken my ID. By now he must have done a background check on who I was. Which meant he knew I had ties to the wrong kind of people. The kind of people who would get a one-way ticket to prison and probably the electric chair.

Last year, a friend of Paolo's had been arrested for driving under the influence, and in less than a few hours, the FBI had come to take him away. He was charged with so many crimes, it would be a lifetime before he was freed from the maximum-security prison he was sent to. He died a few months later, stabbed in a fight. I had overheard Paolo say it was a necessity. But I knew the Outfit killed him, so he'd keep his mouth shut.

"Oh God," I closed my eyes, and my head came to rest against the bar as I held it tight.

What if the FBI came for me? What if I was taken into one of those maximum-security prisons? I wasn't built for that, there was no way I would last a single day inside that place. Not to mention the

Feds, they creeped me out. What if I was murdered like Paolo's friend? I might not know much, but I did know something. The Outfit may protect their own, but they were not above killing to make sure they remained safe. Not to mention I hated those orange jumpsuits they'd look terrible on me.

"Don't I have the right to a phone call?" I shouted, grabbing the guards' attention.

I watched as the asshole who had ogled me came to stand before the cell. "What do you want?"

"My phone call, *Stronzo*." I was pretty sure it was part of my rights — at least all the movies I watched said so.

Officer asshole sighed in frustration but proceeded to take me out of the cell and escorted me all the way toward the phone booth. He remained by my side, an uncomfortable distance from me. I imagined he was doing it on purpose. Officer asshole really did hold a grudge. What was he thinking that I was going to run of again? I knew how to accept defeat.

"Don't I get some privacy?" I offered him my sweetest smile. Hoping he got diabetes from it. The guard's eyes trailed me once more this time landing on my ass. He stepped back giving me some space, albeit not as much as I desired.

"You have five minutes," he gritted out.

I stared at the phone and in that moment, it became my worst enemy. Truth be told, I had no one to call, wasn't even sure why I had requested it. If Paolo had been alive, I would have been forced to call him, even if there were consequences later. But since I didn't have a phone line directly to Hell, I was back to square one.

"Are you going to use that thing or not?" The guard said impatiently.

"I don't know who to call." My cheeks turned pink. I hadn't planned on sharing my reality with him.

A wave of heat warmed my body and anxiety lodged in my chest attaching itself like tar. I dug my nails into my palm and tried to think, but my head was pounding, my heart beating painfully against my chest.

This was it; I was going to be sent to prison, the Feds, who I had no doubt were on their way, would definitely pin some kind of crime on me to punish my family and the Outfit. I might not be involved in their business, but I was part of that world, which unfortunately made me guilty by association. That's when a very, *very,* stupid idea formed in my pounding head.

The kind of idea that tasted like a bitter pill and was hard to swallow. The kind of idea that smelled like shit. I was going to regret this, not just now but possibly for the rest of my life. If it weren't for my mother putting his name in my head, I would never have attempted such a disastrous feat. But beggars couldn't be choosers and right now I was desperate as it got. So, I dialed the number I had committed to memory and listened while it rang continuously.

"What?" A gruff voice answered.

The phone almost slipped from my hands. Four years. My throat constricted and my mouth went dry. Suddenly I forgot how to speak, my lips refusing to move. His voice was the same, and I was not ready for the wave of memories that flooded my head, giving me no chance to fight back.

"H-hi," I whispered.

"Who the fuck is this?" Cassio snapped; sounding pissed off. I closed my eyes and relished in the sound of his voice—

Snap. Out. Of. It.

I willed myself to remember where I was. "It's Frankie—Francesca." I corrected.

"Who?" Cassio's voice was detached like he hadn't stabbed me in the heart with a single word.

"Francesca Biancini." I closed my eyes and swallowed. "Francesca Manci." I corrected myself again. The name left a bitter taste in my mouth. Like the foulest of poisons.

"One minute." The guard shouted.

"Where are you?" Cassio demanded.

"One sec," I put a hand over the phone and asked the guard exactly where I was. "Precinct nine."

There was a long pause, and I could hear the shuffling of sheets, then a female's voice. My heart pulsed painfully in my chest. I tried to ignore it, tried to swallow down the jealousy that welled up inside of me. God, how I regretted calling him. Cassio was obviously busy right now. With a woman. A woman he could be dating. A woman he had probably been sleeping with.

Ugh. I pinched my temple; I could feel the start of a headache. This was a mistake I should never have called him. Why would Cassio help me? He hated me after all.

"You're calling me from prison?" His voice broke through my thoughts.

"Jail," I corrected.

There was another large pause until he said. "Why are you calling me?"

Jesus, how many blows to my self-esteem could I take? "Because, you know, you're the…the only one I could call." Good, now I sounded pathetic. Did I have to admit that to him?

"Times up." The guard walked toward me. Intent on removing the phone from my hand.

"You know what, forget I called, just pretend I don't exist." He was obviously pretty good at doing that.

I inhaled deeply and rested my head against the wall. A shiver raced down my spine and I couldn't help laughing at myself. What did I honestly expect? Calling Cassio was perhaps the worst idea I'd had since getting arrested. I was on a streak tonight, one fuck up after the other.

The guard must have taken pity on me because he remained silent as he escorted me back to the cell. Standing that close to me, I was sure he heard my exchange with Cassio.

Who the fuck is this?

His voice echoed in my head as I sat down on the floor and removed my Jimmy Choo pumps.

Francesca.

Who?

"Any luck?" Kimberly asked, and I opened my eyes to find her sitting forward and resting her elbows on her thighs.

"Guess we'll be cellmates for a while." Was all I said as I rested my head against the wall, yearning for some quiet since I wanted to lick my wounds in peace. As well as replay that short conversation over and over again, beating myself for being so stupid.

Why was I such a failure? Maybe my father had been right when he called me a big disappointment.

3

FRANCESCA

There was a shift in the air like the moment before a storm where everything went still, the air turned cold, and the world turned dark. It would happen all at once, one moment peace and the next chaos.

An icy shiver raced down my back, causing me to tremble, I dug my nails into the palm of my hands readying myself for the force of the storm. Eyes open and searching, they eventually landed on the guards at the end of the corridor. There was a commotion, they argued but then the door was opened, and two men stepped forward.

I sensed him before I even saw him walk into the room. His presence demanded my attention and my eyes refused to look anywhere else but at him.

God! What have you done Francesca?

"Miss Manci." The asshole guard that had leered at me like I was his next meal called.

Then I heard Cassio's voice. Laced with violence and the promise of death, the most gruesome and painful of deaths. I just wondered whose. His tone was professional and detached despite the dark edge to it. "That's her." His head turned toward my direction.

Transfixed, I watched as he walked toward the cell, wishing my eyes would find something else to look at. Instead, they were locked on him. Only him. Like there wasn't anyone else in the room.

I sucked in a deep breath, and it refused to leave, remaining lodged in my lungs, straining it with unwelcome pressure.

Cassio had changed.

He looked older, manlier if it were even possible. He had always been tall, but now he seemed larger than life. The breadth of his shoulders made him look strong and capable. The white casual shirt, and the black trench coat he wore hugged his frame offering me a quality view of his muscles.

Cassio ran his fingers through his messy bed golden brown hair, it was longer than I remember, curling around his ears and falling over his eyes. The strangest urge to run my fingers through it settled over me, and I had to bite the inside of my cheeks to focus on something else.

"Dear heavens." Kimberly came to stand beside me, fingers circling the bars. "What is that?"

I refrained from answering because there was no right answer for her question. Cassio was power incarnate, his head held high, his steps determined, and his back straight as a rod. He was a god in all his glory and might.

With each powerful step he took toward us, I realized that staying here didn't sound so bad after all. Kimberly was starting to seem like a fun companion for the rest of my night.

The closer he got, the smaller the room around me became. Cassio seemed to suck all the air out of the room, pushing and pulling everything in its wake. Like a tornado that had finally touched the ground. Beautiful in all its danger.

Cassio Moretti stopped right in front of me on the other side of the cell. He tilted his head left, studying me like I was the newest attraction at the zoo. His eyes trailed my body, not as invasive and hungry as the guards had been. Cassio's was cold, detached, and...judging.

There was nothing warm about him. His pine-green eyes burned with icy fire, leaving third-degree burns in their wake. He tore through my barriers, even though I fought with everything I had. Nothing could have prepared me for that.

I studied him trying to conjure the same intensity but obviously, I failed. Leaning against the bars to keep myself steady, I offered him a sweet smile, that always worked for me. *Had worked once on him.* But to this new version of him, I was nothing but prey, who had been spotted by its predator.

"Francesca," he drawled.

My name on his lips was both like a curse and a balm soothing my soul. It reached the top of my head and all the way to my curled toes. It was too much. With the effect of the drug, his presence, and the way he looked at me, I was seconds from having a nervous breakdown.

I didn't answer, nor did I move—it was physically impossible. I was in complete shock. Cassio shouldn't have come, nothing in our short conversation indicated he was coming, or that he wanted to. The man didn't even recall who I was.

Cassio ran his thumb under his lower lip, a sign I recalled, that he was annoyed. He ordered the guard to open the cell door, and he reluctantly did so, glaring at me the entire time.

"You've got powerful friends," the guard chuckled as he reached for me, but before his hands could land on mine, Cassio stopped the guard from reaching me. He pulled the man away and offered him a warning look.

"Let's go, Francesca," Cassio ordered as he began to walk away.

I stood there frozen for a while before realizing that was it, just like that, I was freed. I turned just in time to catch the guard locking the cell door with Kimberly still inside. "Hey, your shoes." She picked them up.

"Keep them," I said still dazed with everything that was happening. "Nice meeting you."

"Francesca," Cassio drawled again, this time impatiently. He was already halfway through the corridor.

I took my time reaching him, the bright light bothered my eyes, and I used my hands to shield my sight from its assault. I heard

Cassio tsk, but he said nothing else as we walked out. Cassio led me all the way to a large office I assumed belonged to the chief officer.

The chief officer was old, probably close to his sixties, with graying hair, a protruding belly, and one of those mustaches that curled at the sides. He looked like he belonged in a cartoon instead of a police station. It made me smile, but it quickly died when Cassio glared at me.

"None of this will be mentioned again, her charges will be dropped, and the paperwork will disappear," Cassio ordered in his authoritative tone. "Do you understand?"

To my surprise—but then again, I shouldn't have been—the chief nodded. "Yes, Boss."

"Good." Cassio agreed, seemingly satisfied with the chief's answer.

"Her possessions are here, and after that, you are free to go."

Cassio picked up my clutch and held it out to me, but it slipped through my damp fingers and fell to the floor. I reached down to grab it, but the world spun, and I grabbed the desk to keep me steady. Cursing, he reached down and picked it up for me.

"Hold it, it's not that hard." He offered me the clutch once more, and this time, I held it with both hands.

He gave me a quick glance before leading me toward the exit. I followed closely behind, almost stepping on the back of his black boots once or twice. The moment we stepped outside, the cold autumn air kissed my exposed skin causing me to shiver uncontrollably. I wrapped my arms around myself trying to ward off the wind.

Cassio stopped, and I stood beside him, taking in a view of the parking lot, aside from the few police cars parked there, I saw a black sports car and two other ones.

I shivered again unable to control myself, but it was so damned cold outside. From the corner of my eyes, I noticed Cassio was staring at me. He shook his head in what I imagined was disbelief. "Where is the rest of that thing?"

"It's a special edition, Dolce and Gabbana," I explained matter-of-factly.

"I don't care what it is, Francesca, dressing like that gives men the wrong impression."

"Now wait a minute." I turned on him one finger raised. *The nerve of this guy.* That's when I realized he wasn't criticizing me, he was actually…concerned.

Looking at the night sky, Cassio sighed loudly and then proceeded to remove his trench coat and offered it to me. "Put this on." I was momentarily stunned. "Unless you want to freeze, then I'll gladly let you."

So much for thinking he was being nice. I grabbed the coat forcefully and put it on, regretting it the moment I did. It sat comfortably over my shoulders and offered me the warmth I needed; the only problem was it smelled of him. Of citrus and sandalwood.

"Let's go," he said.

There was only one black sports car parked in the parking lot, and I deduced it was his. Cassio always liked his cars fancy. I ran toward it, barefoot, hurting as though I was stepping on glass. I shouldn't have left my heels behind.

I tried opening the door, but he hadn't unlocked it. I tried it again, but he was taking his sweet ass time in reaching the car. "Can you freaking open it?" I snapped.

Cassio slowly walked toward the driver's side, lifted the car keys so I could see them, then made a show of pressing the button. The car beeped and its lights flashed. Again, I tugged at the handle, and it finally gave way. When I was inside, I closed the door as hard as I could muster.

"Stronzo."

Cassio entered the moment I uttered the word. He closed the door and twisted on his seat facing me. Knowing I had made a mistake, I dug my nails into the palms of my hands and moved away from him.

"Call me that ever again and you'll learn just what an asshole I can be," he snapped.

"No worries, I don't need to be reminded, I already know."

He stared right into my eyes. His pine-green ones were cold, and it was unfair how beautiful they still were. "I should have let you rot in there," he said to himself as he turned on the engine. "The next time, I'll remember to forget you."

I swallowed hard and turned away, so much for trying to rile him up. One did not simply argue with Cassio. He always had something smarter to say.

CASSIO

W<small>HAT A SHIT SHOW</small>.

Tonight, had not gone how I had expected it too.

Fuck. Fuck. Fuck.

I held back the urge to hit the steering wheel, refusing to lose control of the situation, even though I was *this* close to losing my shit. My eyes wandered to the woman in my car, she had her nose shoved into the collar of my coat. Either she didn't care that I caught her smelling my scent or she hadn't realized I was watching her.

Francesca fucking Manci.

She was the last person I expected to hear from, but oddly enough, there was a part of me, small—albeit alive—that had been eager to see her. Like a puppy with its master. Four years and apparently, she still had that effect on me. I must have been Pavlov-ed or some shit. It was the only explanation.

I gripped the wheel tightly and swerved in between the cars in front of mine, pressing on the gas. "Can you go slower?"

I turned to face Francesca. "Why?"

"There's no one chasing us, and last I checked, you're not Dominic Toretto, so chill out."

"I have it under control," I said swerving around another car, she gripped the seatbelt and only because I didn't enjoy that sight on her face, I slowed—only a bit.

Silence settled over us once more, and in the meantime,

Francesca began rummaging through my car, looking around and touching everything. She stopped when she found my gum. Without ceremony, she popped one into her mouth and threw the wrapping paper on the back seat. I clenched my teeth but remained silent.

Unsatisfied with what she had found, Francesca reached for the glove compartment and opened it, my gun fell out, she tried to hold it, but overwhelmed, she let it fall to the floor. Annoyed and slightly amused, I swerved the car left and stopped on the road's shoulder.

"God damn it, Francesca."

"It fell," she snapped as though it was my fault.

I moved toward her with the intention of grabbing the firearm, Francesca jumped back, hitting her back against the door. Her sapphire blue eyes widened, and she sucked in a deep breath.

"What was that?" I pulled away from her, giving Francesca some space.

"Nothing." She brushed it off like she hadn't flinched from me.

"What did you think I was going to do? Hit you?" I sneered.

The look in her eyes told me that was exactly what she had expected. I fisted my hands, anger coursing through my veins, but not at Francesca, at the men who did this to her. "I'm going to pick it up now," I said with a calm I did not possess.

Reaching out slower this time, I reached for the gun, my arm coming in contact with the bare skin of her creamy thigh, and I watched as she shivered. I couldn't help the amused smile that graced my face, but it remained there for only a few seconds, not long enough for her to see.

"I don't hit women, Francesca," I said as I closed the glove compartment. "Not even those who annoy the fuck out of me."

I didn't need that kind of dominance over them, in fact, it sickened me to know there were men out there who enjoyed and partook in this kind of behavior. I took a deep breath, inhaling the scent of sweet cherries, it filled my nose and twisted my insides. Francesca always looked so damned sweet.

What happened to her now?

She didn't look sweet, on the contrary, she looked sensual and sexy, her white dress hugging every curve of her perfect body. Those toned long legs on display drove me insane. Not to mention the pink lipstick that made her full kiss-me lips look even more kissable.

I cleared my throat and focused on the road before me. Francesca chewed loudly and then popped a bubble, the loud POP echoing inside the car. How could a woman infuriate me so much, and in the same moment, have me completely ensnared in her presence? Unable to help myself, I watched Francesca again, taking advantage of the fact that she was looking out the window.

She was still unbearably beautiful, and that dress... blood traveled to my dick, and I couldn't stop myself. The white dress she wore left nothing to the imagination. I could see the large swell of her breasts and her nipples poking through the fabric. I wondered if she was cold or turned on.

Stop that. Focus. Keep your mind where it should be and control yourself.

What was she doing back in my city? Last I checked, she was still living in Indianapolis with her very old—dead husband. How could I have forgotten? Paolo Biancini, Francesca's late husband, had died three weeks ago. I just hadn't expected her to be back so soon after. I thought maybe she wanted to mourn him.

Having Francesca here in my city was dangerous. Too many memories. Too much water under that broken bridge.

"I heard about your husband." The words slipped through my lips. Silence never bothered me, but with her it did. Francesca had always been a chatterbox.

She popped the gum again and turned to face me, something unreadable in her eyes — was it sorrow? I ran my thumb under my lower lip and clenched my teeth hard.

"I'm not in the mood for small talk." She replied eventually.

Great. "I was being polite, Francesca."

"It doesn't suit you." She looked at her nails.

"Nice to know that's what you think about me," I pointed out.

"I don't think about you at all, Cassio." I turned toward her, and she swirled around to face the window, obviously hiding what I would find written all over her face. Warmth pooled in my stomach at the realization that she still thought about me.

Then guilt followed and so did anger, so I focused on the latter and decided not to think about that further. Thinking about what Francesca was thinking was a double-edged blade, and I was bound to be the one getting both ends of it.

When I stared at her again, she was pale as a ghost, a hand on her stomach and eyes closed. "Are you going to be sick?"

"I can handle it," she murmured, but it didn't look like it.

"I swear to God, Francesca, not in my car," I said, not wanting to sound like an asshole, but my baby was only a week old, and I fucking loved it.

"It's not my first time," she snapped. "I'm fine." The lie that slipped through her mouth was obvious to us both.

Which reminded me why I was so awfully and incredibly pissed with the woman beside me. "Hold on," I ordered.

I found the nearest diner just in time. Francesca flew from the car not stopping to see if there was anyone else around us in the dimly lit parking lot. She ran toward the bushes wearing nothing but that flimsy dress and my coat. I parked the car and quickly followed, not daring to leave her alone.

Francesca was heaving hard the second I reached her. "Go away," she barked at me as she leaned downward to throw up again.

"I'm not holding your hair," I said at the same time.

She managed to look up to glare at me, but nausea pulled her back under, and she didn't have time to say whatever smart thing I knew was coming out of that mouth.

I stood there beside her, half looking at Francesca, half watching the parking lot from where we stood. When she was done heaving her soul out, she sighed loudly and stumbled backward. I grabbed her arm and steadied her. She was paler than before, her bones trembling.

"Shit." I cursed as she fought to get away from me. "Let's get you cleaned up," I said and escorted her toward the twenty-four-hour diner.

Three tables were filled, but aside from that, the place was fairly empty. The bathroom was at the back of the room, and I held on to Francesca, knowing she could walk on her own but not putting it to the test. The truth was... holding her felt natural, like something my hands were used to from lives past.

"What are you doing?" she snapped as I opened the women's bathroom door for her and proceeded to follow.

"I don't need you holding my hair." She snapped.

"If I let you go, you're going to pass out."

"I'm fine." She pushed me away and I let her go reluctantly, only to watch her stumble toward the sink. She said that a lot I noticed, but I was starting to realize she didn't say it from the heart.

Closing the door behind me as I retreated from the restrooms, I took the closest booth and ordered a bottle of water and salty chips. By the time Francesca came out of the bathroom, her makeup was less messy, and her long golden hair was tied in a ponytail, offering me a view of her long neck. I shifted trying to accommodate my dick that was constrained by my pants.

"What are we doing, Cassio?" she asked as she took the seat across from me.

"You need water and electrolytes, your blood pressure is too low, and I'm not risking you getting sick inside my car."

She pursed her lips and narrowed her eyes, opened her mouth as if to say something but decided against it. Francesca snatched the bag of chips and popped it open. When had she become so loud? "Eat and drink slowly, or else—"

"I know, Cassio." She sighed. "As I said, not my first time."

This brought me to the matter at hand—or rather a handful of matters we needed to discuss. "Why did you assault a police officer?"

Her jaw dropped and then she quickly picked it up. "It was barely an assault. I kicked his shin when he tried to grab me."

My nostrils flared, and I ran my thumb under my lower lip trying to control irritability. "Why did he grab you?"

She looked at her hands and then rested against her cushioned seat. My coat was large on her and for some reason, the sight caused my blood to race inside my veins. "I freaked out." Then she proceeded to tell me parts—because I knew she was hiding the most important bit of the story.

"How the mighty have fallen." I shook my head.

"Like you care."

"Actually, I do, Francesca." I tapped my fingers against the table staring her deep in the eye. "I can't keep cleaning up your messes like that. You must have been pretty high to do something so stupid."

She pushed the empty bottle and chip bag toward me. "I'm done here."

Well, I wasn't. Not even close. When I got that call from Francesca tonight, I thought it was some sick joke. Hearing her voice after four years had been a physical shock. Enough that I jumped from bed ignoring the woman beside me.

"Who gave you the blow?" Her eyes widen and her cheeks turn pink. Francesca looked around embarrassed and then glared at me for making her so.

"I'm not going to answer that," she snapped.

"I highly recommend that you do." I fisted my hands under the table. *Aggravating woman.*

"Or what? You're going to treat me like one of your men?" She whispered that part. "I'm not going to answer because I don't want to."

I almost chuckled, when had she grown a backbone? Where did the sweet Francesca Manci go? The Outfit's little saint. So poised and perfect.

"Who gave it to you?"

She sighed loudly looking at the ceiling. "Why does it have to be someone? Why can't it be me?" She crossed her arms. "I bought it." The worst part was that there was no trace of a lie on her face.

"That's expensive shit." I pointed, slightly shocked.

"I like expensive shit."

I couldn't help but provoke her, maybe it was to see how far she'd gone, or how far I was willing to go. "Is that why you married Paolo Biancini? For the expensive shit?"

"That and the sex, of course. Can't forget that." She offered me a sweet diabetic smile. "Or that bed we once broke."

My fists were clenched so tight that my knuckles were numb and pale. I asked the question, so the fault was mine alone, and now I had to imagine her in bed with that old fucker. It twisted my stomach and left me wanting to break something.

I could stomach a lot of shit, my hands were coated in blood, and I had a spot in Hell with my name on it. Few things, if any, scared me. But talking to Francesca and learning what had happened to her in these past four years was not something I planned on doing tonight, in a diner at four o'clock in the morning.

We headed back to the car, and I drove her back to her place until she grew all stiff. "Where are you taking me?" She inquired.

"Your home."

"That place is not my home, Cassio," she said with such fierceness that it left me feeling like a fool. With all the bad memories that happened in that house, I wouldn't call that place a home either.

She offered me—begrudgingly—the address to her new place. A neighborhood, I might add, was not to my liking, but I didn't mention that. It wasn't like we were going to see each other again. In fact, I had no plans of seeing her ever again. Tonight, had been a one-time deal. A necessity. A favor.

With her no longer living in Indianapolis, the only way to keep her away from me was avoiding her at all costs. Francesca was too much trouble and as my dick had proven tonight, when it came to her, I was eager for some action.

I couldn't deal with the past right now, with what happened between us, and from her hostility toward me, it seemed neither did she. It was best to ignore it ever happened. Even if the thought of forgetting her didn't sit well with me.

As I parked the car, I pushed aside all thoughts of the past and focused on her. Before she could leave, I locked the doors. Her vivid sapphire eyes flashed toward me, and I had the impression she was about to get on my nerves with her new attitude. "Don't think this will ever happen again, Francesca. I let this one pass because you are obviously grieving, but the next time you are found with blow or any drugs on you, I will deal with you as I deal with my men."

"Trust me, Cassio, I never want to see you again."

"The feeling is mutual." I unlocked the door. She stepped out of the car in a hurry, and I sped away from her building with a bitter taste in my mouth as if I had been running from something.

4

CASSIO

Arabella Moretti, beloved daughter, and loving sister the simple tombstone read. Bella wasn't the kind of girl for flashy things or grand gestures. She had been a simple girl in a world of diamonds and gold. She had been offered a silver spoon but would have rather eaten with a wooden one.

That had been Bella, my little sister.

Soft patters of rain landed on my coat. It was an ugly, depressing day. The bouquet of flowers I had left for her would soon become drenched with rain. What had caught my eye when I arrived this morning, was that a fresh bouquet of white tulips had been placed at my sister's tombstone.

Tulips.

I knew only one person with an obsession with tulips, one person who would go to the greatest lengths to find them even though they were not in season. I tried to push thoughts of her out of my head but waging war with myself was futile. So, I had been torturing myself with visions of Francesca Manci for the past week—no reprieve.

Night after night I placed my head on my pillow only to be invaded with golden blonde hair, dark blue eyes, and the sweet scent of cherries. It left my mouth watering and my dick hard as a fucking stone. Not even Claire, my usual booty call was able to soothe my needs.

Once.

All it took was seeing her once again and my body was already acting like a teenager after discovering his dick served for other purposes other than pissing. It was pathetic and not to mention unnecessary. Francesca had no place in my head, not even to annoy the fuck out of me with that tight mini dress.

Fuck. Me.

It had left nothing to the imagination, it had hugged her body in all the right places. She was nineteen the last time I saw her, and you could already see traces of the woman she was becoming, but holy devil.

The woman was a temptation.

She was the most delicious of sins, and I wanted to commit it over and over again. Soft curves, which demanded to be grabbed by my hands. Wide hips that would look incredible straddling mine. Round breasts that would taste exquisite and mile-long legs that have no trouble wrapping around my waist as I pounded—

"Fuck." I pinched my nose and looked at my shoes, anywhere but the tombstone before me, feeling a bout of shame.

Bella and Francesca had been close friends and that's actually how I met Francesca, through my little sister. When Francesca and I started dating in secret, she had wanted to tell Bella. I was the idiot who told her not to. I was scared, terrified even. Back then, Francesca was already promised to Paolo. Their engagement was set, she even had his ring on her delicate finger.

Francesca didn't want him. She had only met Paolo twice before being offered to him like cattle in a market. We were supposed to have been friends and nothing more, not even that...acquaintances at best. But then, how could I stay away from her?

Meeting Francesca was like meeting an angel after living in the darkness of Hell for centuries. She was the light at the end of a long endless tunnel. The bright light in my cold, dark world.

"What am I going to do, *Bellissima*?" I tapped my shoe on the floor.

The silence that followed was like a knife to the gut. I didn't know why I insisted on coming here every week. My father used to say it was a form of obsession. My brother Vitelli said it was a form of grief. I disagreed. It was guilt, plain and simple.

Still is.

I sighed as my phone chimed, the incoming messages a sign it was going to be a busy day. There were no off days in the Mafia, especially not for a young Capo who was being watched by vultures ready to pick off my carcass the moment I fell. That was not going to happen—unfortunately for them.

The drive to one of my newest clubs took me slightly more than the usual twenty minutes. Pearl Jam blasted on the radio, and while alone, I allowed myself to fully enjoy the music, singing along to vent some of the upcoming stress.

The club, Posh, was empty save for the cleaners and the staff who were getting it ready for the night. I made my way up to my office on the second floor, shut the door with my foot, and then headed toward my desk, which sat before a massive floor-to-ceiling window that offered me a view of the club downstairs.

I took my seat and opened my drawer, picking up one of my favorite knives. I wasn't a knife kind of man, but this one in particular was special because of the person it was going to kill. Grigori Petrovich, Pakhan of the Russian Bratva and my sister's murderer.

I had been saving this blade for this job for four years now, waiting and planning how I was going to savor every moment of stabbing it into his heart. Offering no mercy. Only pain. Like he'd done with my sister. Stabbing her in the gut and leaving her there in the living room to bleed out. So, we could find her later on.

I could still remember the sight, the blood seeping onto the marble floor, painting it red. Her cries, the unrelenting fear in her eyes, the tremor in her hands, and finally, the empty gaze in her eyes, which were once filled with so much warmth.

I swallowed hard while gripping the knife, and closed my eyes, imagining Grigori's face and his own dead eyes when I killed him.

How sweet it would be.

It was a ritual of sorts. Every day, like a prayer I would stare at that knife and imagine the man I'd kill with it. A promise. A vow. Something to keep me going when the days grew long and cold. Even I, used to living in the dark, had days I felt lost. So, my promise to Bella was all I had left. My need for vengeance was stronger than the need for my next breath. Killing Grigori and his ilk was the reason God had put me on this earth.

The war with the Bratva might have started before I was even born, but my father was never ruthless, or cruel. He hadn't been strong enough to end them. My father didn't have the right motivation, as I had now. His untimely death due to a speeding accident made an impact on the Outfit, especially me. Now I was left to clean up his mess and deal with this shit.

I unlocked my phone again and ended up on the same gossip site from yesterday, only to be bombarded with a picture of Francesca and her late husband at a charity gala. I had done a thorough search of her this past week, mostly to scratch an itch. I had no idea why since I had no intentions of seeing her again.

After learning what I did, that Paolo Biancini mistreated Francesca, and allowed her to use drugs, all I wanted to do was kill him all over again. Torture Francesca's late husband for days, making sure he paid for what he did to her.

Paolo had been known to have a foot on the wild side. He ran my drug empire in Indianapolis, overseeing it for me. No wonder she had easy access to it. That didn't mean she should have. Francesca, as his wife and the wife of a *Mafiosi,* should have been protected from the darker aspects of our life.

Except from what I've heard, respect was the last thing she was given. The rumors I'd heard were that Francesca was nothing more than his trophy wife, placed high up on the shelf to collect dust while he fucked his mistresses. When he needed Francesca, he'd take her out and polish her until she looked like he desired.

No wonder I didn't recognize her that night. Something about her had been off, I simply couldn't decide whether Paolo Biancini managed to truly change her or if she was wearing a mask. An armor to protect herself. Neither of those options sat well with me.

Why would you care? Francesca was none of my business, not anymore. Perhaps, if I was being honest, she never had been. She had always belonged to someone else, even in the past when we dated in secret. She had been promised to another—I was the one who wanted a taste of the forbidden fruit. But I wanted what I wanted, and a Moretti always got what he desired one way or the other.

I've heard that repeating the same thing over and over again helped with making it sound truer. So that's what I did. I told myself that I didn't care about Francesca. I didn't. I couldn't.

My eyes closed, and I pinched my nose. When the traitorous thought was gone, I stood and headed toward my liquor cabinet, it was early and I didn't drink, not anymore, not since after Arabella's death. I filled a tumbler with water and used it to wash away the guilt that had lodged in my throat like a boulder.

You broke things off and let her go. You made your bed so now sleep in it.

I spied the bottles still full of liquor and imagined how easy it would be to wash it all away. A few sips, and I could bleach out the sour taste in my mouth. Except I had made a promise. To Bella. To me. To the Outfit.

After my father's death, someone needed to take over, and a grieving, drunkard had no place at the head of the Mafia. I stopped drinking and cleared my head, promising to never drink again. And for four years I didn't.

The ringing of my phone interrupted my thoughts, offering me a much-needed reprieve. "My office now," I hissed, ended the call, and threw my phone on the desk.

Today looked like one of those days that seemed too long and too damned annoying to survive with a clear head. But alas, here I was. The crown may sit heavily upon my head, but I had been groomed for this my entire life. If it were easy, any man would be doing it.

I sat in my chair again and waited, knife in hand. When the door creaked open and my brother's head peeked through, the blade went flying. "I called you three times," I snapped, running my thumb under my lips. The blade wobbled when my brother took it from where it had been embedded in the doorframe and held it closed. "If I wanted you dead, you would be—now sit down."

"You're in a peachy mood today. Is it Claire again? I told you to find someone else to put your little friend in," Vitelli grinned. "One of these days she's going to beg for you to put a ring on that finger."

"As if," I scoffed. Claire was nothing but a booty call, someone I fucked when the need arose. She knew that I knew that. Case solved. No ring on that finger—ever. "First, there is nothing little about me, and second, I called you thrice, Vitelli. *Thrice.*" Vitelli was still grinning like a cat who had his fill of cream. "Why the fuck are you smiling, your mood is making me nauseous."

Vitelli set the knife on my desk and ran his fingers through his bedhead hair. Indicating he had just woken up, and by the wrinkles on his shirt and the marks on his neck, he hadn't been alone. I sighed inwardly; when was he going to grow up?

"My apologies for insulting your manhood, brother—"

"Where were you? When your boss calls, I expect you to answer it, immediately."

"Even if I am inside someone?"

I pinched the bridge of my nose and seriously thought about using that blade on him. "Vitelli, how much do you enjoy keeping your neck attached to your head?"

"Okay... noted, next time I'll answer. What's so urgent you had me come in here so early on a Friday morning?"

"Romeo Ferraro has contacted me," I said simply, but the reaction on my brother's face had mirrored my own when I received the call last night.

"Romeo fucking Ferraro? *Il Diavolo?*"

I scoffed at the name. Devil my ass, the man was flesh and blood like all of us. The only difference was that there were insane men, and then there were men like Romeo Ferraro. He had made a name for himself by killing for the first time at the age of nine, and also his father and most of his underbosses. He'd taken control of New York in less than a few months and was now the undisputed Capo of the *Cosa Nostra*.

"When?" There was excitement in my brother's eyes but also apprehension.

"Yesterday," I answered, leaning back into my seat pretending to possess a calm I did not have. "He wants to set up a meeting. To discuss matters."

"Matters? What could we have to discuss with him?" Vitelli sneered. "The man is deranged. Killed all his men."

"His father's men," I reminded him. "Ferraro has been having problems with the Russians as well, perhaps he finally sees reason and decided to ask for my help."

Vitelli scoffed. "A man like him does not ask for help, Cassio."

"Neither do I." But alas, here I was, agreeing to a meeting with a man I never thought I would talk to—ever.

The Outfit and the *Famiglia* had never seen eye to eye. A few years back, a war between both Mafias had started thanks to a bloody wedding. No one knew who shot first, but in the end, five people had died. Romeo having killed two of them himself.

Peace between New York and Chicago hadn't been something I would have imagined, but despite his shortcomings and infamy, Romeo seemed like a man whom I could deal with. I would rather sit with real monsters than men who hid behind masks.

"There is something else." I tapped my fingers over the table. "Another one of our cargos has been stolen by the Russians, more than the last time."

"How did they know we were transporting it?" Vitelli said and stood up heading towards the liquor cabinet, opened a bottle, and served himself two fingers of Scotch. I didn't bother telling him it was ten in the morning.

"Luciano managed to question one of the culprits."

"What did he say?" Vitelli closed the cork and sipped.

"That our theory about having a spy in our midst is correct. The Russians are receiving info from a man calling himself *Volpe*."

"The fox," Vitelli chuckled. "Doesn't exactly inspire fear."

"Foxes are one of the most cunning animals in the world. Apparently, this spy is one egotistical fucker." I ran my thumb under my lips growing frustrated.

"Should we warn the Commission?"

I had pondered it before, but no, telling the rest of my underbosses would only create unnecessary chaos. "Let Luciano deal with it, for now."

As my enforcer, it was his job, he had eyes and ears in every corner of this city. Not to mention his other skills inside the questioning cell. If anyone could help me find who this *Volpe* was, it had to be Luciano.

"Will you warn Donato Manci?"

"No." The word slipped out effortlessly from my lips. "This stays between us."

Donato Manci, Francesca's father, had been my consigliere for the past four years. He had also been my father's, before his untimely death. The title was a decorative one at best. Everyone knew my true consigliere was Vitelli, but for appearances sake, and peace amongst my men, Donato was the one who played the part.

Unfortunately, I still needed him to maintain the bridge between the younger generations and the old traditionalist one—which Donato ruled over. Despite hating his guts and wishing I could use them to hang him, I needed the fucker and the support he offered me.

"We should just kill him and get this over with."

"Then what, I start a civil war? What do you think his supporters will do when I end him? I'm not Romeo Ferraro, I don't kill my own."

I had a bullet with Donato's name carved on it, and he had an expiration date, all I needed was a cause and a good enough reason to use it. Except the man was loyal to a fault and had never given me any doubt as to where his allegiances lay. He might not like me much either, but we had both learned to live in the same cage together—like two hungry lions.

"He will kill us, mark my words, brother," Vitelli pointed out somberly.

I had thought that, too, once, but Donato had lost his chance when I was weak and grieving. After my father's death—a few months after my sister's—Donato could have taken control of the Outfit. Risen above me and taken the crown and put it on his own head. He had had enough support to do so, but he never did. Instead, he followed me, he stood at my back and watched as I took control. If he wanted me dead, he would have done something already.

My brother and I sat for another hour discussing our future meeting with the New York Capo, as well as the growing problem with the Russians. While we talked, a nagging feeling at the back of my head wouldn't leave me alone.

"Did we ever catch the man who killed Paolo Biancini?" Vitelli frowned at my sudden change in subject.

"No," he said. "The assassin left no traces behind. We think he was a mercenary. Paolo's heart attack was legit, caused by poisoning."

"Aconite." I supplied the name of the poison that truly killed him. "Does anyone know?"

Vitelli shook his head. "We cleared the files and made sure no one would talk." That meant the files were torched and those who knew, now lay six feet under.

"Why would someone kill an old man?" I wondered aloud.

"Because he wasn't that old and was still strong as a horse. Someone wanted to speed up the process." Vitelli tapped the rim of his scotch which now sat untouched.

Someone who would gain a lot from killing the richest man in the Outfit. Most of his profit was redirected to our coffers, since he left no male heirs behind, but I was sure somewhere along the line, some of that money went somewhere else.

"Did we look into it?"

"Not really." Vitelli shrugged. "As I recall, you told me to let it die."

I recall now saying those words, but I had always held a grudge with the man, albeit unbeknownst to him. He had what I most wanted and couldn't have. The only reason he was on my mind was because of Francesca, and honestly, I wouldn't have cared about that idiot if it wasn't for her.

"Why are you thinking about that old fart right now?" Vitelli inquired.

"The shit you say makes me wonder if I punched you too hard when we were children." I couldn't help but chuckle. "Someone has to think about these things." I answered him.

"Do you want me to investigate it?" Vitelli asked as if this was the last thing he wanted to do.

I tapped my fingers against the table and took a deep breath. Was it worth opening that Pandora's box right now? With so much going on, did I really need one more problem to deal with?

Francesca's dilated pupils and a hazy gaze came to mind. Her nausea and messy appearance. Like she didn't give two fucks about what she was doing. As if she didn't care about anything or anyone, especially not herself. Seeing her in that cell, sitting on the floor like a fallen angel, had struck something within me. Thoughts that wouldn't be so easily replaced.

"Yes," I finally answered, both ashamed that I was doing so, and eager to find out more on the subject.

Vitelli nodded, drained the rest of his Scotch, and set the cup down. He made to leave but stopped halfway and turned again to face me. I could see it in his features that he had something to say, it was practically spilling from his mouth, yet he kept silent.

"I don't have all day, Vitelli, so spit it out."

"What are you doing next Friday night?" he asked.

"Working as I always am." Which was not a surprise.

"I..." He paused and looked at the ceiling. It was not like my brother to forget his words.

"You."

"I met someone, she's throwing a small party Friday and I want you to come." He finally spilled the words without stopping to breathe.

My eyes lingered on my brother, and I couldn't help but chuckle. "*You* met someone?"

He narrowed his eyes and clenched his jaw but nodded. "I've been seeing her for weeks now. Three to be specific."

That caught my attention, Vitelli didn't *see* women, he fucked, then left. I couldn't remember the last time he had been with the same woman twice. That's because it never happened. "You?"

"Yes, Cassio? Why is it so hard to believe?"

"Because you are always on my ass to find someone to fuck other than Claire, and here you are, telling me you *met* someone."

He looked at me in exasperation, knowing I had caught him. "She's different, Cassio." His eyes fucking twinkled when he said those words. "One night, it's all that I ask." One night. Could I escape my problems for one night?

"Your problems will still be here in the morning," Vitelli said, reading my mind. "Just come."

"No." The word slipped from my lips before I had a chance to truly process my brother's request.

"Cassio." It sounded awfully like a plea, and I stared at my brother as he sat up straighter in his chair. He seemed… awkward. Vitelli was nervous. "Everyone will be there, and I would like you to meet her, too. She's nice."

"Good for her."

"Can't you for fucking once do something for me?"

"I do it every day, Vitelli. I keep your ass from getting killed. I keep the streets you walk safe, and I keep the money in our bank accounts flowing."

"Fuck, Cassio." He shot from his chair and paced. I watched the scene before me in confusion. "I…like her."

"You like fucking women, Vitelli; you don't like them in particular." That caused him to stop and clenched his fists. I hadn't seen that kind of anger in my brother's eyes in a long time.

"She's different. I really like her. I have been seeing her for three weeks now. Almost a fucking month, Cassio. I didn't know it was fucking possible."

My brother sounded awfully stunned by his confession as he took a deep breath and plopped himself into the chair again. "It's one night."

One night. A lot of things could happen in one night. Distractions allowed for errors, and errors allowed for problems.

Fuck it.

"Text me the address," I said and raised my finger. "For a few hours, nothing more."

Vitelli tried to hide his grin but failed. "Yes, Boss."

5

FRANCESCA

"You're a terrible friend, *chérie*." Antoine kissed both my cheeks and grabbed my hands. He stared at me with his all-seeing eyes and shook his head. "What did I tell you?"

"Sorry." I smiled shyly, tempting him not to be angry at me. "I got carried away."

"You need to answer the phone, Frankie." He pulled me down onto the sofa next to him. "I was worried, you should have called me when you got home."

I knew that. Antoine and Marie had grilled me hundreds of times about answering my damned phone, but I never did. It wasn't intentional, after all, they were the only two people I spoke to.

"I know." My cheeks burned with shame. "I'm all right." *Now.* The word almost slipped through my lips.

Antoine eyed me suspiciously, knowing there was much more to the story, but decided not to press me further, at least not right now. At that moment, Marie arrived with Jasmine tea and a few chocolate bonbons I loved.

Reginald's little head lifted as he sniffed the treats, and he stood to sniff what Marie had brought for us. "I haven't forgotten you, baby." She produced a dog treat from her pocket and offered him the small bone. He barked in excitement and twirled around with the bone in his mouth.

A few seconds later, he came to lay by my feet and rested down to eat his treat as we served ourselves tea. Jasmine scent filled my nose, and I inhaled deeply, enjoying the scent of my favorite drink in the world.

"So, now that she's here," Antoine began. "Tell her the news." He clapped his hands eagerly.

"What news?"

"I'm having a party on Friday."

I looked at my friend suspiciously. Although Marie was not a saint, she and I couldn't be more different. While I indulged in alcohol, the strongest drink she had during the day was coffee. While I lost myself in drugs, she enjoyed meditation. She was the sun, and I was the moon. Yet we fit somehow. Two completely different peas in a pod.

"A party?"

"No need to sound so suspicious." Marie set her teacup on the table. "It's for a good cause."

"You mean a charity then?" That fit her better.

Her father was Remy Bousset, one of the richest men in France, and from what I knew and had overheard, he was one of the Outfit's greatest suppliers. Marie had a falling out with her father after he threatened to disown Antoine for being gay. As a fuck you to her father, she spent his money by giving it to charity—as much as she could.

Antoine and Marie exchanged a glance, then they both looked at me. "I have something to tell you, please don't be mad."

"Why would I?" The truth was, I also had something to say, except I wasn't courageous enough to do so.

"I didn't want to hurt you, and I meant to tell you when it started, but with the move and your father's threats and..." Marie paused, offering me a tight smile. "I'm seeing someone." She announced. I was stunned into silence. "Aren't you going to say something?"

I opened my mouth and then closed it. "As in dating?"

Marie nodded tightly. "It happened the day we moved in, we met at a coffee shop down the street." She bit her lip and looked at me, waiting for my anger to surface. "Our orders were accidentally switched, and one thing led to another, and now..."

"You're seeing him," I mused, still working on believing what I'd heard.

Her cheeks pinken, and she nodded. "It was all so fast, I didn't mean for it to happen like that, I wanted to tell you. "She said again.

"Why didn't you?" I wasn't angry, but I was hurt that my best friend had forgotten to tell me something major had happened in her life.

"Well, *chérie*," Antoine looked at me. "You're not exactly at your best right now." He tapped my hand in the typical Antoine fashion. Spilling whatever was in his head and not caring about it.

He wasn't wrong though, was he?

"I just wish you'd have told me." I pointed out, unable to contain my saddened state.

"Tell me about him." I decided I couldn't judge my friend for keeping a secret when I was, too.

"He's perfect, Frankie." She beamed, and that's when I knew my friend was a goner. Marie rarely involved herself with men.

Although we were part of the same world, hers was filled with all kinds of freedom mine did not possess. She could date whomever she wanted and not be branded a harlot for doing so. She could choose whom to marry and, if she wished, to divorce later. Marie had the choice to make choices.

Men were something else entirely, she had never involved herself with someone, at least not romantically. For her to be doing so now, meant she was really into this sexy guy she was telling me about.

"Does he have a name?"

"It's a surprise. I want you to *know* him and draw your own conclusions." She smiled brightly, as though she was thinking about him at that moment.

"You'll come, right?"

I felt Antoine's eyes on me like he knew something he shouldn't. I knew eventually he would scold me for using again, and I was waiting for the moment the bomb dropped. "I'll come," I said eventually.

Marie sighed and then smiled. She stood to grab her notepad so we could begin the plans for the 'small' party she was having. When she left to grab more tea, I reached down to grab Reggie who was begging for some snuggle time. I sat him beside Antoine and me like a barrier.

Slowly my friend turned, his almond-brown eyes finding mine. "I haven't told her yet."

I sighed. "I will."

"How did you leave the party?" he asked. "You should have called, I was worried."

"I honestly forgot, Antoine." I scratched Reggie's ear to keep myself from looking at him.

I loved my friends, dearly. They stuck with me when I needed them the most. After Paolo's death, all my so-called friends left me. Marie and Antoine had stayed and had followed me all the way to Chicago.

They had seen the true me, the woman behind the mask, the woman who wore one because she no longer knew who lived behind it. The siblings had seen me at my worst, and at my darkest moments.

They had never shown any signs of judgment but telling them I had been arrested for assaulting an officer and drug possession was too far, even for me. It was a new low on my ever-growing list.

Not to mention the one person I had been trying to avoid the entire week. He'd attached himself to my brain like tar. He wouldn't leave me alone, and the worst part was that my brain seemed to want him there. It grew eager every time Cassio showed up. It reminded me of Reginald whenever I arrived home. It was pathetic. Certainly unacceptable.

"You look sour," Antoine said calling me back to earth.

Cassio made me like that. All it took was to think about him and my stomach churned, but not always in a bad way. There were...fluttering. Butterflies that took flight when I thought about him. Butterflies I was going to kill with the strongest pesticide I could find. They had no business being there.

"I was just remembering something," I said. "But don't worry, everything is fine." I took my tea and took a deep sip from the warm liquid. I could feel him narrowing his eyes in suspicion, but he didn't say a word as Marie came back.

"So," she looked at both of us. "Where do we start?"

Two hours later, we had everything planned for a not so small party. Marie had said only a few friends, but the list had gone up to a hundred people. Apparently, her new boyfriend was one popular hottie.

Seeing her happiness stirred something within me that had been dormant for a while, but it also brought with it another feeling I'd rather not experience. Not when it came to her. Jealousy was a horrible thing and was eating away at my insides and leaving me hollow. I didn't want to be that way... to feel what I did. Marie deserved everything she wanted in life. This man she was dating, she deserved to be happy with him, to live out what she had always dreamed of.

She was seldom a romantic, pretending not to care about the men who fell at her feet. But I knew the truth, Marie was waiting for the one, the guy who would sweep her off her feet and carry her into a new life of wonders.

The jealousy I was experiencing had nothing to do with men. It was the purity of her happiness, how her smile reached her ears, her pale skin glowed and her brown eyes burned bright like two bowls of molten sugar. I couldn't recall the last time I looked in the mirror and saw myself that way. At some point, that light that had burned bright at my core, had dimmed and had been put out. Was it during my marriage? Was it before? I couldn't recall and that was what scared me the most.

Marie was talking to her brother, and I excused myself to use the bathroom, Reggie trailing behind me like the good boy he was. Once the door closed, I leaned against it taking deep breaths, trying to calm this wave of anxiety that had hit me out of nowhere, blindsiding me completely. These moments were growing more frequent as the days passed.

I had tried visiting a doctor once, one specifically chosen by Paolo. After all, he didn't want his wife's dirty laundry exposed for anyone to hear. The doctor had given me pills that numbed me, took my pain away, and left me in a haze. Back then, they had been my saving grace, everything I had asked for. It was better to live a life in oblivion and pretend everything was fine.

There was a knock on the door that startled me. "Frankie, you okay?" came Marie's voice.

I stared at the ceiling and sighed.

"Yeah, just getting out."

I flushed the toilet and took my time washing my hands. When I opened the door, my best friend was planted on the other side, both hands on her hips.

She knew. Damn it, Antoine.

Marie didn't say a word, but none were needed, the way she was looking at me spoke volumes. I bypassed her and headed toward the living room to find that her brother was gone. So, he'd dropped the bomb, shit hit the fan, and I had to deal with it.

Marie followed me into the room, took a seat on the couch, and crossed her legs. I did the same, ready for the interrogation to begin. Instead of waiting, I blurted out the truth.

"I used."

"I know, Antoine told me, said you were bat shit crazy." She didn't sound sad or judgmental, but I could see that damned pity in her eyes. I hated that worst of all. "What happened? You were doing so well, Frankie."

Yeah. Then life happened. "I needed some reprieve."

Marie nodded as if she understood but she didn't; she couldn't begin to understand what it meant to need an escape from your life. To run away if only for a fleeting moment. To be someone else.

"I'm glad you left your apartment, but you should have taken baby steps."

I fisted my hands and dug my nails into the palms of my hands. Fighting with Marie right now was the last thing I wanted. "It was once."

She arched her brows slightly and gave me that knowing look that said she knew it wasn't just once. "Remember what we talked about, when you feel the need to use, call me."

But if I had called Marie, she would have told me not to use, and that was the last thing I needed that night. Taking baby steps hadn't worked out. "Doesn't really matter," I said in contempt. "It was the last stash I had and now it's gone. Can we move on from this subject?"

Marie opened her mouth ready to argue back but nodded. "As you wish."

Twisting my hair and bringing it forward, I kept my gaze on my dog who rested at my feet. I wasn't ready to meet Marie's gaze yet and it bothered me that we were back to this. Her always worrying, always suspicious that I was doing something wrong, or possibly dangerous. Marie was going to have a heart attack if she knew I had been arrested. That's why I wasn't going to tell her that.

"I'm trying, Marie," I confessed as I looked at the palm of my hands, more specifically at the indents from my nails. "I really am."

She stood up and came to sit beside me and wrapped her arm around me bringing me in for a side hug. I rested my head on her shoulder and inhaled her patchouli perfume. It was so her, so comforting.

"I'm sorry if this is going to sound terrible," she began, "but I am glad Paolo is dead."

I swallowed hard and kept quiet.

"He was horrible to you."

"He wasn't the only one to blame." I didn't know why I was defending him, but it was the truth. Paolo hadn't broken me entirely, there had been cracks in my armor before I even married him.

"I know, your father is an ass, too."

I couldn't help myself, I chuckled. Ass was a nice way to put it.

"I should probably tell you something." I sat up straighter and patted my clothes, all to keep from looking at her. Marie sat patiently waiting for whatever I had to say. I worked the words in my head searching for the best way to tell her. "My father has found me another husband."

"W-what!" Her eyes widened. "Can he do that?"

I nodded. Donato could do anything he pleased and there was no one who could stop him.

"But you told me a widow has a year to mourn her husband's passing."

I shrugged. "Outfit laws work differently for my father; he bends them to his will when he pleases."

Marie didn't speak for a long while, then said, "Do you know him?"

"No, but it doesn't really matter, the deal is done."

"Frankie." She reached for my hand. "What can we do?"

My heart broke at her use of the word 'we.' She was my friend through thick and thin. "Wait," I said in defeat.

"Don't." She shook me. "You can't give up like that."

There was nothing to be done. Donato had already chosen my next husband, and once again, I had no choice in the matter. It was all a transaction between the buyer and seller. I was the product... cattle.

"We'll figure a way out of this. There must be a way out of it," she said with determination.

I could see the wheel in her head spinning as she tried to figure out a way to free me from yet another arranged marriage. We both knew it was futile because there was no way out, yet I didn't have the heart or the courage right then to tell her that.

I nodded, lacking her conviction for positive thinking.

"Promise me you won't give up.' She squeezed my hand.

"I'll try."

"Francesca," she scolded me. "You're going to be happy and free by the end of this year. Mark my words. Trust me on this, I know what I'm saying."

I chuckled. Not to be a pessimist or anything, but I had experienced happiness and it had ended in heartbreak, the kind that had me searching for those broken pieces years after the damage was done.

Happiness was perhaps a stretch, but freedom... I wanted that above all else. To be able to wake up in the mornings and not have to worry about doing or saying the right things all the time. To be free to choose what clothes to wear and who to be. Freedom to laugh, to shout, to cry, and to remain silent when I damned well pleased.

Most importantly, it was freedom from this act, this character I was playing and didn't know how to stop. An actress was what I had become, and I didn't know how to let go of her.

"We'll figure this out," Marie said again, this time softer.

"Yeah," I agreed but didn't dare get my hopes up.

6
CASSIO

I parked my car before the building in the West Loop and looked upward. From down here, I couldn't see a thing, other than a few lights flashing from one of the apartments, the penthouse to be more specific. I'd changed into more casual clothes for the night, donning a pair of old jeans, a white dress shirt and my second favorite coat, since my other one was currently with Francesca. I wondered if she still snuggled her nose against the collar to inhale my scent. She'd done that a couple of times, I'd noticed, while driving her home.

Unsure why I was thinking about Francesca again—oh yes, my coat—I grabbed it from the back seat and put it on. I made my way into the luxurious lobby and offered my name to the receptionist who let me through without a fuss. Inside the elevator, I stared at the doors and adjusted my sleeves. I hated these gatherings. Always had. I had never been one for small talk. I enjoyed that people often thought me to be unapproachable.

When the elevator finally arrived, I breathed in through my nose and let the air out slowly. Despite my obese bank account, I was a very private man, keeping from the tabloids and the media. The only events I actually enjoyed attending were charity galas, but that was only so I could flaunt my money in the faces of those politicians who thought themselves better than me.

Vitelli's 'small' party was anything but, then again, my brother never did anything half-assed—he enjoyed the scene, the loud voices, and the music. He thrived in environments like these. I was almost suffocated by the cacophony of voices in the room. As I watched my surroundings—always aware of where I was—I noticed most of the faces I knew were members of the Outfit.

Meandering through the crowd, and for the hundredth time wondering what the hell I was doing there, I searched for my brother.

Vitelli wasn't hard to find as a circle of people had formed around him. I stopped short in my tracks as I spotted the woman beside him.

Marie LeRoy was not who I expected her to be. She barely reached my brother's shoulder even though she was wearing blood red heels. Her hair was tied in a slick ponytail, her makeup clean and natural. Her clothes were elegant and chic, wearing a dress that hugged her petite form and landed just below her knees. She was every bit the woman I would never have imagined my brother would date.

Not because she wasn't beautiful — she was, with almond-colored eyes and a beauty mark right above her red lips—but because this was not the kind of woman I had seen my brother with. They were usually… escorts or women he picked up at our clubs.

After my initial shock, I made my way toward the couple, not once failing to notice that my brother had his arm wrapped around her in a possessive manner that warned every man in the near vicinity that she was his. I couldn't help the ghost of a smile that graced my face. Vitelli was so lost in her, he didn't even realize how pussy whipped he'd become. My brother was now taken, and that was hilarious.

The moment he saw me, he pushed through two men surrounding him and pulled Marie along, cutting the conversation short. "Vitelli." I extended my hand, and my brother grabbed my forearm in greeting.

"Brother, this is Marie—"

"Pretty much figured," I said, nodding towards Vitelli's hand on hers.

"So, you're the brother I've heard so much about," she said as a way of greeting.

I shoved my hands into my pockets and nodded. "Do I meet your expectations?"

She smiled, white teeth shining. This woman was so out of my brother's league, it was going to be fun watching him grovel.

"I thought your entrance would have been more dramatic. Guns blazing, bullets ricocheting." Vitelli's hand on her waist clenched. Marie must have noticed she said something wrong because her smile faltered.

So, she knew about the family business.

"Sorry to disappoint," I said lightly, even adding a tight smile. "Next time, I'll think of something more entertaining. We can dim the lights and add some smoke, or is that too much?"

Both of them relaxed and Marie even managed to laugh a bit, I could be entertaining and sociable when I wanted, the thing was I almost never wanted to.

I wondered how much my brother had shared about the lives we lived. If she knew who these people in her house were and what they did for a living?

"*Merde*," Marie cursed. "Would you excuse me for a second?" she asked and left before Vitelli had a chance to answer.

I watched as my brother followed her with his eyes, as she headed toward a group of girls that were trying to pop open a massive bottle of champagne that probably cost more than they earned in a year.

I wondered to myself who had invited that crowd. As I watched the flock of loud women, one of them caught my attention. Her blonde hair was loose and her dress so tight, I could see the outline of her underwear. I knew instantly that it wasn't Francesca, but my stomach tightened either way. When she looked at me and smiled, I finally breathed.

It wasn't her.

Taking my eyes off the blonde chick, I looked around the room. "So, Marie knows about us."

"Her father is Remy Bousset," Vitelli explained, catching me by surprise.

Remy was the Outfit's supplier and one of the oldest in the business. Whatever I needed, the man could find. "When were you going to tell me?"

"When you actually gave a fuck."

I cocked one brow at my brother's attitude.

"Either way, she took her mother's maiden name after some falling out with her father. Apparently, he threatened to disown his own son."

Again, my curiosity pricked. "Why?"

Vitelli looked at his girlfriend—whatever she was—as though she could hear his words. "Because her brother prefers the company of men if you know what I mean."

I nodded in understanding, even if I didn't agree with Remy's actions. The world we lived in was a harsh place and not everyone could survive.

"I haven't told her anything else. She knows about me because she saw my gun, the actual weapon," He smirked. "I would never betray—"

I stopped him right there. "I know you won't, I trust *you*, Vitelli."

"Thank you."

I placed a hand on my brother's shoulders and warned him. "But —don't ever make me doubt that trust. If she ever puts you or our safety in danger, I won't think twice,"

Vitelli tensed under my heavy hand, and looked away and I followed his gaze, which landed on Marie. "She won't," he said with certainty and adoration.

I hoped he was right because if something ever happened, my brother would never be the one to take the brunt of the fall—she would. If I had to, I would kill her to protect Vitelli, no hesitation.

When Marie returned, she was pulled into Vitelli's arms and

chuckled when he whispered something in her ear. "Cassio," she called swatting his brother away. "Vitelli tells me you're single,"

I narrowed my eyes as I glared at my brother. I was and pretended to stay that way until the pressure of marriage and siring an heir grew too heavy for me to carry. "I have a friend I want you to meet, she should have been here by now, but she's always running late."

"I'm not—"

"Oh, there she is." Marie interrupted me and quickly excused herself plunging into the crowd.

When I turned toward my brother, he had his hands up in the air.

"This is not on me," he said quickly.

"Better not be," I snapped.

"She's just a girl, Cassio, what's got your panties in a twist?" Vitelli chuckled. "Plus, it's a change from fucking the same chick all the time."

"Boys, this is my friend, Frankie," Marie said, and I slowly began to turn. When I did, my entire body froze, air got stuck in my lungs, and I gawked like a fool at the woman who stood before me, or better...

At Francesca fucking Manci.

FRANCESCA

"He's nice, Frankie," Marie said as she pulled me from the hallway into her home. "You owe me for being late."

I rolled my eyes and said nothing as I took in the environment around me. It was filled with people...I recognized. I pulled back and came to a stop. "Where did you say you met your guy again?"

"At a coffee shop down the street," Marie said tugging at my hand.

"Yeah," I mumbled. "Okay."

So why did I recognize these people? Well, not all of them, but some were people from my past. Men and women who had frequented the same church as me, had gone to the same weddings, events, and galas.

This was the last place I wanted to be right now. I couldn't be near them; I could already begin to feel their judging gazes on me. Maybe it was in my head, but I could see some of them leaning in to exchange the newest piece of gossip. Our world was a small one, like money, gossip was what made our blood pump. It spread quicker than wildfire and took longer to put out.

Coming here wasn't a good idea. Especially because today hadn't been the best of days. Mother had a relapse, her chemo wasn't working, and she had been in one of her moods. Reginald ate one of my socks and had a stomachache, and to top it all off, Donato had called me again, insisting that I return home.

Marie had planned her party and had been texting me all day. She had been buzzing around me like a bee, as though she knew I wanted to cancel. Things would have been better if I had something to numb my anxiety and settle my nerves.

Tonight, I was nothing but a ticking time bomb waiting to detonate, and I feared the disaster that would follow.

"Will you stop fretting," Marie mumbled as we headed toward the two men she wanted me to meet. This brought me back to the problem at hand. "As I said, he was a perfect gentleman, and you're going to like him. Not to mention he's terribly hot."

"You know I'm not interested," I said, reaching for the servant who was roaming around with shots on her tray. Marie watched me swallow the transparent liquid with narrowed eyes. "I'm detoxing, Marie. No men."

What difference would it make when I was already promised to another? What was the point in putting in all the effort, when in the end, I was going to have another man's ring on my finger? So no, I wasn't interested.

"This is not about what we talked about, is it?" I asked, knowing fully well it was. Marie wasn't going to give up. She loved a lost cause too much.

She smiled dismissively, but I knew the truth. She stopped and turned to face me, grabbed my shoulders, and stared me deep in the eyes. "I don't often say this, and it's probably unadvisable, but have some fun, Frankie. You're a twenty-three-year-old gorgeous bombshell. He's going to fall for you instantly."

I sighed loudly, my shoulders sagging. "I'm not going to escape this, am I?"

"No, you won't." She smiled and we resumed walking toward the back of her living room where the men were.

"How long have you known him?"

"For a few minutes, tops."

I looked at the ceiling and laughed in desperation. Marie was on a roll today. When we cleared most of the crowd and reached the men, a strange sensation settled over me, like a premonition. Or rather a déjà vu. They had their backs to us, both men were tall and broad-shouldered. One had light brown hair that curled around his ears and neck, while the other had a messy mop of dark curls. Even looking at his back, I could tell that the tallest of them didn't look as comfortable as the one beside him. There was a slight tension in his shoulders and the way he tapped his fingers repetitively against his leg.

At least I wasn't the only one who was anxious.

"Boys, this is my friend, Frankie," Marie said, and on cue, they both turned to face me.

My legs stopped, my feet turned to lead, and they kept me from being able to breach the distance between myself and the two men. It was at that moment that I knew I shouldn't have come.

The entire party dissolved around me, blurring at the edges, and then disappearing entirely. My eyes landed on Cassio Moretti. He was standing as still as a statue, and I wasn't sure he was even breathing. I watched as his pine-green eyes turned arctic as he slowly came to realize who was standing before him.

In that couple of seconds, my mind went blank, and then all I could think about was how fast I could run away from the party without being caught. Perhaps I could make it to the door in five seconds tops. Not in these shoes I wouldn't.

Damn it.

Damn him.

It had been a week since I had seen Cassio and to my greatest displeasure, he looked even better now than he did before. "Frankie?" Marie nudged me, and I realized I had been rudely staring at Cassio. "Why are you glaring at my guest?" *Glaring?* Marie whispered pulling me closer towards the group. "Guys this is—"

"Francesca Manci," the second man supplied, and that's when I realized it was Vitelli Moretti, Cassio's younger brother.

"What?" Marie was taken aback. "How do you know her?"

Vitelli came forward and as though not even a single year had gone by, he brought me in for a hug, his strong arms wrapping around me. The action was awkward—on my part—I had no idea what to do, so I patted him lightly on the back until he let go.

"I can't believe it's you," he chuckled lightly.

"Frankie?" Marie arched her brows in a silent question.

"What kind of name is Frankie?" Cassio finally offered, his tone bland and detached.

"Mine," I snapped and offered Marie my attention. "We grew up together, sort of."

"She and my sister were best friends," Vitelli supplied, and I couldn't help but feel a sudden rush of pain in my heart. We hadn't been close; we had been skin and bone. Sisters.

From the corner of my eye, I noticed Cassio's nose flared at the mention of his sister, but he said nothing of the matter.

"I didn't know that." Marie said, looking at me. "Well, Frankie, since you already know each other, I don't need to present you to the *guy*," Marie said speaking closer to me so neither of them would hear.

My insides twisted at that moment. I had completely forgotten what tonight was all about. Me meeting Marie's new boyfriend or whatever they were right now. I stood there perplexed and slightly horrified as she moved toward one of them.

A voice that had been silenced for an eternity came back to life and screamed in my head as I watched my friend reach out, hand outstretched toward one of the Moretti's. Was the man she had been gushing about for an entire week, Cassio? Was he the one that had put those heart-shaped signs in my friend's eyes?

It couldn't be.

Certainly, it wasn't Cassio. I mean... *Cassio?* It didn't make sense. The man who had rescued me from prison and had broken my heart wasn't capable of love. But that was a lie, wasn't it?

I had loved him once. Desperately. Cassio had been the air I breathed, pure and fresh and reviving. And I thought he had loved me too.

The scene before me seemed to take an eternity to unfold and I watched. Eventually, Vitelli reached out and took her hand, interlocked his fingers with Marie's, and brought her closer into his arms.

I sighed. Unfortunately, it was loud enough that it was probably heard by everyone at the party. Annoyed and greatly angered with myself, I plastered a fake smile on my face and pretended I hadn't freaked out a moment ago.

Everything is fine. Everything is fine. Everything is fine.

I sang the mantra in my head, maybe if I said it enough times, I was going to be fine, and survive this party. Then Cassio looked at me with cold eyes. His gaze traveled up my golden heels, all the way to my dark blue dress that was a bit too short for my liking.

Paolo had been the one to buy me this dress and he liked them as short as possible. The dress made me uncomfortable, but I still hadn't gone shopping, so I didn't have much choice in the wardrobe department.

His gaze then roamed upward landing on my chest and my exposed collarbones. Slowly it trailed upwards to eventually meet my eyes. There was something in them aside from the iciness. When his thumb ran under his lower lip, I knew what it was... annoyance.

He was annoyed at me, and we hadn't even exchanged two words. I shot him a sweet smile, pretending I hadn't noticed the gloom and doom emanating from him. He was *not* going to ruin this party for me. I was already nervous as it was, Cassio had no business in making things worse than they already were.

"Did you lose something?" I asked when he wouldn't take his eyes off me. He didn't answer. "If you're going to keep staring, you might as well take a picture, it lasts longer." With that, I excused myself and left, my heart beating against my throat and hands shaking.

How could one man elicit such emotions from me without even opening his mouth? Damn him for existing.

7

FRANCESCA

The alcohol was doing wonders. My head was spinning and everything was hilarious. That heavy weight over my shoulders was nothing but a feather now. A small, albeit insignificant reminder of what had transpired when I arrived.

A server passed me by, and I reached for two shots of fireball. "Shots for *mon chérie*." I placed it in Antoine's hand, almost spilling the contents. He laughed and clinked the cup with me as we drank.

I was going to reach for another one when he pulled me back and sent the server away. "Maybe some water now, *chérie*." He took my cup and set it on the kitchen counter.

"Last one, I promise," I said.

"You said that the last time, you're not convincing me now, *mon amour*." He kissed my cheek and then proceeded to grab a glass from the cabinet and fill it with water. "You're already drunk, Frankie." He pushed the water toward me when I refused like a petulant child.

I hated water, especially since it could possibly make me less drunk and that was not what I wanted nor needed tonight. I didn't care if people were going to judge me, all I wanted was to silence the voices in my head.

Antoine ran his hand across my cheek and removed a few strands of hair that had fallen over my face. The touch might have looked intimate but between us it was common. Antoine was a hugger and a toucher. I was used to it and had even grown dependent on his touch. Like a dog who offered his belly for pats. I leaned against his soothing touch, my skin burning and my head spinning.

Maybe I was drunk.

"What's going on, Frankie?" When he used my name like that, I knew he was on to something.

"I'm having fun."

With his hand still cupping my face, he shook his head. "Francesca, you're trying to get drunk, not have fun. I have seen you like this before and we both know how it ended."

With an IV bag and a needle in my vein. A massive black hole in my memory and bruises from Paolo's fists. I couldn't remember what had happened first, the fighting or the partying, but either way, Antoine was right.

"Don't be so dramatic. A bit of fireball never killed nobody," I teased.

His hand dropped from my face, and he stepped away, placing the half-empty cup on the sink. "So, nothing's going on?"

"If you're worried, don't be." My tone was harsher than I wished it to be. The truth was, something *was* going on, and Antoine had no right in sniffing it out so easily. The man was like a cat after a mouse when it came to drama.

He watched me for a second, looked at something or someone behind me, and smirked. "So, this has nothing to do with the man that has been eye fucking you for the past hour?"

"What?" I choked on my saliva.

Antoine furrowed his brow and offered me a look that said I was either blind or dumb. "The same man you have been staring daggers at all night."

To make his point clearer, he stared at Cassio whom I shamefully knew was standing surrounded by women, one of them was almost hiking up his leg and arms.

"Stop doing that." I slapped his arm.

"Oh, *chérie*, he knows," Antoine waved his hand in dismissal. My cheeks blazed, and I turned so that my back was offered to Cassio.

"So, something is going on." He wiggled his brows.

"He's Vitelli's brother," I explained and for good measure added. "Nothing more." Because with Antoine, nothing could happen with a man without it being "something more."

"Yeah, I know, *chérie*, but that doesn't explain the tension between you two. I'm almost going blind with how thick it is."

I rolled my eyes. *What tension?* I needed something to drink, this subject was making me sober. There was no tension between us, Cassio had been avoiding me, and I had made sure I was as far away from him as humanly possible.

Unsure why I did it, I stared at Cassio in time to catch him already looking at me. From afar, it was hard to tell if he was either bored out of his mind or angry to the point, he wanted to kill someone. It was hard to tell when he did such a good job of lying. From what I recalled; he hated these kinds of events. A part of me was having fun knowing how uncomfortable he was, or rather not by the looks of the woman in his arms.

She said something and he responded causing her to laugh. I swallowed hard wishing I had some strong liquid to wash out that bitter taste in my mouth. Why did I care if she laughed, or that she was all over him for the last hour or so, and he didn't seem to mind? I didn't care, it was not my place.

Before Antoine could stop me, I grabbed another shot and downed it quickly, raised the empty cup in a toast, and set it on the counter, and turned around again, not daring to look long enough to catch Cassio's reaction.

"I sense some history between you two," Antoine pointed, stealing my attention.

"No," I answered all too quickly. "I used to know him."

"He seems intent on getting to know you again," Antoine pointed.

"I'm not interested," I said plainly, but once more a bit too quick for my liking.

True. I had suffered greatly because of him, and four years later I still had some open wounds that refused to heal and scarred me deeply. I didn't want to get involved with Cassio ever again. If he was the last man left on earth and I was the last woman, humanity would end with the both of us.

"Four months is a long time to be celibate," Antoine—who did not know the meaning of celibacy—said.

"Antoine," I chided. "I just lost my husband."

He rolled his eyes. "Paolo is dead, not you. Stop pretending as if your life ended when his did." Antoine had never been a fan of Paolo's and he liked making that clear. "If you want to sleep around then just do it. No one is going to judge you."

But they would. He might know about the Outfit, but he wasn't a part of it. Antoine did not understand that in my world, women did not *fuck* around. The only man they had sexual relationship with was their husbands—when it pleased them to do so.

This time when I did look back, Cassio was gone, and so was the woman in his arms. Unconsciously, my eyes searched the party, but I didn't catch sight of them. A flicker of something a lot like hatred stirred within, and I let it fester for a while. Four years was a long time to overcome our breakup. People didn't even know we had dated, but it still felt like a punch to the stomach.

One thing was to know he was fucking around, and another was witnessing it. I despised how that made me feel little. Cassio always had all the power to manipulate me in his hands, that hadn't changed. Four years later, and I was the one running away with my tail tucked between my legs while he walked with his head held high. Four years and it still stung watching him flirt with another woman.

Why do you care if he's with other women. You should be happy, at least he's not bothering you.

I left Antoine and headed outside. The chilly night air kissed my skin, and I warded it off by hugging myself. It was too cold out here, but it was better than staying in there knowing Cassio and that girl were somewhere in there doing God knew what.

"Francesca?"

I turned around and found that none other than Gianluca Gallo was walking toward me. He hadn't changed much since the last time I saw him at my wedding. He had been my older brother Savio's best friend, and his father was Donato's right-hand man, Enzo. We had grown up together, I hadn't liked him then, and I had a feeling nothing had changed much.

"Gianluca Gallo," I greeted, giving him a polite smile, although this wasn't a pleasant surprise.

"I didn't expect to find you here."

"I could say the same," I returned.

"Sorry about your husband. It is not really a surprise though, the man was ancient," he said plainly.

It wasn't a jab or a joke. Gianluca was never a sensible man. He spoke what came to mind, and he didn't care what people thought about him.

"I've heard you're practically married," I changed the subject.

He chuckled and shook his head. "Nah, we're just fucking around."

"Oh." It wasn't what I had heard. The poor girl was in for a heartbreak.

But I couldn't really blame her, could I? Not when I had fallen for a man who made me fall for him and then threw me away like I was trash.

I reached for the bottle of water I'd brought with me, took a few gulps, and then closed it. Needing something to do with my hands. The alcohol was still in my system, but it was slowly releasing its claws from my mind.

We both stood there in awkward silence, and I didn't know what to do or say. He had never been my favorite person. He had been my brother's friend, never mine, therefore, I never made an effort to talk to him. Gianluca's eyes roamed over my body and an uncomfortable sensation coursed through me.

"You've grown."

"It's the natural process of life," I said simply and watched as he settled his hand inside his jacket pockets and that's when I saw a pack of cigarettes. "You smoke?" I asked.

"I'm trying to stop. You?"

"Yes, to smoking, and no to the stopping." I hadn't had one of those in years.

I didn't like the taste of it in my mouth, or the smell that remained on my fingers. In fact, I didn't like it at all, but I needed something to do, and smoking seemed like a good idea.

Gianluca pulled out a Zippo, and lit up one cigarette, and put the rest of the pack inside his pocket. He took a deep drag and then offered it to me.

I inhaled deeply and let the smoke settle into my lungs. When I exhaled, I ended up coughing. "Shit," I laughed. "It's too strong."

Gianluca smiled and took the cigarette from my hands. "That's weird," he nodded toward the living room. "Never thought Vitelli Moretti would get married." *So, small talk it is. Great.*

I grinned broadly. "Marie is a good girl. I just can't believe she fell for Vitelli of all people."

"Who would have thought," he mused. "Young love grows in the strangest of places."

I reached for the cigarette, and he moved away, I tried again, but Gianluca sidestepped. He pulled it from his mouth and smiled. "If I'd known you would turn out this beautiful, I might have married you back then."

My smile fell. "Who says I would have married you?"

He stepped closer to me and lifted my chin with his fingers, "You wouldn't have had a choice." I slapped his hand away and he laughed, I rolled my eyes. "But now you are no longer pure are you, you have lost your value."

My jaw dropped. "*Vaffanculo*," I snapped. This wasn't fun anymore. I turned to leave, but he grabbed my hand and pulled me back to him. "Let me go, Gianluca," I warned.

"What the fuck did you just say to me?"

I swallowed hard at the anger in his eyes. He gripped my wrists tighter, and I winced. Gianluca took a deep drag and then breathed the smoke out on my face.

I looked away and begged him. "Let go of me, Gianluca."

"We are not done talking, Francesca," he lifted his hand, and I flinched. Gianluca watched me and then laughed. "You know what they used to call him, Paolo 'heavy hands' Biancini."

I had known that my husband did in fact have heavy hands and had experienced just how heavy they were whenever we fought.

"Let go of me, Gianluca," I tried yet again, starting to lose my patience.

"Or what? There's no one out here. The music is loud."

I looked around and noticed we were indeed alone in a very private area. I'd come out here for that and now I realized my mistake. Panic flourished like flowers in spring.

"If I wanted, I could kiss you right here."

I pulled back, but he brought me forward, wrapping his arm around me. I leaned back, trying my hardest to stay away.

"I always wanted to taste you; did you know that?"

I swallowed bile.

"To know if the girl next door tasted as sweet as she looked," he laughed. "Well, not as sweet anymore, are you?" He pressed me tighter against him.

From behind Gianluca, I saw Cassio marching toward us in a madman's haste. I could see a bright fire burning in his eyes. He was going to rip Gianluca's head off.

"Cassio, don't!" Someone shouted.

8

FRANCESCA

It was all I heard before Cassio and Gianluca collided. I was knocked back, stumbled, and almost fell. Gianluca was now on the floor, Cassio over him throwing punch after punch, hitting him wherever he could. Gianluca wasn't putting up much of a fight, and even if he could, no one could beat Cassio. I stood there watching the scene before me, unable to move.

"You okay?" Vitelli stood before me, checking on me.

"Yeah," I assured him and when he was sure I was indeed alright he left me standing there.

He reached the two men and pulled Cassio from Gianluca. In the process, Cassio ended up elbowing his brother in the face. His head snapped back, and his nose instantly began bleeding.

Someone gasped beside me, and I turned to find Marie staring at the fight, her hands covering her mouth, eyes almost popping out of their sockets. Sometimes I forgot she wasn't Outfit and wasn't used to this kind of violence.

A crowd had gathered around us and people were starting to stare. I dug my nails into the palm of my hands feeling guilty for what I had created. This was all my fault. I bit my lip, too, trying to focus on the pain instead of the shame.

Eventually, a bloody-faced Vitelli managed to pull Cassio back, he vibrated with anger. His hands were bloody, and his face contorted with pure, unending rage.

"Oh God," Marie made to go toward Vitelli, but I pulled her back.

"He'll be fine."

"But he's bleeding," she cried out.

"Marie, don't."

"His brother hit him," she whined in shock. I spun her so she faced me.

"Cassio Moretti is a dangerous man. Don't ever doubt that." It was advice I'd take to heart as well. "Don't give him any reason to hate you."

We both looked back at the scene when they began to shout at each other. Vitelli was still holding Cassio, locking his arms over his brother's large body. Cassio was still trying to reach for Gianluca who smugly wiped his bloody lips and smiled.

"*Ti ucciderò*," Cassio promised to kill Gianluca, and by the look in his eyes, I really thought he would.

"Get the fuck out of here, Gianluca," Vitelli shouted.

He wiped his bloody hands on his pants, rolled his shoulders, and held his head high. His left eye was already beginning to close, but he didn't seem to care.

Then to my horror, he looked at me, then back at Cassio. He shook his head as a sly smile graced his busted face. Gianluca walked away from the two Morettis, passing by Marie and me. He stopped, tipped his head, and winked.

"Evening, ladies," he greeted and then finally left.

I couldn't stop staring at Cassio, who had his eyes locked on mine. Had he been watching me this entire time? I thought he was busy with that blonde girl he had been talking to almost all night.

"You should leave," Vitelli said to his brother.

"So now you're telling me what to do?"

"Haven't you done enough?" he raised a hand to his nose and cursed when it came away bloody.

The two men came toward us, and Cassio stared me down, probably thinking about all the ways he could murder me. He wasn't alone in that sentiment either. Anger boiled in my veins as I noticed the entire party had stopped to watch us. Cassio ran his fingers through his hair like nothing had happened.

"Come on, we are leaving," he said, I didn't move. "Francesca, come on; I'm taking you home."

"I can call a taxi," I said irritably.

I felt Marie's and Vitelli's eyes on us, but Cassio once more didn't seem to be bothered. "God only knows what other kind of trouble you're going to get yourself into."

I clenched my jaw and dug my nails into my palms, he wasn't going to expose me out here, was he? Cassio wasn't that crazy… or he was. I didn't know him anymore. Even when I did, he'd always had one less screw in his brain.

"Francesca," Cassio bit out impatiently

It was useless to argue with him, and I was too shaken to do so. Instead, I kissed my friend goodbye and thanked Vitelli for the party. The couple watched us leave. My shoulders grew tense and my face hot as we passed through the crowd.

I felt a hand on my back twisting the fabric of my dress and pulling me back.

"You did nothing wrong, Francesca." Cassio's breath tickled my ear, causing a shiver to race down my back.

We walked toward the elevator, while all the guests stared at us, and Cassio walked leisurely while I wanted to be out of here as fast as possible. I felt their judging eyes on me, and my cheeks burned with embarrassment. When we finally reached the elevator, the car was already there.

We stood as far away as possible from each other inside the elevator, and I still didn't understand why he was taking me home. The last time we talked—or exchanged words—Cassio didn't seem inclined to be around me.

I didn't judge him because the sentiment was reciprocated. I didn't want to be around him even if it meant walking home, on my own, in the dark Chicago streets. I would risk that kind of danger over Cassio Moretti any day.

"Do you ever wear clothes, or do you simply forget them?" he asked, tone detached, but I knew he was looking for a fight.

"Do you ever behave, or do you like beating the shit out of people for kicks?"

"Do you kiss your mamma with that mouth?"

Cassio didn't know about my *mamma*, still, the jab hit my guts and it became hard to breathe inside the small car, where his scent circled the air, giving me no choice but to breathe him in.

"Are you always a mess, or just when you're desperate for attention or drugs?"

"Fuck you, Cassio."

As soon as the doors opened, I marched out and walked away with no direction in mind, but anywhere away from him was a victory. Cassio wanted a fight, but I wasn't in the mood. Not after what happened.

Before I noticed what was happening, Cassio spun me around and pressed my body against the wall. He didn't give me a chance to escape as he caged me in, one hand above my head and the other next to my neck.

I sucked in a deep breath and regretted it the second his citrus and sandalwood scent filled my nose. He was too close. His strong unrelenting body was dangerously pressed against mine, and I could feel the volts of electricity cursing through his veins.

Cassio was alive.

"Don't piss me off right now, Francesca." His hot breath touched my skin, tickling my cheeks. "Because if you push me, I'll fight back."

In my drunken haze, mixed with the cigarette which had lowered my blood pressure, my mind ceased to function. It gave me the kind of courage I did not usually possess. It awakened something in me that only came to life when he was near. Cassio was pissed—well, his bad because so was I.

"Or what, Cassio?" I snapped, pushing against his unyielding chest. *Why was it so hard?* Cassio didn't give an inch. "I'm not afraid of you."

His smile was pure venom. "You're not very smart, are you, *Principessa?*"

"Don't call me that, Cassio," I snapped, pushing him once more.

"Or what, *Principessa?*" he taunted.

"You're no better than Gianluca," the words slipped out of my mouth before I could stop them.

I instantly regretted them. I wasn't the kind of person who needed to hurt others in order to feel better about myself. Cassio stepped away turning his back on me.

My apology was stuck in my throat, and I couldn't utter it. So instead, I swallowed it down. I was tired of being treated that way, of men thinking they could do whatever they pleased just because I was physically weaker than them.

I stood there unsure if he was still going to take me home, and when I finally regained my composure, I found Cassio standing by his black sports car. He waited outside the driver's door.

"Get in the car," he ordered.

I did not want to prolong this any further, so I did get in the car. Cassio followed soon after. The silence that surrounded us was so uncomfortable I couldn't stop fidgeting, turning my rings repeatedly, and digging my nail into the palms of my hand. Cassio didn't look like a man who was easily offended, but I had managed to do so.

I might still hate him for what he did all those years ago, but I wasn't this person. I couldn't be mean, not even to him, and I hated that most of all. I was sure Cassio wouldn't have apologized.

"The words just slipped out," I said after a while.

"I'll take your apology."

I held the urge to roll my eyes. "It's an explanation, Cassio, not an apology."

"Whatever." He kept on driving.

After a while, as my nerves settled, so did the adrenaline, and my hands began to shake. Cassio stared at them for a while and heated up the car but it had nothing to do with the cold and everything to do with what happened.

"Where are you taking me?"

"Your house, where else?"

"Can you drop me somewhere else?"

"I'm not your chauffeur, Francesca."

Didn't seem like that given it was the second time he was taking me home. "There's a diner near my place just drop me there."

Cassio stared at me like I had spoken to him in some other language. "No."

I fisted my hands and begged for patience. Instead of fighting, which I knew he still wanted to, I offered him the truth. "I can't go home right now."

He stared at me, his green arctic eyes breaching through my walls and reading with clarity what was written all over me. I didn't want to be alone. That was the truth. Not after what happened tonight.

Cassio didn't utter a word as he drove through Chicago until we reached a massive skyscraper. He drove into the garage and parked the car in a designated spot. Unsure what to do and slightly conscious of myself, I opened the door and waited for him.

The elevator led us to the twenty-fifth floor, every second in there with him was excruciating. I kept wondering why I put myself in these situations. Tonight, I couldn't even blame it on the drugs. Although I had drunk more than a normal person should, I was sober now. As sober as I could be. This was all my fault.

What was I doing here? I should have asked Cassio to drop me at my place and be done with the night. With him. Cassio had made it clear that he didn't want to see me, and I didn't want to see him. So why were we here?

Once the doors opened, he removed a key card and swiped through his door. He opened it for me, and I stepped inside, clutching my purse for dear life, as if it could shield me from him. I was so out of place, it hurt.

If Cassio had noticed, which I knew he did, he said nothing, he allowed me to explore, but I remained there, like a statue. "Come," he said after a while.

He led me through the massive living room—which was at least thrice the size of my entire apartment. I followed him up a set of stairs and through a corridor. He stopped at the third door to the right and turned to face me.

His expression was hard to read, but I could see his shoulders were tense and his eyes were colder than they naturally were. He was not pleased.

"You can stay here tonight. There are towels in the bathroom if you need any." He spoke through clenched teeth. If it bothered him so much, why was he doing this? "Don't ever mention this, do you understand?"

"Trust me, I won't."

"Good because this is the last time I will save you, Francesca." With that he turned and walked away. I watched until he disappeared at the end of the corridor.

My room was clean and spacious, my bed alone was large enough to fit a family. The room was decorated in tons of white and gray, making it look cold and impersonal. Despite that, it was beautiful, with floor-to-ceiling windows that offered me a view of Lake Michigan.

After wiping away my make-up and tying my hair into a bun, I stood by the window, watching the city outside. Once again, it struck me that I was in Cassio Moretti's apartment.

Why had he brought me here? Why had I accepted it? I didn't want to be alone right now, but that didn't mean I wanted to be with him. In fact, Cassio was the last person I should be with.

It was for one night, and one night only. Now that I was back in Chicago and my best friend was dating his brother, I was bound to see him. It was best we dealt with this like adults.

There was no point in pretending we liked each other. One of us would have to cave and be the adult here, and it looked like it would have to be me. Only because I didn't want to be miserable every time we saw each other.

I left the room, heading toward his. I was about to knock on the door when courage failed me. Then I lifted my hand and knocked once, twice, and was about to do so a third time when the door opened.

My knees wobbled, and my eyes had a hard time focusing on his face. Cassio stood before me half-naked, his chest on display. I stared and... stared. It was hard. He was hard, his chest was. I mean his packs... he had six of them and a V muscle that slipped into his pants. His skin was tanned... golden like he had spent all of his summer in Capri, sunbathing.

I was rambling in my head, but he was so... juicy. I had seen Paolo shirtless countless times, but he had been pale and pouchy. The only other comparisons had been the men from Hollywood movies, and Cassio could easily be one of them.

And that tattoo. Right on his left pectoral, a small writing in cursive which I couldn't read given the dimness of the light. Was it hot in here? I was certainly sweating.

"You're drooling, *Principessa*."

"No, I'm not." I finally managed to look into his eyes and saw a flicker of heat.

"You are." He crossed his arms and flexed his muscles. I narrowed my eyes realizing he was doing it on purpose.

"I. Am. Not."

"Then what's that trailing down your chin?" Like an idiot, I reached to wipe it off, but there was nothing there.

My cheeks blazed, and I forgot what I'd come here to do. Instead, I turned around and ran back to my room. Locked the door and hit my head against it.

"Great, Francesca," I cursed. "You did great."

9

CASSIO

Numbers stared back at me causing my head to spin, I'd been looking at them for the past two hours and still nothing seemed to get into my brain. It was early Saturday, the club was closed for now, but the crew was already working hard to get it ready for opening hours. I skimmed through some of the files, in case something else caught my attention, but honestly, nothing would. Numbers had never been my strength, but they were one of the many evils of this job.

Pulling my chair back with a loud sigh, I stood and stretched my back like an old man and cracked my neck, working at the small knots that had formed over the last few hours. I checked my phone, it was still ten o'clock, and the day already showed signs of being a monotonous one.

Mobsters lived a pretty calm life, all things considered. Most of the time, my job consisted of looking at our numbers, brokering deals with fellow mobsters, and attending boring meetings to discuss more deals with fellow mobsters. I couldn't recall the last time I'd pulled out my gun and used it. The poor thing was gathering dust these days.

Aside from the war with the Russians, everything was flowing as it should. Which I couldn't complain about, but it gave me ulcers. I knew they were planning something and sitting here looking at numbers wasn't going to help me.

I had Luciano and some of his men look into the spy situation, but until now, he hadn't come up with a single lead. The Russians were still attacking and stealing our cargo, and there was nothing I could do but shoot them on the spot, like the rats they were. I ran my thumb under my lip as annoyance coursed through my veins.

Was it *that* hard to find a spy? *Volpe,* as the fucker liked to be called. The situation was under control until now, but eventually, I wouldn't be able to keep it a secret anymore. I would have to tell my underbosses and then all hell would break loose. A spy was the worst kind of traitor, one the Outfit would gladly dismember and feed to the vultures.

A knock on my door pulled me from my thoughts and I turned from where I was standing by the floor-to-ceiling window—watching the club from above.

"Come in," I shouted, my head starting to pound with the beginnings of a headache.

Donato Manci walked into my office wearing one of his old Brioni suits. He was the stereotypical mobster, with a generous Italian nose, balding head and healthy build. The man was so fat, I wondered how he still managed to walk.

"Cassio, *come stai?*" I had been good until he arrived.

"*Bene,*" I grunted out. "What do you need?"

It was rare that he visited me here, we usually talked via phone or video calls. He wasn't ailing or anything, he was just a lazy fucker. I didn't mind, the more he stayed away from my business, the better things flowed.

Donato and I butted heads almost always and it was tiring. He knew I hated him, and I had a feeling he hated me, too, but he was loyal to the Outfit—which meant he had to be loyal to me.

He pulled one of the chairs before my desk and sat his heavy self on it, the poor thing groaned. "I don't have all day, Donato." I made myself clear I wasn't interested in talking.

I had work to do, work I hadn't been able to do because I couldn't help thinking about his daughter.

"I've heard the Russians attacked another one of our cargos," he said.

"Yes." There was no point in lying.

"They are growing bolder." Donato shook his head. "When is our next shipment coming? We should—"

"Donato," I stopped him. "I'm sure you haven't come here to discuss that, so let's cut to the chase."

Although he was my consigliere and these were the things we should be talking about, I knew he hadn't come here for this. We had had a meeting three days ago. He knew when our next shipment was, and when the next one after that was coming. He wanted something and he was testing the waters first.

"Have you heard my daughter is back in town?" The change in subject took me by surprise, but I had time to hide it.

"I might have." The same way I might have been dreaming about what it would be like to have her around my cock, screaming my name... "Why?"

He didn't show any kind of emotion, but his eyes were shimmering with subdued rage. "She refuses to come home."

"Some widows live on their own," I reminded him. "It's not law that they return home." And I wouldn't blame her for not doing so.

He gritted his teeth, and he was beginning to vibrate. "And what a shame that is," he spat. "Francesca is my daughter, therefore mine to deal with."

"So why are you here?" I ran my thumb under my lower lip, wondering what his head would look like with a bullet in it.

Donato looked at the door and then back at me. He seemed to ponder whatever he had to say, and I realized he was scared to do so. "You know I treat you like son, that I trust you above all," Donato said looking deep into my eyes.

"I know," I said despite knowing it was all a scene.

Donato took a deep breath and finally confessed. "Francesca is sick, she has been for a while." The words slipped from his mouth and despite being momentarily shocked, I could hear the malice in his voice. Something wasn't right.

"Sick?" I asked unbelieving.

"That's why Paolo and I had a falling out. He never cared for my daughter as he should have."

I almost fell back laughing, but instead, managed to keep quiet. He was right about one thing, Paolo never cared for her as he should have, but neither had Donato, and I couldn't understand why all of a sudden, his fatherly instincts were kicking in.

"She needs to come home, Cassio, so we can treat her." He sounded almost worried, which *almost* struck a chord in my heart, but then I knew he was playing at something here.

"Did you know Paolo had her taking pills, all kinds of them?" Donato said. "He had a friend who prescribed her these drugs. I tried to stop it, but Paolo wouldn't let me talk to my daughter."

Donato went on and on, rambling about Francesca's life in Indianapolis, and it baffled me how much I hadn't known. Then again, why would I? I had promised myself to forget her, and although that hadn't happened, I did my best to ignore her existence. Regret pooled in my stomach, making me nauseous. If what Donato was saying was true, then I had to do something.

"Did you know her husband was embezzling money from us?" Once more I was hooked. Why hadn't I heard of that before? "The money she's living on is my money."

I didn't fail to notice that he said *mine* instead of ours. In the Outfit, when a man died without leaving male heirs behind, the money always returned to our coffers. It was the way, always had been. That was why most widows returned to their parents' houses to be married again.

It made sense now why Donato wanted his daughter to go home. It had nothing to do with her being sick. Donato couldn't fool me, I knew he was going to show his true colors eventually, and he did. He wanted her money. Donato wasn't a poor man, but then again, he didn't have to be in order to be greedy. Too much power bred ambition—the kind that usually led a man to an early grave.

"We should question her, send Luciano," he ordered me again.

I clenched my jaw trying to rein in the anger. "And do what, Donato?" I threw at him. Did he really want our enforcer to beat his daughter up because of an assumption?

Albeit it was a very serious one, I didn't beat women, not even those who annoyed the fuck out of me. I had never been that man. I wasn't like my consigliere or Francesca's late husband.

"We are not the Bratva. We don't go after women." I made myself crystal clear. Each word punctuated with determination.

If Donato touched a single finger on Francesca, he would lose that finger.

"So, you won't send anyone after her?" His nostrils flared.

"I'll deal with it."

What are you doing, Cassio?

A cold shiver raced down my back, what was I supposed to do with her? The money wasn't hers to begin with, but if I took it from her, then Francesca would be forced to go back to her father's, and that... I wasn't sure I could put her through that.

"I'll deal with it," I said again, convincing myself there was an explanation for all of this. The money had to have come from somewhere.

"Paolo was killed," Donato said after a beat of silence.

I managed last minute to hide my surprise. "And how would you know that?"

"Because the fucker was in league with the Bratva," he said calmly like it was the most obvious thing in the world. "Where do you think all his money came from?"

Drugs.

Donato must have read my mind because he said. "Where do you think he got all those drugs from? He dealt with both us and the Russians."

"Those are serious accusations, Donato." I pointed. "A dead man cannot defend himself."

He shrugged like it meant nothing. "The money must have come from somewhere."

I stared Donato down until he looked away, and still I looked. What was his play here? Why accuse a dead man of treason? Why did he want his daughter so much?

Money.

I knew that, but why did Donato need the money if he was already the second richest family in the Outfit—behind mine?

"There is one more thing,"

I groaned inwardly. "Yes."

"I intend for Francesca to be married as soon as her mourning period is over. She should not be on her own."

My guts twisted so painfully that I was forced to shift in my chair. "Marry her?" The words sounded pathetically weak.

He nodded. "I already have someone in mind, the deal is still on hold, but she will be married by the end of the year."

"That is before her mourning period is over." I pointed, fists clenched and jaws tight.

"A few months here and there won't make a difference." Donato shrugged.

This was the one thing I couldn't stop him from doing. As Capo, I had power over many things, but not this. I couldn't intervene in family business, not even if I desired to.

"If she's sick as you pointed out, then maybe you should wait." I sounded desperate and it made me angry at myself.

"Francesca needs a man in her life, someone to lead her and tell her what to do. Alone, she will only self-destruct."

He wasn't wrong there. Francesca had always been a people's person. Always flourished when she was around others, but her marriage to Paolo had broken her. What would happen if she married again, to a man just as vile as the first?

"Are you seeking my blessing?" I tried to keep my voice calm. If he was, he wouldn't find it here.

Donato pondered it for a while, then shook his head. "I only thought it would be the right thing to do, warn my Capo," he explained.

"Who is she to be married to?" I asked out of curiosity.

Donato smiled. "I'd rather not ruin the surprise."

I could order him to say the name of the man who was going to marry Francesca before the year was over, but I felt awfully sick and wanted this conversation to end. So instead of looking further into it, I reminded myself that Francesca was not mine. That she hated me and would never want anything to do with me— not after I broke her heart. So, I let the subject go.

Donato left my office leaving those thoughts marinating in my head, and they started to give me indigestion. I couldn't stop analyzing every angle.

I knew Paolo and Donato had become estranged over the years. That had been one of the reasons Francesca never visited Chicago. Something had drawn them apart, and I needed to figure out what it was. And there was only one person who could help me with that. The one person I had promised to not see again, and the one person I was desperately wanting to.

Instead of leaving my office and doing something crazy, I called my brother. This time, Vitelli picked up on the third ring.

"I want Paolo's bank statement and everything he has invested in in the last few years," I told Vitelli.

"Well, hello to you, too," he teased.

I took a deep sigh. "Just send it to my phone when you have it."

"It's Sunday."

"And tomorrow is Monday and the day after is Tuesday. I'm aware of the days in a week."

"You want them now?"

"Yes, and you're already late." I traced my fingers against the edge of the table.

"This smells like trouble." It didn't smell, it was trouble.

"Move your ass, Vitelli, I'm already late, and I plan to solve this now."

"It's Sunday," he pointed out again. "Can't you at least wait— fine, I'll send it to your email," he grunted.

"And, Vitelli, keep this between us. I don't want people to know about it." I could practically hear all the unasked questions in his head.

"What is this about, Cassio? What happened Friday, you almost had a coronary when you saw Gianluca touching Francesca."

"Goodbye, Vitelli," I said simply, eliciting a sigh of frustration from him.

"What's going on between you and Francesca Manci?" How was my brother so perceptive?

"Not that I owe you any explanations, but there is nothing between us, she's a potential loose end, and I don't like loose ends. I want to make sure she won't be a problem in the future."

"She a Manci, her middle name is trouble."

And you can't be more right about that. Francesca had trouble written all over her in big bold neon letters.

10

FRANCESCA

Weekends were supposed to be the universal days when a person could finally rest or have fun. We were not supposed to be haunted by our problems, there was supposed to be some kind of law preventing that kind of stuff.

Problems were only meant to appear and be solved during business hours, from Monday to Friday, preferably from 10 a.m. to 4 p.m. so I could at least have my me time later. But as with everything in my life, the timing when things happened always seemed to be off.

It was seven in the morning, and my head had been pounding from all the alcohol, my body still buzzing from all the physical activity it had endured when my phone rang. I didn't pick it up, I never answered the numbers I hadn't registered in my phone. I wasn't going to risk picking it up and Donato being the person on the other side of the line, so I let it ring.

It eventually stopped but then it started again, by then, my sleep was already interrupted, and I was looking to let out some pent-up rage. I pitied the person who called me by mistake, I even pitied Donato because I was going to unleash hell on him. But when I picked up, I wasn't expecting to hear that voice.

"Hello? Francesca?" It was boyish yet manly. It was rough, yet still gentle, it was pubescent. My voice got stuck in my throat, and I was speechless. Literally unable to speak.

Four years. That was the last time I heard my little brother's voice. Not little anymore I realized, Marco wasn't the little boy I left all those years ago.

"Francesca, are you there?"

"Hmm." That was the only word that was able to leave my mouth.

"She told me to call you. I—I didn't know what to do so I called." He sounded guilty and unsure, and my heart ached to hear my brother like that.

"Okay?" I wasn't following what was happening, it still took me by surprise that my little brother was calling me at seven in the morning on a Saturday.

"Mother fainted."

I shot from my bed sitting up, the quick movement making me dizzy, and I had to close my eyes for a couple of seconds to focus on his words. My mother hadn't told Marco, he didn't know about the cancer.

"Where is she now? Where is Don—father?" The word was bitter against my mouth.

"At his mistress' he won't be back until noon."

"Shit." Son of a bitch. I despised the man, I hoped he contracted some STDs.

"I don't, I shouldn't have—"

"Marco. It's okay. Take her to the hospital, and I'll meet you guys there."

Why was he so awkward about this? I was his sister, he was my little brother, regardless of what happened. I left my bed and headed to my wardrobe, choosing the first piece of clothing I found.

"Francesca. Father won't be... I shouldn't have called."

"He doesn't have to know. Please, just meet me at the hospital, everything is going to be fine."

It took me a while longer to reach the hospital than I would've wished. I had to wake up my neighbor next door, Mrs. Margaret, who was always so polite and nice, and had to beg her to look after Reginald. As always, the old lady was glad to do so.

Once the taxi pulled over at the hospital, I ran from it, almost forgetting to pay the poor man. A part of me was freaking out and wanting to run toward the street instead of toward the hospital. I didn't want to go in there and learn my mother didn't make it. As I ran through the oncology center toward Dr. Conrad's wing, my heart was beating hard against my chest.

The sight of my brother almost brought me to my knees. Over the last few years, I had stopped expecting to see him. Whenever my mother came to visit me in Indianapolis, and promised to bring Marco, I knew it was a lie, he would never come.

The first year after my marriage, we tried to have him come over almost every month, but Donato always refused. He wouldn't have his son around me after he and Paolo fought. So, when he called today, that same flicker of hope ignited inside of me, but I pushed it aside before it turned into a spark. I didn't expect him to come.

When his eyes met mine, for a confusing second, I didn't recognize him. He was my brother, same blond hair, same eyes, and same skin color, but he had grown up, was almost taller than me, and was already more fit than I ever would be. But there was something in the way he stood and looked at me that was too cold, too jaded to be my little Marco. The boy who drove me crazy, whose diapers I had changed and tucked into bed, was no longer.

"Francesca," he greeted me like a stranger, no hugs no kisses, no *I missed you*. I stopped and held myself back. Held the urge to reach for him, to hold him. "She's inside. The doctor won't tell me anything, says I'm not an adult." There was frustration and anger in his voice. I stood there awkwardly, not knowing how to speak to my own brother.

"I'll talk to him. We can talk later if that's okay." He shrugged.

I entered the room where my mother was being kept, she was lying down on a bed with machines connected to her and an oxygen tube coming out of her nose. My eyes darted to the machine monitoring her heartbeats, and apparently her heart was steady but seeing her in that state did nothing to appease my nerves.

"Miss Manci."

"Francesca," I corrected the doctor. "What happened?"

"Let's take a seat, shall we?" Sitting only made it worse. I was already restless, and I needed something to calm me down, so I began to pace the room.

"What happened?"

"Your mother's body was very weak, and the chemo has made it weaker."

"Isn't it supposed to be helping?" I stopped and looked at him.

"Yes, but it also takes its toll. That's why I suggested the home-care system."

"That's not viable." My asshole of a father–who's currently fucking another woman–doesn't want to help his dying wife.

"Then we'll have to hospitalize her. The sessions will only get worse, and she will only grow weaker. Episodes like this will keep happening. Has she been eating? Taking her meds? Resting?"

"I don't... know. I don't know."

I haven't seen her since the first few chemo sessions. But looking at my mother resting on that bed with tubes and machines all over her, I knew my answer... no, she hadn't. She needed people to take care of her, people to be constantly around her, making sure she took her meds, that she ate, and that she rested. That was why she had come to me. So that I could make these decisions. I loved her for trusting me but hated the weight she'd thrown on my shoulders.

"I'll sign whatever paperwork you need me to. Just... help her."

"We will, Francesca. I'll have the papers brought in for you to sign." He patted my shoulder. It was the right decision, right? She would have help in the hospital, while at home, she would have none, so why didn't I feel better about it? Why didn't I feel the weight lifting off my shoulders? I walked toward my mother and took her hand in mine. I was shocked at how cold and skinny it was.

"It's going to be okay, Mamma."

Seconds later, Dr. Conrad brought me the papers and I signed them. Some part of me felt guilty for doing it. Like I was giving the responsibility to someone else, but I swore to myself I would be here every hour of every day. I wouldn't leave her side until she got out of here as strong as a horse.

When I finally left the room, I was surprised yet again, when I found Marco leaning against the wall, that same jaded look on his face.

"Coffee?" I asked. Jesus, he was thirteen, what did thirteen-year-olds drink these days?

Maybe he was a tea kind of person, or he just didn't like anything, by the look on his face, it felt like he didn't feel like drinking anything. I dug my nails into the palms of my hands as anxiety filled me up to the brink of explosion. "Or, if you like, we could just sit, you don't have to drink anything. Or, if you don't, you don't have to." *Please say something.*

"Coffee's fine," was all he said as we walked down the corridor.

"Oh, great." I sighed.

We sat in the hospital's canteen; it was my second cup of coffee while he hadn't touched his first one. I began pulling at my lip when a tiny smile appeared on his perpetual jaded face.

"What?" I asked, smiling too.

"You're not going to faint, are you?"

"Is it that obvious?"

"That you're nervous?" he inquired, a flicker of light in his eyes. "Yes."

"Oh," I chuckled nervously. "At least that's out of the way. What gave me away?" He stopped and pondered my question.

"Your legs won't stop tapping, you've bitten your lip raw, you've dug your nails so deep into your palms they'll start bleeding," he explained. "And this is your second cup of coffee in less than two minutes," he answered matter of fact.

I was a nerve ball, so what?

The boy before me was a complete stranger, to me and I was a complete stranger to him. I had no idea what to say and there was a lot I wanted to. Marco used to be the one person I knew I could speak freely with. Even being ten years younger, we were close, and I missed him so much. So, fucking much, that my heart was threatening to explode right now.

"You've grown observant."

"I've grown." He stated.

Silence stretched between us again.

"I know she's sick, so there's no need to lie to me like they have been doing for the past few months."

"I—I wasn't." I totally was.

"Spare me. Everyone thinks I'm a kid, but I'm not, Francesca. I've seen things boys my age has never even dreamed of. I'm not scared of death."

I looked at my brother, his jadedness, his coldness, and his ability to stand still. He had never been like that. He was always running around and causing trouble. What happened to him? What were the things he saw? My traitorous mind took me to the one place I shouldn't have gone. *Had he killed? Had he become a Made Man?*

"I didn't say you were. Mamma asked me to keep it from you and we haven't exactly spoken these past few years. If you have questions, I'll answer them. I promise." He looked at me as if he didn't really believe me.

"How bad?"

"I don't know," I answered.

"What stage?"

"Four."

"How long have you known?" He grilled me, question after question.

"Marco—"

"How long?"

I sighed in defeat. "A month now."

He grunted, which sounded like he was somewhat satisfied. I wasn't going to lie, I meant it. But there were also things I wasn't ready to talk to him about like the fact that my mother was worse than she had been when I first saw her. That she was only going to get worse, and that there were challenging times ahead of us. *Us.* It was weird thinking about him here with me.

"I can't stay any longer." He looked back at the doors like he was expecting someone to show up. Probably one of Donato's guards.

"I know."

"Father won't allow me to stay. He doesn't even know I'm here."

"I know, and I won't be the one to tell him. He doesn't know I'm here either," I promised him.

"I have to go; he will be coming home anytime soon."

"Oh, okay."

Marco stood up, and in this moment, he looked like the adult, and I looked like the child, waiting to be guided. Just like before, we didn't kiss, neither did we hug. He simply started walking off.

"Will you come visit?" I asked. "Mother," I added, I didn't want to scare him off right now. If my father found out he was here with my mother, it wouldn't be as bad as if he was seen with me.

He shrugged, "I'll try."

Sunday was the worst day yet. It finally struck me that my mother was truly sick and that she was hospitalized for real. Seeing and hearing those machines in her room had left me dizzy. I spent my day with her trying to make her as comfortable and as cozy as possible. I'd bought her my favorite flowers—purple tulips—and placed them all around the room. Mamma had always loved flowers, just like I did, and it was something we both had bonded over in my youth.

When Dr. Conrad finally sent me home after watching my mother like a hawk all day, I stopped at the flower shop near my house and bought a few more to decorate my place. When I finally reached my apartment, my head was aching, and my body was vibrating with anxiety—in a way I hadn't experienced in a long time. Withdrawal was the worst part because you craved drugs more than anything, more than life itself. As I entered my apartment, my hands were shaking, and my mouth was salivating. I dropped the flowers on the counter and raced to the bathroom to throw up except nothing came out.

I heaved and heaved bile until my stomach twisted in pain. I sat there resting against the wall, my palms damp and sweat racing down my back. I wanted to use, I was desperate for it, but my last stash had been taken by the police and my prescribed pills were ending. Paolo was the one who usually supplied me with both, so I had no idea how to go searching for drugs. I could hit a club, but I was too tired and too drained to do so. The last thing I wanted was to go out.

After washing my mouth and hands, I headed toward the kitchen to greet my puppy. Dogs were loyal. Dogs loved you. Dogs were always happy to see you no matter what. That's why I would spend the rest of my life surrounded by dogs and not men. No matter how much I wanted a family, I would never allow myself to fall in love ever again.

Love only brought heartache and pain. The kind of sorrow that tore through the body and destroyed everything in its path. Leaving only blood and destruction in its wake. I was never going to go through that ever again. Love was a rock tied to your feet, that dragged you down, drowning you in the endless sea.

Arranging the flowers into a vase, I set them on the counter and observed my work, then my eyes landed on the pile of boxes I still hadn't had the courage to open. I needed wine, a lot of it. Except when I opened the fridge, there was none left. Damn it.

With my lack of coke, the alcohol was going faster than expected. I will have to go to the supermarket sometime soon. I needed to do something, I couldn't stay in here, even if I was tired. My head and my insides were just too alive, and my body would have to deal with it. In the weirdest turn of events, I changed into my gym clothes. Maybe taking Reginald for a walk would quiet my anxiety. *Maybe I could find someone to sell me some blow.*

Someone knocked at the door.

I frowned at the piece of wood. The knock sounded again, angrier this time. A thousand thoughts cursed through my mind. Tucking my shoulders and straightening my back, I reached for my door. I opened it while the person was about to knock a third time.

"Ugh. It's you." It was easy to mask my relief with annoyance.

"Trust me, it is not where I wanted to be either." Cassio took a step as if he was about to come inside, but I blocked his path. He eyed me from head to toe taking in my outfit, my short shorts, and my cropped zip hoodie.

"Wait a minute, how did you get in here? Please tell me you didn't kill someone. You didn't kill someone, right?"

Cassio looked at me for a couple of seconds and didn't answer. My heart began to beat faster. I always knew what he was, but sometimes I kept forgetting that the man before me was nothing but a cold-hearted killer and would've done anything to get what he wanted, no matter the consequences.

"Through the front door like most people do. Can I come in?" He stepped forward again, trying to push me back, but I stopped him.

"No." Of course not! "Cassio, did you just kill someone?"

"Jesus, Francesca, chill out. I asked your neighbor to let me inside. Which reminds me, you live in a shitty neighborhood in a shitty apartment, what did you expect?" That my neighbor wouldn't let a stranger into the building.

"Let me in." He planted the palm of his hand on my door.

"Why would I do that?"

He sighed in frustration. And because he was so fucking polite, he shoved the door aside and stepped into my apartment as if he owned the place.

"Hey, I didn't let you in," I complained following Cassio inside.

"This place is a mess."

"It's called style, look it up."

"Thanks, I'm good."

"Have you come all the way here to criticize my apartment or do you actually have something to say worth hearing? Because, if not, I'm running late for Reginald's appointment." Which meant his daily walk that I was about to do before he arrived.

"Reginald?" he asked suspiciously.

"Yes, my baby." I flashed him a grin. Cassio looked at me, as I smiled at him. His brows furrowed so intensely that his forehead wrinkled.

"Baby?" He asked more to himself than to me. He looked shocked. In that moment, his cold unfazed expression subsided with complete perplexity. He looked at me again from head to toe, lingering on my body with such intent that the room began to turn hotter. I knew I should end the charade there, but I was enjoying the look on his face. Everyone knew my marriage had been a fruitless one.

Tip tapping came from the hallway taking his attention from me. Reginald, my baby, came running toward us. His skinny body wiggling with excitement, he was most definitely the worst guard dog in existence.

"What the hell is that!" Cassio remained paralyzed, looking down skeptically at Reginald. I picked him up in one swift motion settling him in my arms, and he began to wiggle, I gave him one kiss on his cold muzzle.

"This is Reginald," I said matter of fact.

"That is your baby?"

"Yes," I answered simply. And I could measure the amount of sudden relief that filled him. Why should he even care? The action made me suddenly very angry. "I really have more important things to do than chitchatting with you. As odd as it sounds. If you'll excuse me." I tried to pass him by, but the apartment was too small for the two of us, he was already taking up too much space, and he hadn't even left the entrance.

"Sit down, Francesca, you are not leaving," he said with all the calm and coldness in the world, something I imagine he learned over the years. It was incredible what a calm and detached tone of voice could accomplish. People thought shouting was the answer, but it wasn't. "You better remember who I am, Francesca."

"Oh, trust me, I haven't forgotten." *How can I?*

He came inside eyeing my apartment with both interest and disdain. Taking in the boxes I still hadn't opened and the complete mess I'd made of things. *What a grand surprise.*

He took a seat on my stool, forcing me to stand in my kitchen looking at him. He didn't sit on the sofa, which meant this wasn't going to be something fun to discuss. I settled Reginald on the floor and leaned against the kitchen counter putting as much space between us as possible. I hated that he was here for less than five minutes, and I was already nervous. With all that had happened in the last two days, this was the last thing that I needed.

His eyes trailed to something behind me, and Cassio stood, walked toward it, and grabbed one of my orange pill bottles. It was hard to judge at that moment what was going on in his head, but I could tell from his clenched jaws that it wasn't pleasant.

"What did I tell you about the drugs?"

I didn't answer.

"What. Did. I. Say?" His voice was deadly calm.

I flinched.

"There would be consequences," I whispered.

"Shit, Francesca," he hit the bottle against the counter. "When are you going to get it together?" He growled angrily. "I can't keep dealing with your shit all the time."

"I didn't ask you to," I argued. "You were the one who came barging in. Why are you here, Cassio? I have more important things to... hey, what are you doing?"

"Who gave you this?" His voice was no longer calm. "Who the fuck gave you this?"

"Paolo." I snapped. "One of his friends was a doctor."

"This is heavy shit, Francesca." He shoved the bottle into his pocket exactly where I would never dare reach.

"I know, that's the point."

He picked up a piece of paper and then grabbed a pen from the nearby table and wrote a number. "If you don't make an appointment by Wednesday, I'll come back here and force you into a clinic."

I laughed. "Have you lost your fucking mind?" I crossed my arms.

He spun around so fast that I stumbled back. "I don't deal in requests, I deal in orders, and you will abide by them."

"I am not one of your men, Cassio."

"No," he agreed shaking his head. "You are much worse. I have given you a choice," he said with a scary calmness.

"You can't force me." I dug my nails deeper into my palms.

"Test me and you'll find out what I am capable of, Francesca. Speaking of which," he ran his thumb under his lip. A sign he was pissed. "We have to talk."

"I have nothing else to say to you."

"Sit down, Francesca."

I didn't.

"How long have you been using?" he inquired coldly.

"That's kind of insensitive to ask, don't you think?"

He offered me a look that told me he wasn't in the mood for games.

"Well, if you wish to know, I started using the day I was married. I took some of my mother's pills. From there on, I tried other things, I don't discriminate."

He was silent for a while, drinking my words in, having him in my small apartment was too much. His presence was too consuming. His scent was starting to cling to the walls around me.

It had been a day since I last saw him, and I needed more time to process everything that had happened. Seeing him fight Gianluca Gallo had been a massive turn-on—which explained how obviously deranged I was. Who would react that way?

And his body... I still can't forget how perfectly sculpted he was, like one of Michelangelo's artworks. *Focus, Francesca, that's not important right now.*

"What do you want, Cassio?" I snapped out of my trance before it took me places it shouldn't.

"To talk about your husband." Well, that was like an ice-cold bucket of water poured over my head.

"Do you want some whiskey? You drink whiskey, right? It's the only thing that's left. I would've offered vodka, but I drank it."

I was rambling, but I took the whiskey, and two glasses, and filled them, handing one to him. Cassio looked at me but said nothing, he didn't even reach for his cup. *Fine.* I downed both without even making a face, I was that good.

"Are you nervous?" Yeah, after what happened, I was.

"I'm tired, stressed, and annoyed, all I wanted was to enjoy a day with my dog, and you've ruined it."

"Trust me, Francesca, I haven't even begun to ruin your day."

"Great!" I cheered. Just fucking great. "Could you get to it then so I can go back to my life?"

He took the bottle and moved it away from me as far away as he could put it. "Paolo Biancini," he began, "your late husband, embezzled money from the Outfit, meaning all the money that's currently in your bank account does not belong to you."

I laughed.

He didn't. He was serious.

"So, what? You're saying he stole?"

"Yes and no."

"Well then, by all means, please tell me." My blood was beginning to boil. He didn't seem a bit phased by all of this.

"The money is clean, it was his, but there is no telling where it came from."

"And how is that my problem?" Cassio tapped his fingers against the table. "Cassio, I didn't... I didn't know." I didn't steal from the Outfit. I would never do that; I knew what happened to people who did, and it was the kind of horror no one should go through.

"Your father wanted to send our enforcer."

The alcohol suddenly didn't taste so nice, and it twisted inside my stomach, wanting to come back up again. Why was I so surprised? Why did it still hurt to hear that my father would've sent the enforcer to beat the shit out of me for something I didn't do? I worried at my lips and wished I had something to do, to hold. My hands were sitting there, idly doing nothing, and I had an impression they were shaking.

"And you didn't?" I asked.

"I don't beat innocent women."

"Who says I'm innocent?" He raised a brow doubtingly.

"Of this you are."

"So, what now?" I hated how weak my voice sounded.

"That money now belongs to your father, as his daughter you are his. He has every right to take it."

For some miracle, the alcohol remained in my stomach. My pressure reached so low I almost fainted, thank God I was sitting or else I would have toppled over. Cassio was still looking at me with that same unfazed expression. I wanted to hit him, see if something ever made him change.

"I'm not moving back in with him," I said outraged. "I'm not giving up on my freedom. He ruined my life once; I will not let him ruin it twice."

There was no way I was letting go of this small sliver of freedom I had found for myself, even if it only meant I had a year to enjoy it. "Plus, I don't think my father would like to have a whore in his house, I don't imagine it would be good for his reputation."

"Why would you say that?" he asked simply, with... was it discomfort I saw? Did he really look that annoyed by my choice of words? I huffed, annoyed as well. Was he living under a rock? Did he not know what my father thought of me? I bet Donato had made it quite clear to everyone what kind of a daughter I was.

"How many?"

"How many what?" My brows furrowed.

"You know what I am asking. How many since your husband? I know you have a lover. How many since him?"

I choked and found it hard to swallow. I had to hold on to a laugh. Did he really think I had a lover? It would be easier to end world hunger than for me to ever be with a man again. This was just too much. "Why?" I crossed my arms.

"How many, Francesca?"

"There was only him." Despite the fun I was having, I told the truth.

"I don't believe you."

"Well, that's too bad," I shrugged.

"How many, Francesca?" he snapped.

"I don't know, I don't remember, there were so many of them. I was high most of the time, so I don't really recall."

He was on me in seconds, he had pinned me against the fridge, one hand on my neck but he wasn't squeezing or hurting. He just held me as if he needed to hurt me but couldn't make himself do it. His tall frame was hulking over mine in a dominant way, but it didn't scare me, he never had.

"Don't provoke me," he hissed.

"Don't ask questions you don't wish to know the answers," I answered, dripping venom.

Just then, I realized how close our bodies were. One of his knees was in between mine and his hand was over my head. His muscular body was inches from touching me, but I could feel the heat oozing from him. Even being a cold asshole, Cassio radiated heat like a furnace. My body couldn't help but react to his, I wanted to get closer to feel his heat, to let myself burn. My breathing accelerated and my breasts felt heavy. Everything began to feel too hot. Too much.

Our gaze met for a single second and for a moment I was transported back to a time when we were only Cassio and Francesca and there was nothing in between us. His cold green eyes grew dark like his irises was bleeding into his pupils.

I licked my lips, hungry for something I had been denied for so long.

"Did they make you scream, *Principessa*?" His head dropped lower. "Did they fuck you till you couldn't walk anymore?" His head dropped again until his lips were inches from mine.

I had the urge to lick my lips, but I didn't have to, he did it for me. His tongue darted from his mouth, and licked my lower lip, biting it gently.

I had been sexually oppressed for such so long that a moan escaped my lips before I could hold it back. Cassio chuckled, like the asshole he was. I was giving him power, power that he was going to wield over me if I wasn't careful enough.

Cassio dipped his head even lower. "Fuck it," he cut the distance between us and smashed his lips against mine.

I was so stunned for a second, that I didn't know what to do, but Cassio kept his lips on mine until he breached my barriers and I softened into him. His lips were warm and wet against mine, just like I remembered. I didn't hesitate in kissing him back, one of my hands grabbed his hair, tugging it and pulling him closer at the same time. Unsure whether I needed him closer or farther away from me.

Cassio still tasted the same... like all my sins and my dreams, all wrapped up in one. It lasted for what felt like an eternity. I was floating in time as he pushed me harder against the fridge. One of his hands settled on my waist while the other still gripped my neck. With his thumb, he caressed me gently, a contrast between the way he was fucking my mouth. Cassio shoved one leg in between mine and the contact drew fire, my skin burning. He pressed against my core, and I moaned into his mouth. I had been deprived of this for so long it was pathetic.

Sensing my need, he moved his leg higher, so that it pressed against my core in the most delicious of manners. I rubbed myself against it in desperation, seeking the kind of release only he could offer me in that moment. My panties became drenched as wetness pooled between my legs. At the back of my head, the voices screamed for me to stop, but I couldn't, it was physically impossible right now.

"I hate you." I kissed him.

Cassio pulled back. "That only makes me harder." He moved his leg even higher, and I moaned, head falling back against the fridge. His scent surrounding me, his strong arms holding me and his leg in between mine were too much. Still, I begged for more.

"Just like that, *Principessa*," he groaned in my ear, "are you going to come for me right here?"

"Yes," I moaned, and if it were even possible, he shoved me harder against the fridge, the friction between us increasing, and I couldn't stop myself, it was too late to go back now. "Cassio," I cried, begging him to stop since I had lost all sense of reason.

He kissed me instead, long, and hard, this time there was nothing gentle about the way he was handling me. His hands were rough on my body, one of them skimming up my waist toward the underside of my breast where he caressed me and then slipped his hand under my top. The moment his calloused hand touched my feverish skin, my back arched, and I moaned into his mouth.

Cassio was playing me like a puppeteer, moving my strings and controlling me with his mouth, hands, and legs.

The start of my orgasm was on the horizon, I could see it clearly. He pinched one nipple and twisted it gently, in contrast to what his mouth was doing too mine. "I'm so close," I panted.

We broke apart then, I gasped for air, but all I did was breathe him in. Cassio shoved his head into the nape of my neck and nuzzled it, groaning loudly.

Then he stepped away and wiped his lip with his thumb, I almost fell to the floor, my legs hardly keeping me upward. I was panting hard, trying to understand what had just happened between us. The arctic look in his eyes froze me into place. He was fuming.

"You have a month to figure things out or you'll have to go back to your father's." The words were venomous.

Then, like he hadn't just crashed his lips to mine and kissed me like he was drowning, and I was his oxygen and like he hadn't just deprived me from my first orgasm in years, he turned and walked out of my apartment. The door closed with a bang, I slid to the floor and placed a hand over my face. My body was still burning, my panties were drenched, and my core still begged for attention.

What had I done? Cassio was the one person I should have never allowed back in my life and here I was kissing him and riding his leg like nothing happened between us.

I tucked my head into my hands. "Oh God." I was so screwed.

11

FRANCESCA

It was odd how comfortable I had grown in this place in the last few weeks since my mother had been hospitalized. Everyone in the oncology wing knew me and called me by my name. They even knew my favorite Jell-O flavor—cherry, of course.

I stopped by the desk and leaned against the counter. Martha was the nurse on call today. It was safe to assume I had become friends with all of them. The best part—the only good part about coming here every day—was these people.

"Hey, Martha." I greeted her and placed a Tupperware container on top of the counter.

"Darling," Martha beamed when she saw me. "Please tell me those are your famous blueberry muffins."

"The one and only." I chuckled when she placed her hands over her chest. "I brought some for you and the girls," I said as she approached me and opened the lid.

The scent of freshly baked muffins filled the air. Martha grabbed one and then called for Jenny who was passing by. The two of them ate a muffin each and sighed taking their first bites.

"Where did you learn to bake like that, Frankie?" Jenny asked as she savored her second muffin.

"I had a lot of free time on my hands, so I decided to take some classes."

Paolo disliked having me bake, he thought it was beneath me, but since he was gone most of the time, I used those moments to learn from our cook, Erica. She taught me most of what I knew, and it became a form of therapy. Those hours when there was nothing but the dough before me, the voices in my head would silence and I would simply exist in that moment. There was no anxiety, no pressure. Just me, Erica, and whatever we were cooking or baking for the day.

"Well, girl, if you keep bringing us these treats, I'll be rolling out of here like a ball." I chuckled and then picked up the Tupperware and offered it to the other two nurses who passed us by. "How's my mother?" I whispered, as though she could hear me from all the way here.

"In a mood," Martha warned. "Refused to eat and she yelled at Dr. Conrad twice."

I sighed and closed my eyes for a few seconds. Most days were bad, but then there were some that were completely terrible. Mamma never seemed to be in a good mood, and lately, the only days she did smile were when my brother came along. Those days were rare, but I knew he was trying. With my father on his ass, it was hard to spare a few minutes to spend with my mother.

"Wish me luck." I smiled and the two nurses smiled back. They knew how hard Mamma could be, but still, they were great professionals.

When I entered the room, my mother was sleeping, but the soft noise must have alerted her because her eyes shot open, and she turned to face me. It was still a shock seeing the bright Pucci scarf around her bald head.

"Savio?" My mother's weak voice snapped me from my magazine.

"No, Mamma, it's me, Francesca." I corrected her.

"Oh." Her blue eyes settled on me.

"Jesus, please, settle down, no need to be so excited." I watched the machines just to make sure everything was okay. Not that I understood much of what was going on, but at least her heart was beating.

"I'm not," she countered dryly.

"Truthful as always." I sighed and headed toward my usual place beside her bed.

Dr. Conrad said things could and would get worse, he also warned me that my mother could lose some of her memory. Which explained why she was calling for her dead son? It pained me every time, to remind her Savio wasn't coming, but at least she would quickly forget that, too.

I picked up the food tray and inspected what they had brought up for her to eat. Mamma never ate much, but with chemo and the strong medication, she needed more food in her body. I often cooked for her, but she refused that, too. She was a hard woman to please.

"Mamma, you have to eat something."

"I'm not hungry," she rebuked like a petulant child.

"Well, you'll have to eat it anyway."

"*Cazzo*, Francesca, I'm not hungry." That was also new. The swearing and the cursing. They were getting more common as the days passed, and I seemed to annoy her more.

"One banana, and I swear I'll leave you alone."

"If that's what it takes for you to leave, then I'll take all of them."

"You're a ray of sunshine." I kissed her cheek and gave her the banana, and she swatted me away.

The doctor had told me her mood would be one of the first thing to be affected. He didn't know I was already used to them. I had been the one closest to her when growing up, therefore, I had been the subject of my mother's hateful words all my life. Even now, I did my best to ignore them. I knew she was passing through a hard phase, she needed someone to unload her rage on, and if that helped her feel better, then I would be here for her.

She ate her banana slowly and it was obvious she didn't want it. After a few bites, I took it from her and finished the thing myself.

"When is Savio coming?"

"He won't be coming today."

"And Marco?" she asked hopefully.

"It's just me, Mamma, like always." I tried to sound enthusiastic about it, but I knew she wouldn't be. Her boys were her world, always had been.

"Don't you have a life?"

"I-I..." Her question took me by surprise and I was actually speechless. "My husband passed away, Mamma."

"I know that, Francesca, I am not senile," she snapped. My jaw dropped. *Then stop asking me about your dead son.* "Shouldn't you be out there instead of in here?"

"I have nothing else to do," I answered honestly. No life to go back to other than this.

"That's sad, Francesca," she stated, and I had to agree. "You're young, you should be out there looking for a husband."

I sighed loudly. It wasn't the first time she had said such a thing. My mother didn't know that Donato already had someone lined up for me to marry when my mourning period was over. He was *that* fast.

"Yes, Mamma," I agreed and turned my attention toward the new tulips I had brought yesterday.

I arranged them quietly and felt my mother's eyes trailing me the entire time as I did so. Like cooking, they offered me a kind of bliss that I could only find in drugs and alcohol. Since my pills were almost over and my stash was gone, I had to content myself with these little things. Which ended with me cooking too much food every day and buying so many flowers my apartment looked like a florist shop.

Mamma was right, I needed something to do with my life.

"Has your father come to visit?" Mamma asked when I finally stopped fussing about the flowers and sat by her bed.

"I'm sorry."

"That's a no, then. I figured he would be too occupied with his whore." The venom in her voice was the same as when I was twelve years old.

"Why do you even care? You don't even love him, it's a blessing that he ignores you."

My mother looked at me as if I had punched her in the face and as if I had spoken a blasphemy.

"Is that what you thought of your husband? Is that why you let him humiliate you as he did? Parade you around like a cheap whore."

"Please, Mother, I'm not cheap. You and Daddy raised me to be an expensive whore." I threw back at her, and my mother gasped in full shock.

"Isn't it? Wasn't that what he called me? A whore. You let him do it. Your own daughter." My blood was boiling, and I don't know where that anger came from. Oh, wait, yes, I knew. From the fact she was actually mad at me, for my father calling me a whore and treating me like I was the trash stuck to his shoes.

She scoffed. "You don't understand."

"No, Mamma, I don't."

We were back to our silence, and I flipped through the pages of my magazine, not really looking at them. I felt her staring at me, making it harder to concentrate. I settled the magazine on my lap and looked at her.

"I do love your father," she said simply. *Love.* As in present as in still loves and not loved in the past. "Don't make that face at me, I know what you are thinking. I know the man that he is, what he's done—"

"Including ruining my life," I pointed.

"When you love, Francesca, when you really love, you can't help yourself. You don't pick and choose the parts you love about a person; you love them for who and what they are. I know you have hated me for it and maybe you always will, but because I love him, there are things that I will always forgive him for."

"He did despicable things, Mamma," I reminded her.

"Yes, he did," she agreed. "You'll learn one day, that to love is to forgive. That to love is to understand your lover's limitations and not hate them for it but to help them through them."

"Yet he never changed," I grumbled.

I stared at my mother dumbfounded by what she was telling me. What she said was right, a person had to change because they wanted to, and in that moment, sitting with my mother in a hospital room, I realized I had to change, too. I blamed her and my father for so many things in my life. I even blamed Cassio and Paolo, but I never stopped to look at myself. At the damage I had created. The thought sat like a heavy stone in my stomach, and it followed me through the day.

"Honestly, I feel like I am talking to myself," Marie said snapping her fingers and bringing me back to reality.

"Sorry, I got distracted."

Marie gave me one of those looks where she doubted what I was saying but wasn't going to press me about it. We were having coffee at a small little place near her apartment. We'd just come back from a walk at the park, and Reginald was curled at my feet. I secretly wished I were him.

"Is Vitelli coming?" I nibbled on a piece of my doughnut, not really hungry for it.

"No, he had work to do today, he's been busy lately," Marie said. "It's all Cassio's fault."

I couldn't agree more.

"Frankie, what's going on?" She picked up a piece of her chocolate croissant and nibbled on it.

"What?" I settled the doughnut on my plate, and picked up my jasmine tea, to take a sip. The better question was what *wasn't* going on. "I kissed Cassio," The words jumped out of my mouth. *So much for forgetting that.*

Marie slowly placed her croissant on the table and stared at me. "*Excusez moi?*" Her jaw dropped and then when she picked it up, she added aghast. "You what?"

"Well, he was the one to kiss me first, but then I kissed him back."

"I knew it." Why did she sound so gleeful? "Explain, and don't think about leaving anything out."

"There is nothing much to say, one moment he was there and then he kissed me." I sipped my tea leisurely.

"Frankie, that's shit. Feed me more. I need more!"

"Shhh." I widen my eyes commanding her to behave. My cheeks were already blazing, and I was mortified that I'd kissed Cassio when it was supposed to be the last thing we did. I was supposed to hate him!

I didn't know where to start, there were parts of my life which Marie didn't know. Parts like Arabella Moretti's death, my engagement to Paolo, and my relationship with Cassio. I'd kept those things hidden in an attempt to lessen the hurt. Except four years had gone by and the wounds were still festering. Why couldn't I move on?

"Cassio and I used to date… in secret," I confessed.

Marie's eyes widened. "Oh, GOD." Her jaws dropped. "Wait, why in secret?"

"I was already promised to Paolo, our engagement had been set, but then I met Cassio, and I wasn't going to be married for years, and I thought…" I sighed deeply. "I thought nothing was going to happen."

Marie nodded in understanding. "Except it did." She pointed out.

"We fell in love, or I did," I explained. "We dated for two years, and Cassio made me believe he was going to fight for me." I shrugged like it didn't matter. Like what I was saying wasn't like stabbing myself with a sharp knife. "Then one day he broke up with me."

"You're shitting me." Marie was in shock.

I shook my head. "He said he didn't love me and that we were a mistake." To this day I can still remember the words Cassio had said to me. They had been tattooed in my brain, and I was never going to forget them. Not even if I tried.

"What an asshole," Marie pointed with gusto. "He dumped you just like that?"

I shrugged again. "As I said, I was promised. I thought he loved me enough to save me, but apparently he didn't, and I was too blind and stupid not to realize it."

Marie looked at me as if I were a lost puppy in need of a home and some cuddles. She reached for my hand and squeezed it. Then suspicion showed in her almond-colored eyes, and she dropped my hand. "So why did he kiss you?"

Good question. Why? Why did Cassio kiss me?

"Does this have anything to do with that guy at the party?" Marie inquired connecting the dots I hadn't seen myself. "Was he jealous or something?"

"Of me?" I laughed. "Please, as if." I stared at the yellowish colored tea and wracked my brain trying to understand what happened that night. "It's hard to know," I confessed. "One moment he's acting nice, and then the other, he's pushing me away."

"Hot and cold?"

"Cold. Freezing cold." I remembered the way he looked at me, always with those cold pine-green eyes. Except, that day he kissed me, there had been heat in them, so much heat it burned my insides.

A strange ache settled in my heart. I couldn't allow that. "It's been four years. I should have forgotten him," I said to the tea, not being able to look at my friend.

"Clearly you haven't," she pointed out what I didn't want to admit myself.

After psychoanalyzing everything about the kiss, Marie allowed me to change the subject. I was tired of trying to understand why he'd kissed me, or why he saved me from Gianluca, or why he saved me from jail, or why he took me to his house? Or why he did all those nice things? If he hated me so much, why was he always there when I needed someone?

Cassio had let me go all those years ago, and it was my fault for bringing him back into my life once more, but I was supposed to be a one-time deal. We had agreed on never seeing each other again.

Yet here I was, with a massive headache, as I'd tried to figure out what to do next. Staying away from Cassio was the only choice I had. I just prayed he'd stay away from me as well. I couldn't deal with another problem right now, and Cassio was certainly the largest of them all.

12

CASSIO

The headache started at the back of my head and traced a path all the way to my eyes. They were going to pop out at any second. These meetings always took longer than expected. That was what happened when all of my underbosses joined under one roof to discuss business. Today was no exception, hours had gone by, and it felt like I had aged years.

To me, this was always the most boring part of the job. My father always made sure I was present for these meetings, even when I was a child, and barely understood what these men were saying. Barely understood what it was to be a *Mafiosi*. I'd sit on the floor behind his chair playing with my Hot Wheels and pretending I was elsewhere.

Sitting in a chair for hours was torture. My body was always craving to move, stand, and pace. My mind was always working faster than it should. Thoughts sprouting at a million miles an hour. I had to learn to be still, to sit and listen, and then listen some more. To pretend that I gave a shit to most of what these men said.

"We cannot allow the Russians to take our territories," Luca, one of my younger underbosses said. "We have been controlling things in Minneapolis so far."

"Things in Oklahoma have been dire," Carlo, the underboss of

Oklahoma intervened. "Our cargos have been stolen before we can receive them from Texas."

I sighed, it had been going back and forth since the beginning of this meeting. "How many have they taken?" I asked Carlo.

"Until now, we lost three shipments and almost a quarter of our product, if my men hadn't intervened before."

"It's almost as if they know when and where to attack." Matteo Nuzio, underboss of Ohio, pointed out astutely. I glanced at my brother who was cleaning his nails with his knife. When he heard what Matteo said, he looked at me, too.

"Is there a possibility we might have a spy amongst us?" Luca asked tentatively.

I didn't want to say no, but saying yes would also mean telling my men about the fact that we did have a spy. Code name *Volpe*. These were the men I was supposed to trust, but I feared that in telling them, I would scare this fox away and lose all chances of catching him before more damage was done.

"And who do you suppose it is?" Donato said from where he sat to my right, a place that should have belonged to my brother. "Are you accusing good Italian men of treason?"

Luca's nostrils flared, like me, he didn't like Donato. "I suggested no such thing, Donato, I was simply pointing out that—"

"A spy is amongst us," Donato supplied. "That you believe it must be one of us because only we give the orders."

Luca opened his mouth to speak, but I intervened. "There is no point in arguing," I said tiredly. "The problem with the Russian expansion in our territory remains. And their Pakhan, Grigori Petrovich, is still in hiding."

Speaking that name was physically revolting. The thought that my sister's killer was still out there and fucking with me... it made me see red.

"Grigori must pay with his life," Carlo stated, and the other men nodded.

"And he will." I deadpan even though my blood was boiling, my rage ignited.

It took another hour or so before the meeting finally ended, and I sat there as my underbosses filed out of the room. Donato remained sitting on his chair looking at my brother who was back to cleaning his nails. The animosity between them both was as clear as day. I stacked some of the papers I'd brought, numbers of our growing business'. While the Russians were growing bolder and stealing our cargo, I learned to never put all my money on a single horse.

The Outfit invested in diverse sectors, varying from real estate to pharmaceuticals to drugs to stolen cars to countless other markets. While some were taking a toll, others were multiplying like bunnies.

When it became clear Donato wouldn't leave, I turned my attention toward him. "Is there something else?"

"I fear Luca was right," he sighed loudly. "We might have a spy amongst us."

One of my brows shot up, Vitelli, I knew, had his curiosity pricked. "You say that with an awful lot of conviction."

"Think about it, Cassio."

"Boss," I corrected him.

Donato pursed his lips but started again. "Think about it, *Boss*. They had four years to act but only now they seem to be doing so."

I said nothing.

"Grigori tried to have you and your brother killed, too, the day he killed Bella, but he failed. When your father died, it was the time to attack, and he didn't. Why is that?"

"I don't fucking know, Donato, I haven't talked to the man," I spat. Grigori had tried to kill my siblings and me. He managed to kill Arabella, but Vitelli and I survived. Ever since then, Grigori had been ruling from the shadows.

"He didn't have the right incentivization," Vitelli said surprising us both. "What? I listen from time to time."

"That doesn't answer my question, how do you know there's a spy amongst us?" I tapped my fingers against the table.

Donato slowly and with difficulty rose from his chair, the poor thing groaning. "I'm no fool, I have been on this earth longer than you, I see and hear things," he said with a knowing smile. "In case you've forgotten, I am still your consigliere."

I narrowed my eyes and watched as Donato left the room. The moment the door closed behind him; Vitelli broke down in laughter. I turned my glare at him trying to understand what was so damned funny. "He just pulled your ear as though you were a naughty child." He laughed.

It certainly had felt like that. So, what if Donato knew I was keeping information from him?

"Shut up, Vitelli."

"Did you see his face—"

"Vitelli, shut it or I'll do it for you."

"Yes, *Boss*," he offered me with a salute.

I rose from my chair as well, pulled on the sleeves of my dress shirt, and took a deep breath. I might fucking hate him, but Donato was right, Grigori could have come after me right after I took control of the Outfit, and he didn't. So why now? What was propelling him to steal my shit and attack my territory? The answer was simple, and Vitelli had been right, something or better yet, someone was giving him the right incentivization. Grigori was just the hungry dog, and there must be a master behind him.

Vitelli lounged in one of my armchairs, he popped a beer open, brought the bottle to his lips, and savored the beverage before putting it down on his knee. I looked at my cup of cold water and took a sip as well before placing it on the center table.

It was Sunday and Vitelli had insisted we for once have a family lunch, as it used to be tradition before it all came crashing down. We had been sitting in complete silence while we waited for his girlfriend to show up. My brother wanted me to spend some time with her to "get to know her better." Which was unnecessary, I already knew all the important things I needed to know. All I cared about was if she was loyal to Vitelli. From what I gathered; the girl was.

"Until when are you going to keep up that charade?" Vitelli asked as he picked up his beer and pointed toward my water.

"It's not a charade," I pointed out. "I don't drink."

"You don't have to prove yourself anymore," Vitelli said. "You are boss, no one is going to take that from you."

I scoffed. "There will always be someone trying to take it from me, Vitelli. As long as I live, there will be greedy men coming after what we have."

"Why are you always so grim?" he teased.

"It's called being realistic."

"I'd say pessimistic." He argued.

I rolled my eyes and reached for the water. "Where is your girlfriend again?"

"Already bored of my company?" He joked. I sighed loudly as if to say yes, but that only caused him to laugh. "She's getting ready. You know how girls are."

The fact that my brother didn't correct me when I said "girlfriend" was concerning, and it made me wonder if he even noticed.

"What could be taking her so goddamned long?"

"Do you have something better to do?"

"As a matter of fact, yes, I do—"

"Work doesn't count, Cassio," Vitelli argued. "It's Sunday, for once let it go." His phone rang and Vitelli stood to take the call from Marie. It seemed something happened because he looked at me and then sighed loudly.

I didn't like the look on his face and disliked even more the words that would follow out of his mouth. "Yeah, she can come."

She?

Vitelli pocketed his phone and looked at me with unsettling eyes. "Francesca Manci is coming over."

Fuck.

The last time I'd seen her, things hadn't gone exactly how I had planned them. I had intended to question her about Paolo and the money he embezzled from the Outfit. Then I ended up kissing her, which wasn't part of the script. Kissing her had been a mistake. The sanest one I'd ever committed.

"Is it going to be a problem?" Vitelli eyed me suspiciously.

"Why would it be?" I snapped.

"Let us not forget the last time you two were in a room together."

And how could I forget that? I had my tongue down her throat, for God's sake. An image of that day popped into my mind as though I was there all over again. Francesca's soft and warm lips against mine. The sweet taste of cherry in my mouth, her breathy moans echoing in my ear as she rode my leg with abandon.

I had been a fucking asshole. I knew she had been close, a few seconds longer and she would have shattered, but I didn't want it to be like that. I wanted to be in her when she orgasmed.

As if that was ever going to happen.

I kept forgetting that Francesca was out of reach. Not mine. Not even if I wished for her to be. She was bound to marry another man, one that wasn't me and never would be. Even if I wanted her, I would have to control myself. She was not my problem to deal with.

Not mine.

FRANCESCA

W<small>HAT AM</small> I <small>DOING HERE</small>?

The car stopped and Marie opened the door, stepping out of it. "Marie, this is not a good idea."

"It's going to be all right," she assured me and patted her cream-colored dress that fit her perfectly.

I looked at my ensemble, an off-the-shoulder green dress that was a bit too short. It was not exactly the choice I would have made for Sunday lunch, but since my boxes were still packed and I hadn't had time to find something better, the green dress it was.

"You look fine," she said rushing me out of the cab.

"I'm not worried about that," I said as I finally stepped out.

Vitelli lived in a large condo, nothing close to the size of Marie's, but from the outside, it looked cozy. Like somewhere you'd live with your family and would raise your children. At least the lunch would be held in his place and not Cassio's.

Ugh.

That name.

It had been two weeks since I'd last seen him. Or better yet, since he kissed me, almost gave me my first orgasm in years, and then left. Ah, and let us not forget the ultimatum he'd given me. One month to return to Donato's house. One month of freedom before everything was stripped away from me. If I didn't hate Cassio then, I hated him now.

"You're glaring again," Marie pointed out.

I smoothed my features as we walked into the lobby, our heels clacking against the black polished stone. Marie led the way and hit the button for Vitelli's floor. I rubbed my hands back and forth against the fabric of my dress trying to wipe away the sweat.

"You're making me nervous," she said.

"You shouldn't have forced me to come," I answered back.

"You were holed up in that apartment of yours, sleeping—again."

True. I was tired. Spending my days at the hospital was tiring, and all I wanted to do when I had some time to myself was sleep my fears away. I still hadn't told Marie or Antoine about my mother. I didn't know why, maybe not saying it wouldn't make it real.

I took a deep breath, but it did nothing to calm my heart. Before I knew it, the elevator doors opened, and we stepped into Vitelli's apartment. He was the only one standing in the hallway. He greeted Marie with a kiss that had me looking away, not wanting to intrude on their PDA.

"I'm glad you could make it, Frankie." Vitelli grabbed my hand and kissed my knuckles like a true gentleman. "Make yourself at home. *Si?*"

"*Si, grazie,*" I thanked him.

"Cassio is somewhere, he had some calls to make, but he's going to be back for lunch."

I sighed in relief, finally some good news, at least I had a few minutes to myself. Marie pulled me along and began showing me around the place.

Vitelli's bachelor pad was incredible, decorated in tons of white and grays, with a large living area and a kitchen that left my hands itching to use it. I bet he'd never used it in his life. The one-story apartment was twice the size of mine, and it contained an outside balcony with a jacuzzi and a small garden—which looked suspiciously well-kept.

"We had sex there," Marie pointed with pink cheeks.

"Good to know," I laughed.

We sat in the living area and when Cassio proceeded not to show up, I began to tense up even more. Which was odd, given I should be doing the exact opposite. I excused myself and headed toward the bathroom. I locked the door and opened my purse.

I loved Marie, I really did, but I couldn't do this without some help, my hands were shaking as I opened the orange bottle I still had, there were two pills left. My last two pills. Without a second thought, I popped them and swallowed them dry. Shoving the pill bottle back inside my purse I flushed the toilet just for appearances sake.

When I opened the door, the devil stared back at me. I had two seconds before he shoved me inside the bathroom again and locked the door behind him.

"What are you doing." I cried out in surprise.

"Where are they?"

"What?" I frowned.

He opened his hand. "The drugs."

My jaw dropped, and I had no idea what to do but stare at him. Cassio took my purse from my hand and opened it. I tried to fight him, but the bathroom was too small, and he was simply too big and powerful. He proceeded to remove the orange bottle and growled. His back was to me, but I could tell I had poked the bear with a very short stick.

He turned to face me showing me the bottle. "Why, Francesca?" Why did he sound so wounded?

"How would you even know?" I snapped still trying to figure it out.

"I watched you," he said simply. "It wasn't so hard to tell."

"Y-you watched me?"

His nostrils flared; he hadn't meant to admit that out loud. He took my hand in his and this time it was so gentle I was stunned into letting him hold it. He turned it so my palm was face up, with his thumb, he smoothed the indentations I'd left in them.

"You hurt yourself when you're nervous," he said, his voice was smooth and low. "Why?"

I looked into his pine-green eyes surprised to find they weren't cold, but they weren't blazing either. "It helps," I confessed. "It numbs the need to use."

"Yet, you did use."

I looked away and pulled my hand back and pressed it tightly to my body ignoring the way it still tingled. "Why do you care?" I had asked this question so many times.

"Why do you think?" he snapped. "Fuck, Francesca, why do you think!"

"Cassio," I said softly. "Open the door."

"Not until you tell me why you used."

I sighed in frustration. He wasn't going to let me out and Marie and Vitelli probably suspected something was happening. I had two options, either tell him the truth or lie, and the second one would never work on Cassio Moretti. He could always read me easily.

I crossed my arms. "Because I was nervous. I needed to take some of the edge off."

"Why were you nervous?" He took a step toward me, crowding my space. "Tell me, *Principessa*."

I hated how the Italian endearment on his lips sounded so sexual and hot. How it made my legs quiver and the butterflies in my stomach flutter. I needed to kill those damned butterflies before they led me into trouble once again.

"I already answered your question, now let me go, Cassio. This is not funny."

"I'm not laughing, am I?"

I rolled my eyes. He took yet another step closer, and I hit the counter. Cassio's hands landed on either side of my hips. They were far from me, but still, I felt their heat burning my skin as though they were on me. He leaned down, a lock of hair falling over his eyes. I had the unnatural urge to rake my fingers through his hair, so I dug my nails into the palms of my hands.

"You're doing it again," he whispered, or at least it sounded like he was.

How did he know?

"I am always aware of you, Francesca, even when I shouldn't. Even when I don't want to."

"Why are you telling me this?"

"Why are you so nervous?" He asked ignoring my question.

My head spun with the change in subject. His scent was invading my space, and I couldn't think straight. My eyes darted to his lips, and I wanted nothing more than to end the distance between us and kiss him—

"No," I shook my head. "Get out, Cassio."

Amusement flickered in his eyes, and he smiled. It was so beautiful like the setting of the sun over the sea. I'd forgotten how pretty it was. I had a feeling he didn't do that often, not anymore.

"I want to fucking kiss you, Francesca," he confessed.

I wanted him to fucking kiss me, but we both knew that was the wrong thing to do. This was the past all over again. We were playing with fire, and we would both burn.

"Why?" I whispered.

"Because I always want to fucking kiss you." He cupped my cheeks, forcing me to look into his eyes. The green was almost gone, replaced by lust.

I wasn't given a chance to answer him because there was a knock on the door keeping us from messing up. "Frankie, are you okay?" Marie's voice sounded through the door.

Cassio slowly stepped away, giving me some space to breathe. He ran his fingers through his hair and ran his thumb under his lower lip.

"I'm fine," I answered as my eyes met his. "I'll be out in a sec." I waited until I heard the clacking of her heels and let my shoulders sag. "You can't do this," I snapped pushing him back. "We can't do this." I pointed in between us.

I side-stepped Cassio, and unlocked the door, checking both ways before shutting it as I left. Cassio couldn't play with me like that. I wasn't his toy to be used whenever he felt like it.

13

FRANCESCA

I watered my last flower and then settled on the floor beside Reggie. "So, Reggie, what are we watching tonight? Reality show or Clueless?" Reggie hid his little muzzle under his paw. Okay then, his answer couldn't be clearer.

After a few minutes surfing the TV channels, I squealed in content when I saw *Star Wars: Empire Strikes Back* was on. What could I do, I was a sucker for those.

"It's you and me, Reggie." I scratched his little ears and then reached for my bowl of chips.

A bag of chips and two more Star Wars movies later, my eyelids grew heavy. Even though I spent a lot of time in the hospital, it was oddly very tiring. I had hoped to get some sleep during the weekend but that didn't go as planned. Not when Marie had dragged me to Vitelli's place for lunch.

To say it had been awkward was an understatement. Cassio had avoided me like the plague, barely looking at me like I had offended him or something. I couldn't tell if he was pissed or if he was relieved. Either way, that was the longest lunch I'd had in my life, and at the first chance of escape, I entered a cab and returned home.

Reggie rearranged himself on my leg and yawned deeply causing me to do so as well. Once he was comfortable enough, he resumed his deep slumber. My neck fell back against the sofa, and I looked toward the corridor that led to my room. *Too far.* I groaned inwardly and decided it wasn't worth it. Slowly, my eyes began to close, and I finally lost the battle giving in to sleep.

A loud banging noise woke me up with a start. Reggie, who on my lap, jumped. Instantly, my heart began to speed up as I tried to situate myself. The first thing I saw were the boxes, which reminded me I was still in my living room. Still drunk on sleep, I knelt trying to get my bearings. I squinted my eyes as I looked at the television which was still on.

The loud banging sounded through the room again. Someone was trying to tear off my door.

I let out a yelp. This time it was louder, which caused Reggie to bark, his little frame trembling. With my heart beating fast, I stood up. None of my neighbors were loud, in fact, they were weirdly silent. My eyes darted to the clock on the wall. *3:45.* Another bang. I jumped back knowing without a doubt the sound wasn't coming from my neighbors. Quickly, I picked up Reggie, trying to make him stop barking. I stood there in the middle of my living room, my eyes glued to the door.

Inhaling deeply, I tried to calm myself but once the air got stuck in my throat, I knew there was no point in it.

Someone banged on my door again. I closed my eyes, caught between opening it or staying where I was. I knew my father was after me, that he wanted to drag me back home. What if he had sent one of his men?

The door trembled, and I knew eventually the person would break in, I searched for my phone trying to think of someone to call. The first person that popped into my mind was Cassio, but I refused to call him again. If it were one of Donato's men then there was no point in pretending, I wasn't home, he was going to enter either I wanted to or not.

"I'm coming!" I shouted once they knocked again on my door. No reason to delay the inevitable.

Before I could even open it completely, the door was shoved against me, and I stumbled back. I watched horrified as a man entered my apartment, more like fell inside. I didn't even have the time to process what just happened, as he lay slumped on the floor his back facing me as he tried to stand up. An entirely new kind of fear took over me.

Who the hell was he?!

I took a couple of steps back trying to put some distance between me and the stranger. Reggie, who was far from a guard dog, was hiding somewhere by now. I looked at the man lying on my floor, he wore a black shirt and black pants, and his hair was dark, but I figured it was because he was soaked.

"*Principessa*," I heard the whisper. He tried getting up again, placing his big masculine hands on the floor but failed miserably. "Shit!" he grunted.

Slowly, I watched as the man turned around lying on his back. It took me exactly five seconds to realize who was lying on my floor—bleeding. Then the endearment processed in my head.

"Cassio!" I cried out kneeling on the floor.

I practically flew toward him, forgetting all about my previous fears, as though that never happened. I removed the hair from his face and pressed my fingers to his neck trying to feel his pulse. I knew he was alive, but I needed to know just how much danger he was in. It was then that I also realized it was not water that coated his clothes, it was blood to.

Blood on his beautiful face. Blood on his neck, hair, and hands, blood everywhere.

He tried sitting up and so, I slipped my arm under his, moving him against the wall, so that he could lean on it. Once I moved away, I noticed my hands were stained by blood. The front side of his shirt had a wide tear right on his abdomen, and as gently as I could, I pulled it up. Suddenly I felt really dizzy, my head began to spin, and my blood pressure dropped. With one hand against the wall, I tried steadying myself. *There is blood...there is blood coming out of him.*

I inhaled deeply five times and then counted to ten, and finally opened my eyes. This was not the time to freak out. Cassio had taken on a sickly color that worried me, his face white and his lips blue.

"Cassio! Cassio, wake up." I shook his face with my hands. He grunted but complied finally opening his eyes.

A pained smile marked his beautiful face. "*Principessa,*" he called again, his hand moving towards mine and gripping it hard.

"Yes, Cassio. It's me. I need to call the doctor." I tried to stand but he pulled me down. I was surprised by the amount of force he had.

"No," he gritted out.

"Cassio, you're bleeding," I pleaded almost like a cry. "You're hurt."

"Help me stand."

"Cassio," I complained again but he was having none of it, he tried to stand once more and before he could slip and hurt himself even further, I helped him up.

"Sink," he gritted out and practically shoved me toward the kitchen.

He shot forward leaning against the counter, doubled over my sink, and began to throw up. Not knowing what to do I kept my hand on his back in case he slipped or fell. *I don't know what to do!* I quickly reached for a glass and filled it with water until it almost spilled. My hands were shaking so much that most of it fell on the floor.

"Fuck." He swore again and pushed himself away from the sink. He turned around and leaned against it.

"Here." I handed him the glass of water and he took it from me gulping it down. I couldn't make myself look away from the tear on his shirt and what lay underneath it. Or think about the fact he was bleeding, and I was still standing here, instead of calling a doctor.

The *clink* of the glass against the counter snapped me out of it, and I looked back at him. Cassio had closed his eyes and was breathing hard. I didn't know if he was going to faint or be sick again.

I moved toward him once more, but he turned around and puked again.

"Okay, I'm good now," he said after he cleaned his hand and my sink as well. He turned to face me.

"GOOD?" I shouted. "You're bleeding," I pointed, my voice wavered.

He looked at his hands and then pulled at his black shirt which would've been bloody if the color didn't hide it well. He let it fall back until it stuck to his skin.

"It's not mine," Cassio noted. His voice was slightly altered, and I wondered if this was the effect of blood loss or if he was drunk. He was certainly slurring a lot.

"I'm pretty sure it is." I pointed to his wound.

"Shit," he said again as he looked down at it.

"I need to call the doctor." I tried once more to reach for my phone, but he grabbed me. "Cassio, stop! I need to ca—"

"No doctors." His voice was oddly serious now.

"Then let me call your brother at least."

"Don't!" he practically snapped. "No Vitelli," Cassio ordered and then he hiccuped.

"Are you drunk?" The question left my lips, yet it sounded so stupid when the man was bleeding. This was the last thing I needed to worry about.

"No." Pause. "I don't know." He dropped his head "Fuck, Francesca, I fucked up." He shoved his head into his hands and began shaking it, and all I could hear now was mumbling as his hand blocked most of the sound.

"Cassio, we need to stop the bleeding," I said but he didn't seem to hear me. Moving toward him, I slowly put my hand on his arm, he was freezing. As always, my instinct to help set in and I focused on just that—helping him.

The moment my hands touched his skin, he shivered and dropped his arms, allowing me to look at his face. Even like this, he was achingly beautiful. His deep green eyes focused on me. His full lips were slightly parched. There was blood on his strong, defined jaw and caking his lovely light brown locks. The man had no business looking this good while he was dying.

"We need to stop the bleeding," I said again, this time he nodded understanding what I just said. "I don't know what to do, Cassio," I confessed, every ounce of the fear I was feeling apparent in my tone.

"No doctors. No Vitelli," he said again. He sounded awfully worried, and so I nodded, even if I didn't agree with it.

"Then show me what to do," I whispered.

14

FRANCESCA

Cassio began removing his shirt, and I helped pull the wet fabric from his freezing skin. Once discarded on the floor, I looked back at him and tried not to freak out. I bit my tongue as hard as I could to keep me from crying. His entire abdomen was coated with blood and to make matters even worse, a large bruise was starting to form on his ribs and on his hip bone.

"It's not mine," he repeated for the fifth time since I helped him to the bathroom.

Even with him carrying most of his weight, it took us a long time to reach my room. Cassio grunted all of the way here which gave me cause to think the wound on his abdomen wasn't the only thing wrong with him. When we finally arrived, it took me another few minutes to shove him inside my bathroom. He wanted to lie down on my bed, but I strongly refused him.

"Well, I have to clean it either way," I snapped, I couldn't help myself, I was scared.

I stepped back trying to look at his wound, assessing what the hell I was supposed to do. Thankfully, it wasn't large, but I didn't know if it was deep. Dread filled me when I realized I would need to touch it.

Before I could move, Cassio pressed his fingers against it, and groaned loudly.

"What are you doing!" I swatted his hand away.

"It's not that deep. Do you have band-aids?"

"Band-aids, Cassio? You want me to give you band-aids?" I asked, unbelieving.

"Adhesive tape works, too."

I ran my hands across my face. "You've got to be kidding me," I whispered so only I could hear.

Having no clue what to do, I began searching through my mini first aid kit and took out all of the things I thought could be useful. Cassio was now shivering beside me which added to my growing list of worries.

I didn't stop to think anymore, I just set myself to work. I took the cotton swabs and the antiseptic–hopefully, Grey's taught me something– then I set them aside again, remembering I needed to clean my hands. The act was hard since he was taking almost all the space in the bathroom. Once I was done, I dried them quickly on the towel and picked up the swab again. Swallowing hard, I pressed it against his wound. Cassio let out a hiss, and I looked back at him.

"Sorry," I apologized but there was nothing I could do.

I focused on the process of cleaning it as best as I could, and eventually, he stopped hissing. Once I judged it to be clean enough, I sprayed the antiseptic, earning a new hiss. From there, I took the largest band-aid I found and placed it over his wound, then opened another one and did the same.

Cassio was still covered in blood, I needed to clean him up, so I moved toward my shower stall and turned on the faucet and left it there so it could warm up. Once I turned back to him, I noticed he was looking at me, his face was blank as if he were miles away and not here.

"Cassio, you need to warm up," I spoke softly reaching for him. The only indication that he heard me was a slight nod. He didn't move as I had expected him to. "You need to remove your clothes." I pointed out.

Cassio didn't move, so without any hesitation, I began removing his clothes. With his shirt gone, it only left his pants and shoes. Face blazing, I knelt on the floor and began unbuckling his belt and then unzipped his jeans.

Thank God Cassio was somewhere deep in his head, lost in his thoughts. I wouldn't be able to do all this if he were one hundred percent conscious. There was a lot to look at which made it really hard not to do so. Despite his situation and the wound on his abdomen, Cassio was beautiful. Toned abs, strong arms, and powerful thighs, all of them defined like he had been made of stone instead of flesh and bone.

When the time came to remove his boxers, I froze but he needed to shower, and I needed to clean his clothes, so he had something to wear. Closing my eyes, I reached for his boxers and pulled them down. I had seen Paolo naked before, it shouldn't have been a surprise, but Cassio was a manly *man*. Thankfully he said nothing as I took his briefs and set them together with the dirty clothes.

The mirror was beginning to fog, and I could see the small puffs of steam coming from the shower. I quickly tested the water so that he wouldn't scald his skin. Sliding my arm underneath his good side, I helped him into the shower. Most of the water hit me first but I didn't care. Once I was done helping him in, I stepped back out, already sodden. He closed his eyes once the first jets of hot water fell over him. I looked at his band-aids and they were still firmly attached to his skin.

I glanced at his clothes and then at him, unsure whether or not it was a sane idea. "Cassio, I need to wash your clothes, I'll be right back, okay?"

Cassio nodded, just like he had been doing all this time, but he didn't talk. I waited a few more minutes just to make sure he wasn't going to collapse inside the bathroom. I closed the glass door and picked up his clothes from the floor. Quickly, I left the bathroom, leaving the bathroom door open was a good idea, I needed to hear him if something happened.

I ran from my room and into the laundry area, shoved his clothes in the washing machine, and threw washing powder inside.

"Fuck!" I cursed when the machine didn't turn on quickly enough. By the time it did, my nerves were already eating me up.

"Cassio," I called, once I reached my room once more.

Nothing.

"Cassio," I tried again.

I reached the bathroom in record time but halted once I saw him sitting on the floor. Why was I so stupid?! I shouldn't have left him. I should have brought my phone with me, I needed to call 911, and I didn't care about the consequences. I opened the glass door bracing for the worst.

Cassio was sitting with his head bowed between his knees. Water poured over him, the skin on his back was gleaming in an angry red. I stepped inside the shower cursing when the scalding water touched me. Quickly, I turned the cold faucet on. *I had turned it on.* I recall making sure the water wasn't too hot.

"Cassio." I crouched beside him. The sight of him was haunting. His powerful frame seemed so small right now.

I placed my hand on his upper arm, his skin burning. Slowly he turned toward me and when he opened his eyes, I finally allowed myself to breathe. I knew he was alive, but the thoughts of something worse happening just kept coming back. I looked at the white tiled floor and noticed the water was still coming out in a pinkish hue.

"I'm going to wash you, okay?" Not waiting for his answer, I reached for a loofah and began cleaning him up.

"I killed them." He finally spoke again, startling me.

"Who, Cassio?" I asked as I cleaned him.

"All of them."

Okay. Breathe, Francesca.

My heartbeat increased, and I tried to ignore it. I knew what Cassio was, and I knew what being Capo meant. You didn't get to rule the Outfit unless you were worthy of that title, and I knew Cassio didn't keep it by being nice.

"I lost it, Francesca, I killed his men."

"Who's, Cassio?" I asked worriedly.

"Grigori Petrovich. I found them at a bar and killed them all," he whispered.

"It's okay," was all I managed to say. What he was telling me was definitely Outfit business, but for me, it was all gibberish.

"No, Francesca, you don't understand! I killed his men today," he said and that was all of it.

When I was done washing him, he finally stood up, almost towering over me. I yanked the towel from the bar and began gently patting him, avoiding the area where I had patched him up. He didn't complain but neither did he speak.

"To bed now," I ordered him, and he didn't complain either. I led him toward my bedroom and pulled the duvets on my bed.

Out of respect, I looked away from his nakedness, but mainly because I was a coward. In the end, I took one small peek at his peach-shaped ass and then quickly closed my eyes.

"You can look if you want," he said with a smile. My eyes widened; he was facing me. I did everything not to look down. "What's pretty is meant to be seen."

"God," I rolled my eyes. "You must have hit your head pretty hard. Go to bed, Cassio."

He sat on the edge and slowly slid in. His wince was the only indication that he was in pain. I pulled up the blankets covering him up carefully. The amount of time it took me to turn off the bathroom light was the amount of time it took him to fall asleep. I sighed deeply, not knowing what to do now. Reggie and that big heart of his curled right beside Cassio and closed his eyes, too.

5:08. The clock read.

I sat on my sofa, foot tapping anxiously against the floor. Forty minutes ago, I had put Cassio to sleep. More than one hour ago, he stormed into my apartment. My head snapped toward where the stains of blood had been.

After he fell asleep, I managed to clean the mess left in his wake and also changed from my wet clothes. The moment I sat on the sofa it all came crashing down. I was shaking, and I couldn't tell if it was the fear of what just happened or if I wanted to use. Who was I kidding? I knew that both options were correct.

Thankfully there was nothing in my apartment that I could use, but on the downside, I had no painkillers he could take once he woke up.

My mind was still trying to wrap around the fact that none other than Cassio was sleeping in my bed. Today I experienced a kind of fear I hadn't experienced in a *long time*. The kind that had crushed me once.

I couldn't lose anyone else, not like I had lost Arabella, my best friend. It was undeniable that I still obviously cared for Cassio. I would always do so, no matter what he'd done to me, a part of me would always care. I don't know what I would have done if he had—

"No," I whispered.

He's alive, I reminded myself. He was alive, breathing, and safe. Or at least that's what I hoped. I had no idea of the extent of his bruises, or if they were serious. Most of all, I had no idea if he was safe. Cassio didn't just freak me out of my mind—possibly giving me a heart attack—he told me things tonight that were undoubtedly very sensitive. He wasn't just Cassio, if it were that, then my life would be easier. Cassio was Capo of the Outfit.

I looked at the phone once again.

I shouldn't, I really shouldn't, he asked me not to. What if I didn't? What if something really bad happened and I didn't do something to avoid it?

I reached for the phone.

The phone rang thrice before it was picked up. "Frankie?" A very sleepy Marie answered the phone.

"Can you put Vitelli on the phone?"

"Frankie it's," there was a pause. "It's 5 a.m. Is everything all right?"

"Marie, I need to talk to Vitelli, now." I hated to snap at my friend, but it was urgent.

"Francesca," he called me back to earth.

"Shit." I cursed; I hadn't reached this part in my head. In fact, I didn't even know I was going to call him until two seconds ago. "Okay," I said more to myself than to him. I heard Marie's voice in the background, and I knew she was thinking the worst right now. *Better end this misery.*

"I think Cassio screwed up. Screwed up big." I heard covers being shifted on the other end of the line.

"What do you mean, where's my brother?" The worry in his tone was apparent, and I hated myself for being the one to bring him bad news.

"He's here, but he's hurt." There was no reason to lie. A long silence followed then.

"Here where? I'm leaving right now."

"No. No. No." I stood up. "You can't come, he made me promise not to tell you."

"Francesca." He growled. "Where's my brother?"

"He's in my apartment. He's safe." *I think.*

"Your apartment?" he asked with the same amount of disbelief I was still feeling. Then I proceeded to tell him everything.

"What kind of meds do you have there?" he asked when I was done talking.

"None," I whined. None since I took my last two pills yesterday. Aside from that, I only had my mini kit, and it was a pitiful little thing.

"Okay, that's fine." He assured me. "When you check his bandages make sure it's not getting infected. If it keeps bleeding nonstop, put some sugar on his wound. That should stop it. Do you have chamomile or turmeric?"

"Hmm, yeah. I have both."

"Give him as much chamomile tea as you can, it will help with the muscle pain, and make some turmeric tea as well, it should serve as a painkiller."

How the hell did he know all of that?

"Francesca?"

"Hmm."

"Don't let him walk around or anything with too much physical exertion, from what you told me, I think he must have cracked his ribs."

"Okay." I made a mental note of all he just told me. "Vitelli, what if it doesn't stop bleeding?" I asked because it was the one thing that worried me the most.

"Then you take him to the ER and call me. I'll deal with the rest. It will be all right, Francesca. Just call me when he wakes up. Marie will text you, my number. Okay?"

No. It was not okay.

"Yeah." Another pause before I sighed again. "Vitelli, one more thing."

"Don't tell me it gets worse," he protested.

"Sorry," I admitted. "He kept telling me he killed them, over and over again. When I asked him who, he started talking nonsense. He did mention something about a Grigori Petrovich and something about a bar," I told him almost everything, earning me a long vivid line of curses.

"Fuck!" he shouted. "Okay, I'll post some guards at your building in case something happens."

"Will something happen?" I gripped the phone harder.

"I don't know, we never know with the Russians, just... call me if something happens."

"Okay," I assured him and that was the end of it.

I dropped the phone on my sofa and headed toward my door, then locked it once more. It was a foolish thing to do if the Russians wanted to get in, they would, but at least it gave me a sense of safety. I then headed into the kitchen and took a knife from the counter. Turning all my lights off, I headed back to my room where I found Cassio sleeping soundly in my bed.

I checked his bandage, there was no blood seeping from the wound but that didn't mean it wouldn't get infected. I stared at his torso and the massive bruise forming over it and then unable to look at it any longer I turned away. Anger boiled in my blood and rage coiled in the depths of my soul. I wanted the men who hurt him to pay.

15

CASSIO

"What is going on between you and Francesca Manci?"

I wiped my bloody hands on the towel and kept my eyes on it, ignoring Vitelli completely. Pain radiated from where I had broken my rib, but I ignored it. The skin where I had gotten ten stitches was beginning to itch as well, but like the ribs, I ignored them.

"Since I know you haven't gone deaf, I'll take your silence as my answer."

Closing my eyes and taking a deep breath, I gave him my attention. "Drop it" my eyes ordered him, but knowing my brother, that only fueled his imagination.

"So, there is something going on?" he whispered even though there was no need to.

I turned my attention toward the dead Russian in the room. He was strapped to a metal chair, his face busted, and bullet holes made him look like Swiss cheese——a courtesy of yours truly.

Interrogations had always been Luciano's forte, his area of expertise. But after what happened last week, I needed to vent some remnant pent-up rage from that night. Attacking that Russian bar had been a bad idea, but they were growing on my nerves, and after I learned that they killed two of my men in a brawl, I lost my shit.

In my rage, I'd forgotten my promise to myself and had drunk two shots of vodka before pulling my gun out and killing the Russian fuckers. All of them were affiliated to the Bratva. I didn't let a single one live. Although I felt guilty for drinking, I knew I was getting closer to avenging my sister.

"Vitelli," I sighed again. "Don't you think we have more troubling issues to discuss other than my sex life?"

He grinned like a motherfucker. "So, you two, hmm?" He wiggled his brows.

I stared at the ceiling and contemplated if God would forgive me for committing fratricide. Sometimes I wondered how he was still breathing. Vitelli had a gift of pissing people off, constantly, always getting on their last nerves.

Ignoring my brother and his questions, I turned to my enforcer who was still in the room. "Take the body and dump it where the Russians will find it."

"We are poking the bear," Vitelli finally dropped the Francesca matter. "Grigori will come for us."

"I'm counting on it," I said. "We can't kill him if he remains locked up in his fort," I explained.

Grigori Petrovich had been hiding in his mansion ever since he killed my sister. His place was highly protected, making the White House look like child's play. Which was why it made it so difficult to kill the man.

"We need to lure him out," I said running my thumb under my lower lip—pensively.

"What about this *Volpe*?" Vitelli reminded me of the spy.

I looked at the dead Russians.

I clenched my hands and said to Luciano. "I want you to send a message," I said with a calm I did not possess. "Tell Grigori I'm coming for him, and that I know who his spy is."

"But we don't know." Vitelli shot out.

"He doesn't need to know that," I said. "All we need is for him to believe it. And that's how we are going to lure him out."

"Using his own spy?"

I nodded. "This is what we are going to do."

Then I proceeded to explain my plan. From what we learned in tonight's interrogation, was that the *Volpe* was amongst my higher ranks. Something I already suspected. So, my plan consisted of two parts. I would give each of my underbosses an order, a message of sorts. About the cargo I was sending, a time and place for it, etc. Then, all I had to do was wait for the Russians to show up, and I would know who betrayed me.

If this fox thought himself cunning, then he was in for a treat because I was about to hunt him down as if it were a rabid dog. When I found him, because I would, then I'd skin him alive and tear him piece by piece.

After discussing the plan thoroughly, I headed upstairs to my office. Once inside, I headed toward the cabinet and poured Vitelli ——who had followed me——a glass of whiskey while I took a bottle of water.

"Who do you suspect the spy is?" he asked, setting his tumbler on the table.

I stopped by the floor-to-ceiling window and observed the empty room below. It was still early. The club wouldn't open for hours. I pondered Vitelli's question. "I have my suspicions."

"I think it's Donato." His answer did not surprise me, not in the least. "Just think about it before you dismiss it. He's a slimy fucker."

I cocked one brow. "The Outfit is full of slimy fuckers."

Vitelli shook his head. "Not like him."

"What would he have to gain?" I mused.

"What would anyone have to gain by allying with the Russians?"

Power.

I thought about it but kept it quiet. That's when I saw the glimmer in my brother's eyes and knew whatever he was about to say was probably going to hit a nerve.

"You should be careful with Francesca."

I knew he would come back to that. "I'm not in the mood, Vitelli."

"I'm just saying." He picked his drink up and stared at it. "She's his daughter."

"Vitelli," I warned. "Enough."

He sighed and leaned back. I wasn't going to talk about her with him. Francesca had been on my mind since…always. I couldn't—even if I tried—forget her. Ever since I kissed her, it was hard forgetting her taste. Cherry. Francesca tasted as sweet as cherries. She was my favorite treat.

"You know she was married to Paolo Biancini."

That was a fact I wanted to forget. "And?"

"And," he deadpanned. "He and Donato had a falling out. You never wondered why?"

All the damned time. Lately more than before. "What are you getting at?" He turned the whiskey in his cup and took a while to speak his mind. "Spit it out."

"Maybe you should talk to her," he suggested. "She might know something."

Vitelli left me with that thought and it didn't sit well with me. I didn't want to involve Francesca more than I already had. Going to her place after what happened at the Russian bar was a mistake. I put her in danger. If anything happened to her, I would never forgive myself.

The clock struck five, I still had work to do, but Francesca was on my mind and when she was there, I was a goner. I looked at my computer seeing all I had to do and stood up. I had to see her. It was a bad idea, but I couldn't stop myself.

So, I left.

It took me twenty minutes to reach the hospital, from what Vince —the guard I had designated to follow her since the night I saved her from jail—said, she was still with her mother. I had known about Domenica Manci's illness for a while now, ever since Francesca began visiting the hospital every day. I grew curious, so I investigated it.

The sight of her almost brought me down to my knees, and like a perverted fuck, I watched Francesca walk out of the hospital. It was early autumn, and she wore a purple floral dress that offered me a privileged view of her legs. What was she thinking, she was going to catch a cold this way. I couldn't help looking at her legs and imagine them wrapped around my waist as I–

I shook that image away and focused on the task at hand. It wouldn't do having her affect me this way every time I saw her. Francesca was like a blazing star, much like the sun. She was heat, she was light. Her beauty was blinding. And here I was, a black hole, a tragedy in the making.

She was walking my way, so I left the shadows. The moment Francesca saw me she halted. She looked both ways, probably thinking about running, but there was nowhere she could go that I wouldn't follow.

One by one her feet moved my way; I stood there still, trying to get my bearings. A gust of wind hit her, and her scent traveled my way, and I breathed it in greedily.

Francesca stopped before me and hugged herself. "What are you doing here?" she grilled me.

Good question, what are you doing here, Cassio?

I watched as her enticing sapphire eyes narrowed and she looked both ways, then past me, and then finally she met my eyes. Francesca opened her mouth and then closed it.

"We need to talk," I blurted before she had something else to say.

"Talk," she scoffed. "I don't think that's a good idea."

"I wasn't asking, Francesca." My voice sounded harsher than I desired.

She had this effect on me, I couldn't control myself when I was so damned near her. Her eyes, her scent, her smart mouth, her beauty, it was too much. So, anger was the only way to ward off these... feelings I had whenever I was close.

"I have nothing left to say to you." She was digging her nails into the palms of her hand, and I hated she was hurting herself because of me.

"There's a coffee shop down the street," I said, ignoring her observation.

"I'm tired, Cassio," she said weakly, and I almost caved then.

Francesca, despite her alluring beauty, did look exhausted. She looked thinner and paler, and there were deep circles under her eyes. Her hair was tied in a messy bun, held up by a pen, which I had the urge to pull out and watch as it fell over her shoulders, I always loved her hair.

"It won't take too long."

"The last time we talked it didn't end so well," she stated.

Was this how she thought about our kiss? As a mistake? It hadn't been one of my best moments, but the kiss had been stellar. I knew she thought so as well, Francesca had melted into me like butter on a hot piece of toast.

Mistake, my ass.

"Come," I said and turned to walk away.

16

FRANCESCA

Stronzo.

Did he really expect me to follow him? "I'm not a dog." I snapped.

Cassio glanced back and cocked one brow. I rolled my eyes. He was not going to let this go.

One thing I still remember about him was that Cassio could be persistent. It could take seconds, minutes, hours or even years but he always got what he wanted. I was exhausted, and Mamma wasn't doing any better. Although the nurses tried to keep me company and make my days brighter, it was like the sun had stopped shining.

Sighing out loud so he could hear my frustration, I took the first step toward him. A wave of cold air hit me, and I shivered, I'd forgotten my coat in Mamma's room and was too lazy to go back for it. Now I was paying the price.

"Do you ever check the weather?" He complained but removed his suit jacket and offered it to me.

I begrudgingly grabbed it from his hand and put it on. Cassio looked forward and I took that as a chance to shove my nose into his jacket and inhaled his intoxicating scent.

Night had struck Chicago, and usually, I wouldn't be this relaxed walking in the streets, but shamefully, I was. Cassio's presence still made me feel safe. It was something I tried to deny even now as we walked together, but the truth was harsh.

Even a few steps away from me, I felt like the safest person in the world. It wasn't only because Cassio was the head of the Outfit, but because he was...Cassio. Tall and proud and powerful. No one would dare approach him. Especially not with the gun I knew he kept hidden on him like all Made Men did.

I looked at him, really looked. It had been two weeks since he barged into my apartment half-dead. For someone who had been bleeding continuously, with a massive wound to his abdomen, Cassio seemed...fine. Not that I didn't want him to be, but if it were me, I would have been in bed—resting. Licking my wounds.

I would be lying if I didn't say I had been worried sick. I had almost called Vitelli. Cassio hadn't showed up again, and while a part of me was grateful, another wanted to see him again. Which was confusing since I was supposed to hate him.

The coffee shop was just around the corner as he had said. Cassio chose a table and told me to sit while he ordered for us. When he came back, he sat opposite of me. Silence lingered in the space between us like sticky tar. Not long after, a waitress came by with our order.

"What's this?"

"Jasmine tea and a chocolate filled doughnut." His tone was detached.

He pushed the two toward me and I looked at them not believing what I saw. "I'm pretty sure I got it right," he said.

Cassio had. His sister and I used to go to the same coffee shop every Wednesday, and Cassio was forced to tag along at first—to keep an eye on us. After, when we began dating in secret, it became a ritual of sorts. He came along for an entirely different reason.

"You did." My voice sounded defeated.

I watched as he sipped on his espresso. Jasmine filled my nose, and the sight of the doughnut made my stomach rumble. It had been hours since I last ate something. So, I took his offering and relished the taste of both tea and pastry.

Cassio set his cup down. "I'm sorry about your mother."

The teacup slipped from my hand and burning liquid splashed on my hand. "Shit," I cursed and wiped it away, rubbing my hand where the burn mark was.

I looked at Cassio who was watching me closely. "How would you know?" I asked, still in pain.

"It's my business to know everything."

Then it hit me, fire pumped through my veins. "How did you know I was at the hospital? Did you have me followed?"

Mischief flickered in his eyes. "I won't apologize for it."

Stronzzo. "Why, Cassio?"

"This is important."

"I disagree." I leaned against the chair. "How long have you been following me? Don't I at least get to know that?" I asked when he didn't answer my first question.

"Since that first night."

Oh.

I wanted to be angry, I really did, but that wave of anger never hit me. The thought of knowing someone had my back and would protect me in case something happened, left me feeling less...afraid.

"How's your mother?"

I was baffled for a while, of course he knew about her, if he had me followed then he would know everything. As he said, it was his business. Yet there was a sudden relief as a small weight was lifted from my shoulders. Someone else knew about my mother, I wasn't alone in this anymore.

"The cancer is very aggressive," I confessed. "Mamma is a difficult patient."

"I wouldn't wish that upon anyone," he said sincerely, and it warmed me up a bit.

"We have matters to discuss," he said setting his cup on the table, and I laced my hands, just to keep them busy. Our small talk was over then.

The last time Cassio had charged into my apartment to "discuss matters" we ended up kissing, then he proceeded to give me an ultimatum.

"I'm not going back to my father's." I made myself clear, fear making me feel bolder.

Cassio watched me for a while and then to my surprise he said. "I don't expect you to." I raised one brow. "I shouldn't have asked that of you."

Woah. Okay. "Is this an apology?"

He scoffed. "I don't do apologies."

"Well, it sounded like one," I deadpanned.

"We share the same sentiment toward your father, that's why I'm here," he explained. "To talk about him."

The doughnut turned too acid in my stomach. "I have nothing to say about him."

"I think you do." He leaned back in the chair. "More importantly, I think your husband did too." Why did the word *husband* sound like an accusation? Like Cassio was mad at me or something?

"I never involved myself in their business, Cassio," I said, needing to remind him.

"But you must have heard something," he said.

"I barely saw him as it was, Paolo hated Donato."

"And why is that?" He sounded awfully intrigued.

I shrugged. "Why does anyone? Donato is an easy man to hate."

Cassio nodded, looked at his coffee, and then at me. I watched as he tapped his fingers on the table and pensively stared for a while. Lowering his voice he confessed, "Your husband was assassinated, Francesca."

I sucked in a deep breath. "W-what?"

"He was poisoned. That's what caused his heart to stop," Cassio explained, but I was still stuck in his first confession.

Killed. "Why?"

I never loved Paolo, but it was disconcerting to hear that he had been killed. "That's what I want to know."

I shook my head. "Are you suspecting me?"

Cassio remained calm as he said, "Belladonna is considered a woman's weapon."

"I never loved him, but I would never kill the man," I hissed.

Cassio looked smugly pleased with my answer. "Why did your father and Paolo fight?"

I shrugged. "Paolo always said my father was a snake that couldn't be trusted. That he was too ambitious, too greedy. That if he had the means, he would set the world on fire and watch us all burn."

I had agreed with him.

Cassio nodded. "So, you never loved him?" The question took me by surprise. Was that all that he heard?

"How could I?" I answered honestly.

"He was your husband." Cassio pointed out.

"Yes," I agreed. "What are you fishing for, Cassio?"

He smiled and hid it quickly. "Nothing." He denied me the truth, but I knew him better than that.

"Do you miss him?" He continued with the weird questions.

"Why all these questions?"

"Just answer me?"

Since I had nothing left to lose right now I did. "No."

"Good. He never deserved you," Cassio said decidedly.

"And you did?"

He went silent for a while. "Let's go, it's getting late." He stood up from his chair.

I scoffed. He wasn't going to answer it, but I already knew the answer. *Yes.*

Once, there had been a time when Cassio had been my everything, now he was just someone I used to know. Someone who kept on popping back into my life, making it hard to forget him.

As if I ever did in the first place.

Cassio insisted on driving me back to my place, and because I was tired and mentally drained from our conversation, I accepted, even if he hadn't been offering.

When we arrived, Cassio opened the car door for me and

escorted me back to my apartment. I looked back, trying to find the guard he had posted on me.

"He's not here," Cassio said, realizing what I was doing.

"So, he doesn't sleep on my doorstep?" I teased. "What a bad spy he is."

"Vince keeps his distance," Cassio explained, his lack of mirth bothered me.

I finally reached my door and removed my keys to open it. Cassio remained there with me. My hands shook, and a shiver raced down my back as I recalled the last time he was here.

I turned to face him. "Thanks for driving me."

Cassio was on me before I had the chance to react. He kissed me hard, and I dropped the key on the floor. His lips slammed into mine and before I knew what was best, I let him in. His tongue invaded my mouth and made sweet love to me.

In that moment, Cassio became everything, and I kissed him like my life depended on it. His hands landed on my waist and snaked toward my back as he pulled me in closer.

When he broke the kiss, he shoved his head against my neck and sucked on it, probably leaving a mark. I didn't care, in that moment, all I could think about was that I needed more.

"Your gun is pressing against me."

Cassio smiled against my skin. "That's not my gun, *Principessa*."

Holy God. I gulped and my head lulled back as he nibbled on my neck and jaw and then bit my lip. With my back against my apartment door, I had nowhere to run to. Not that I would want to.

"Cassio," I panted. "What are we doing?" He kissed me again, and I forgot that we were in the middle of a corridor where people could see us.

"I should go." His voice caressed my skin.

"You should." I agreed.

His forehead rested against mine, and I dove into the frigid green waters of his eyes. They were mesmerizing, holding me captive. "I really should," he said but kissed me once more. Pulling me toward him, a flash of memory assaulted me. The last time he was here, our kiss, my almost orgasm. Then a wave of shame hit me, and I pushed him away.

"You can't do that." Tears stung my eyes. "You can't come back into my life after four years and pretend nothing happened."

Cassio stepped back and ran his fingers through his hair. "You were the one who called me that night, Francesca."

"And I regret that more than anything."

His nostrils flared and he nodded. "This was a mistake."

"Yes." I couldn't have agreed more.

"So why were you grinding on my dick, *Principessa*?"

My eyes widened at his crass response. "Fuck you, Cassio." I picked my key up from the floor and turned my back to him.

"You almost did," he snapped.

Yeah, and he didn't have to remind me of that. My door opened and I slipped in, not daring to look at him again, I smashed it shut and shouted, knowing he was still there. "I don't ever want to see you again."

Cassio slammed his hand against the door, he then turned and left. I remained there looking through the peephole almost expecting him to come back and finish what he started.

What? No. That's not what I wanted.

I ran my finger over my swollen lip and closed my eyes. His taste still lingered in my mouth, coffee and Cassio. So, I ran to the bathroom and brushed my teeth twice. When I was done, I opened a bottle of wine and stared at it for a while. I couldn't deal with this, not with a clear head. I needed to forget this night ever happened.

Forget. This was all I needed to do and then life would go back to normal.

17

FRANCESCA

When I looked to the side, Mamma had finally closed her eyes, her book lay resting on her lap. I took it and placed it on the table beside her bed. It was eight o'clock and I was tired. I picked up my things and gave one last look at the tulips I'd bought today. They were in full bloom now.

I left the room and almost bumped into Dr. Conrad. "Francesca, everything all right?"

I smiled, "Mamma was great today."

"As I told you, we take one—"

"Day at a time," I supplied.

"Why don't you come and have a coffee with me downstairs. There is something I would like to discuss with you."

Since I had nothing better to do on a Friday night, I followed Dr. Conrad into the cafeteria.

We sat at one of the round tables and he bought me a large cup of coffee, somehow, he figured I needed it. He waited until I practically drained the whole thing before he started.

"Have you ever thought about being a candidate for a liver transplant?"

"Can I?" I asked in surprise.

My mother was on the UNOS transplant list, but because of her stage and her complications, it wasn't looking so good for her.

"Of course, you can, we would have to run some tests to see if you're healthy, but judging from your age, I don't see why you wouldn't be."

I stilled.

"You would have to undergo a series of tests and a diet, we have to make sure you haven't been ingesting too much alcohol and of course, no drugs, but those are things we can check off."

He went on explaining a series of exams I should do in order to be a viable donor to my mother, but I stopped when he mentioned the drugs. I didn't stop him. I didn't have the heart to do so. The first person who had a good impression of me was going to be truly disappointed, but then I was good at that. Maybe that was why my mother never felt the need to care for me. She knew I wasn't worth it.

"—your father did them and he was out of here in no time."

"Wait... hold on. What did you just say?" I interrupted him.

"I'm sorry, Francesca, I shouldn't have said that. It was a mistake."

Dr. Conrad was about to stand up when I grabbed his hand. It was the first time I ever did something like this out of pure despair.

"What did you say? My father underwent the exams?"

"Yes." He answered gingerly.

"Were they negative?"

"I can't disclose that."

"Please, Doctor. I just need to know." I pleaded.

He sighed. But I knew the answer. If the doctor was here talking to me and suggesting the transplant, was it because my father was negative? Which was good, right? It meant he couldn't be a donor, and for some reason, I wouldn't want his organ inside my mother. He was rotten inside, and I didn't want a part of him in her.

"I'm sorry, Francesca. He was a match." Dr. Conrad confessed.

"It's fine..."

Wait. What?

"Positive?" I asked.

"I've said too much already. He asked to keep it a secret, I shouldn't be telling you this, but I believe it would help your mother if the donor was someone from her family. The list could take months, sometimes years."

He was positive. My father was a match. *A MATCH.* And he still didn't agree to the transplant. I couldn't believe what I was hearing. Days ago, my mother had poured out her heart, telling me how much she loved the man, while he didn't even care about her.

"I have to go."

I didn't know how I got here, but once the taxi stopped, I paid the driver and stepped out. The street before my father's house was empty aside from the two guards posted by the gates. I stared at them for a while, knowing this was a terrible idea but not caring enough to stop.

My blood was boiling, my nails dug deep into my palms as I tried to keep my anger at bay. I had no idea what I was going to say to Donato Manci, but I knew I had to say something.

As I walked toward the gates, one of the guards came forward, his hand on his gun. "Francesca Manci. Open the damned gate before I make a scene." I stopped by the guest entrance. The guard inspected me from head to toe like I was some knucklehead. "Didn't you hear me?"

"Is he expecting you?" one of the idiots asked.

"I'm his daughter." The words tasted rotten in my mouth, making me want to throw up.

He spoke into his radio and after a few seconds, he opened the gates. I took a deep breath and stepped through them and walked the path toward the house. Not stopping to analyze my surroundings.

"Francesca." I knew the voice; it had been with me since I was a kid. I didn't stop to talk to my old guard. "What are you doing?"

"Not now, Umberto." My voice came out harsher than I wanted to.

"You shouldn't have come." That made me stop. I looked into his eyes and saw the plea in them.

"Where is he?" I asked softly.

"Francesca, he's not in a good mood," he warned, trying to make me change my mind.

"Neither am I," I pointed out. "Where is he, Umberto? I'm going in there whether you want it or not."

"He's in his office." Umberto sighed in defeat. "Enzo and Gianluca are there with him. Be careful, Francesca."

Upon hearing Gianluca's name, I shivered. Them being here wouldn't stop me, but it made me falter for a second.

I marched toward Donato's office and didn't stop to knock or introduce myself. If I did, I might lose my courage, I simply pulled the doors open and stepped inside.

Donato was sitting in his office chair. He looked ten years older, his shirt strained against his belly and his thin hair did nothing to hide his balding head. He wore a Hugo Boss suit that looked two sizes too small. The scent of cigars and whiskey filled my nose, and sure enough, I saw both of them near him.

He had been talking to Enzo when I stepped in. Both his men looked at me, as did Marco whose eyes shot wide.

"What is this?" he barked when he saw me. "Who let you in?"

"I don't need to be let in, *father*. This is my home after all, isn't it?"

All eyes were on me like this was some grand spectacle. My father looked both enraged and annoyed. Enzo and Gianluca were both watching me with interest, the kind I did not want to attract.

"Francesca," my father said, my name on his lips were offensive.

"We have matters to discuss."

"Is that how you talk to your father?" he snapped. "Have you learned nothing?"

"Yes, *father*, I did learn quite a few things lately." I chuckled dryly.

"I see you have finally figured out how to use that brain of yours." He mocked.

"Took me a while, but better late than never." I replied.

"I see your husband forgot to teach you manners, I'll make sure to remedy that."

"No need, I'm not here to stay," I pointed out. "You can get off your high horse."

Gianluca whistled and Enzo shook his head and looked at me like I had committed the worst mistake ever. No one had ever dared talk to Donato that way, at least no *woman* ever had. But if he thought I was going to cower from him, then he was wrong. Women in the Outfit were taught never to raise their voices to their husbands and fathers. Pity I didn't give a shit.

I was used to the heavy hand of my late husband. After a while, his threats and beatings lost their power over me. The pain would still linger afterward, but the fear that once gripped me tightly lost its power.

"If you know what's best for you, you'll shut that whore's mouth of yours."

I chuckled dryly. "That's old, *Papa*," I provoked. "You thought I was a whore when I was five and wore a church dress. When I was fifteen and wore long dresses. It's time to come up with another name for me, don't you think?"

"My sharp-tongued daughter," he smiled murderously.

I smiled.

"What do you want, Francesca? I have better things to do than listen to whatever comes out of your mouth."

"You disgust me, Donato." I lifted my head and stared at him down my nose. "You are a fucking asshole; you have no right to call yourself a man. You are nothing but a coward—"

His chair scrapped against the floor and hit the wall behind him. Donato was up on his feet in an instant coming my way. My sweet little brother got up, too, and stood between my father and me.

"Get the fuck out of my face, boy!" But Marco stood his ground.

"Does he know?" I kept on going, once I opened my mouth I couldn't stop. It was like opening the doors to a dam. "Does he know you could have given mother your liver, but you refused?"

"What?" Marco looked at me.

"Marco," Donato warned but he didn't move. He raised his hand and Marco flinched ready for the blow.

"Go ahead, hit him you coward. Hit your son for being a better man than you will ever be," I provoked him further, knowing I was poking the bear with a very short stick.

Donato pushed Marco aside and he fell on the floor before he could reach me again. Enzo grabbed hold of my brother and didn't let go. Donato stopped before me and grabbed my face with his meaty fingers.

"So brave, aren't you?" He dug his fingers deeper. "So noble." His putrid breath made me sick. He let go of me, and I didn't have time to react before he slapped me hard.

I fell to the floor, hitting my knees, pain shot through them causing me to cry out. I clutched my left cheek; it felt like a million tiny needles were entering my skin. I didn't give him the satisfaction of staying down. I stood up and stared right back at him, making sure Donato knew that in my heart, I carried enough hatred for him that I could fill an ocean.

"Out," he snapped. "Before I kill you."

"No," I shouted. I turned to Marco, my brother had been thrashing in Enzo's arms, but he didn't have the strength to break free.

That's when my father removed his gun from its holster and pointed at me. Air got stuck in my lungs and my heart stopped beating. I stared at the barrel of the gun, the black hole looking back. Donato's finger was on the trigger. In the distance, I heard someone screaming, but the sound of my pulse was too loud in my ears.

"You won't shoot," I managed, my voice calmer then I expected.

"Won't I?" he smiled.

"Y-you need me," I croaked, and that's when I realized he did need me, he was going to marry me off in a few months, he couldn't simply shoot me.

Cassio might have changed his mind about forcing me back to my father's house, but in the end, it wouldn't matter, Donato would have what he wanted in the first place. Which was me.

He lowered the gun. "The next time I see you it will be at your wedding. Now get out of my face."

I turned to leave knowing it was better to, at the door I stopped and turned around to face him again. Donato was heading back to his seat and threw the gun on the table.

"I don't care what you do to me, as long as you die a painful and agonizing death."

Without looking back, I left the room. My hands shook, and my cheek hurt from where he slapped me. I knew I was moments from having a panic attack. I had gambled with my life, and I could have lost.

I heard the crashing of glass against the wall and Donato was screaming. I choked on a sob and left the house, not stopping to talk to Umberto who had been waiting for me on the porch.

"Francesca." Umberto grabbed my upper arm making me stop. He looked older, too. His forehead was filled with wrinkles and his once dark hair was now peppered with gray strands.

"I'm fine," I said as my lungs fought to function.

He looked at me from head to toe and his gaze stopped on my cheek. Umberto had seen my father beat me countless times when I was young. He had tried to stop him once and he had been punished for it. I begged him to never try again.

"Let me take a look at it." He tried to touch me, but I pulled away.

"I'm fine." I tried to sound as though I were. Maybe if I said it a hundred times, I would truly be fine. "I need to leave, Umberto."

"Let me take you—"

"No," I snapped and then took a deep breath. "No," I said again, trying to conjure a smile. "Thank you, but I need to be alone right now," I assured him.

Umberto walked me toward the gate, and I did my best not to lean into him and seek his comfort. When I was a kid, I used to dream that he was my father. He'd always treated me as a father should, with love and affection.

When the gates closed, I watched them for a while. Umberto remained on the other side looking at me. I knew he wanted to follow, but he had sworn an oath to my father and the Outfit. Not wanting to make things harder on him, I turned and began walking with no destination in mind.

Night had fallen, and the sun was no longer offering its warmth. The streets near Donato's house were deserted.

The longer I walked, the quicker the scenes from tonight replayed in my head. My cheek was still burning, and I was pretty sure one of his rings had cut my skin. I didn't dare check if I was bleeding.

Suddenly it all went black and all I saw was the barrel of a gun. My heart hit my ribcage beating painfully against it. No matter how deeply I inhaled, air wouldn't fill my lungs. My body vibrated with pain. I fumbled with my phone and dialed the number that had been stuck in my head.

18

CASSIO

I sat at the table with the Ferraro brothers, Romeo Ferraro, Capo of the *Cosa Nostra,* sat directly before me while his brother, Apollo, sat before Vitelli. There was also another man with them, one everyone in the Mafia knew of—Nero "The Reaper" Albiatti. A beast of a man.

Romeo Ferraro looked at me with those disconcerting blue eyes of his. I had blood on my hands, but the Capo before me had his drenched in it. Story was, he had killed his own father and stabbed the man repeatedly to death. It was also rumored that he killed his first man at the age of nine in a church. That's how he earned the name *il Diavolo.* The devil. Few men dared sit in a room with him; even fewer were courageous enough to do business with the Devil. I was one of those few.

Romeo Ferraro didn't scare me. Neither did his brother Apollo who wouldn't stop grinning from the moment we sat to dine. Now I understood why they called him the Joker. The fucker never seemed to do anything but smile. Not a sweet one or a happy one either. There was malice in it, something dark and twisted. Something even I didn't want to discover.

Vitelli was right, maybe I was a mad man for doing business with the infamous brothers from New York, but desperate times called for desperate measures. On both sides, that was—Romeo was just as willing for a partnership with me as I was with him. We were different sides of the same coin. Two Capos doing what they must to keep their people and territory safe.

The only reason Romeo was here in Chicago doing business with me wasn't because I was desperate. It was because despite his sociopathic tendencies, the man was loyal to his blood, especially his family. Something I could relate to. Respect even.

"Now that dinner is over," I began.

"I would still like dessert. I heard the cannoli in this place is to die for," Apollo Ferraro said with a grin. The man was much like my brother, which was aggravating to say the least.

"Apollo," Romeo snapped.

"What?" Apollo asked innocently. "It was a joke."

"Refrain from making them," Romeo said coldly. His brother rolled his eyes, but given he was right, I had the waitress bring him some of the famous cannoli. It *was* to die for.

"I've heard your problem with the Bratva has escalated," Romeo said as he turned his cufflinks. The man was dressed as if he had been headed to a wedding instead of a meeting. I, too, was dressed in a suit, yet he made me feel underdressed for the occasion.

"I've heard you lost part of your territory in Boston," I threw back. Putting two alphas in a room was not a good idea. Romeo didn't answer, but his brother's smile turned feral. Instead of provoking him further, I offered an olive branch. "What matters is how we pay them back. You didn't come all this way to hear from me what I know about you and vice versa. You came to talk business."

"We are talking business," Apollo said. The kid spoke too much when he should stay silent. "You have access to routes in Texas and products that come from Mexico," Apollo pointed out.

"We want half of that product shipped to us," Romeo explained. "In exchange, you'll have half of our products that come from Europe."

That sounded viable, the cocaine I imported from Mexico was

one of the best in the market but there were other drugs, like LSD and Molly which held more value because Romeo retained that market up in the east, and his product was known to be the best, hence the high price.

"I want access to Remy Bousset," Romeo said as he leaned back on his chair taking his tumbler of scotch with him.

"No," I said without hesitation. Remy was my contact.

Romeo didn't seem pleased with my refusal. It seemed the man wasn't used to hearing that word. I couldn't blame him; I didn't like it either.

"I'll give you one of my contacts in Vegas, I know you have been trying to do business out there."

Fuck. He rubbed salt against my open wound. I had been trying to do business with the Camorra since before I became Capo of the Outfit. They were a closed-off bunch, even more so than the *Cosa Nostra.*

I looked at Vitelli, but I had already made up my mind. Remy was one man while Vegas was filled with opportunities to make more money. Yet in this moment, he was acting as my consigliere, and I valued his opinion. My brother offered me a tight nod. He was oddly quiet tonight. Probably anxious about having the Reaper and the Devil in the same room. I felt as comfortable as if I were lounging in my apartment.

"I can only present you to the man, if he decides to do business or not, that's up to him," I warned.

"Oh, he will," Romeo said with entitlement, something only a man with power like he possessed would say.

I liked him. He was the kind of man that did not give a fuck about what others thought of him and was beyond the rumors that circled him as well. What if he killed his father? Maybe the fucker needed to be gone. So what if his hands were bloody to the elbows? Mine were, too. We were all wolves in a world full of sheep, some just loved feasting more than others.

Romeo was that wolf.

With dinner over, talk of business was discussed freely. The

Ferraro's seemed completely open to this alliance and were more willing than I had expected. While he was richer than me by some millions, he was a man of principle, unlike most rich pansy asses I knew.

Romeo was in the middle of explaining to me how he managed to turn his family's company, Legion Corp, into one of the largest in America when my phone rang. I pretended it wasn't doing so and shoved it in my pocket. It went to voice mail, but the person insisted and called me back shortly after.

"Life of a Capo," Romeo said.

"I need to take this," I said pulling the phone.

Excusing myself I headed toward a more private area of the restaurant. Nero Albiatti—the Reaper—watched me closely while I answered the phone.

"Yes?" There was sobbing on the other side of the line. I pulled the phone away and stared at the number.

"Ca-Cassio."

"Francesca?" I whispered in surprise.

"So-sorry," she sobbed.

A cold shiver raced down my back, and I stared at the table where the men were back to having a conversation. My brother stared at me probably realizing something was wrong.

"What happened?" I asked looking away from him.

"I..." she cried. "F-Forget it." She ended the call.

Pissed off and worried, I stared at the phone and then called her again. "What the fuck is going on?" I snapped once she answered the phone.

I ran my thumb under my lower lip trying to calm down. That's when Vitelli stood up and began walking toward me.

"Can you at least tell me where you are?" I heard her silence and then she told me no. I cursed inward, looked up at the ceiling and tried not to lose my composure.

"Stay where you are," I ordered. "I'm coming to get you."

Listening to Francesca cry left me enraged. I had the need to strangle someone. Something had happened and someone was going to pay for hurting her.

"I have to go," I told Vitelli as he approached me.

"Right now, in the middle of a meeting?" he asked me skeptically.

"Yes," I answered as I made my way towards the table. "Gentlemen, I'm sorry, but I must leave. As you said, life of a Capo." I extended my hand towards Romeo. "My brother will escort you back to your jet," I explained.

"You're leaving?" Apollo sounded offended.

Romeo took my hand, despite his brother's outrage, and shook it. "Until next time, Moretti, we have lots to discuss."

I picked up my jacket from behind the chair and put it on. Vitelli followed me as I exited the restaurant. "Take them straight to their jet —no detours," I said.

"Where are you going?"

"Just do as you're told, Vitelli, don't fucking question me right now."

"Yes, Capo," he said with an attitude that would have earned him a punch if I weren't in a hurry.

I entered my car and turned the engine of my Porsche 911 roaring it to life. I called Vince as soon as the phone connected to the Bluetooth. "Where is Francesca?" were my first words.

"She left the hospital Boss," he said, sounding guilty.

I pinched my nose. "And where the hell did she go?"

Silence.

"Vince?" I tried to maintain my calm. "You better know where she is?"

"She was at her father's, Boss. I have eyes on her right now."

Thank fuck. If he didn't, then Vince would have to suffer for it.

My heart was beating as fast as my Porsche. Why she was near her father's house? I could not tell, but I knew something had happened between them. It must have been bad enough for her to call me. We weren't exactly on the best of terms.

I drove towards Donato's neighborhood in a hurry, swerving

through the traffic like a maniac. It was night, and despite Vince having his eyes on her, I was afraid that something might happen.

She was a beacon in the dark night, her blonde hair shining bright, lighting her up like a fallen star. I would have recognized Francesca anywhere. She was walking fast—head down. Good thing I had specifically told her to stay put.

I parked my car and quickly got out. "Francesca," I called out.

She jumped, dropped her phone on the ground, and placed a hand on her chest. I approached her slowly; Francesca swayed, and I quickly moved to steady her.

She looked at me but averted her gaze instantly. "What are you doing here?" She sounded surprised.

"What do you mean?" I was still holding on to her, she was freezing. "You called, Francesca."

"You shouldn't have come." She looked at her hands and then used one to wipe a tear away. Then she winced making it even worse.

I removed my jacket and was about to place it around her shoulders when she flinched. "Shit," I hissed. "I'm not going to hurt you." I tried to keep my anger at bay.

She nodded and winced at the same time. This time, I slowly placed my jacket around her shoulders and pulled it close. Francesca was still not looking at me.

"You shouldn't have come," she said again.

"It doesn't matter," I stated. "I'm here now."

Gently, I reached out for her. Placing two fingers under her chin, I turned her face toward me. Francesca did not meet my eyes.

That's when I saw it.

I inhaled deeply; seeing nothing but red. Francesca moved away from my touch like she was ashamed. Her left cheek was bruised and scratched.

"Who. Touched. You?" Were the only words I could conjure.

Francesca looked at me then, her big sapphire eyes filled with more unshed tears. I fisted my hands as my blood ran hot in my veins. Someone had touched Francesca. Someone was going to die.

"I'm not worth your problems." Her voice was weak. Defeated.

Shit.

That hit me hard. Right to the chest, worse than a bullet wound. I reached for her again and this time Francesca didn't flinch, which was a fucking miracle. Sometimes I wished her husband was still alive, only so I could torture him for what he did to her.

I grabbed her hand, she stared at it like it was the strangest thing I'd ever done. "Let's go. I'm taking you home."

Francesca followed me back to the car and when I closed her door, I took a deep breath before entering as well. She didn't complain when I said I was taking her to my place. Instead, Francesca remained quiet, staring out the window.

Once we arrived at my apartment, she looked so small and thin. Vulnerable. She was breathing hard and kept on digging her nails into the palms of her hands.

"Come." I helped her toward the room she had slept in the last time she'd been here, and guided her to the bathroom.

I turned on the light and quickly headed back to my room where I kept the first aid kit. When I returned, Francesca was staring at her hands which were still shaking.

Placing the kit on the counter beside her, I warned her before moving closer to her. "I'm going to lift you up." I placed my hands on her soft curves.

Francesca sucked in a breath, but it had nothing to do with fear—I hoped. She had removed my jacket, her skin was still cold, but a spark traveled through my body. When I glanced up at her, she was watching me as well.

"You can let go now," she said gently.

"Yeah." I looked at my hand and fought to tear it away from her. Then I set out to do what I had planned. "This is going to hurt."

"I'm used to it," she scoffed.

"Well, you shouldn't be." I picked up the towel and placed it under the faucet.

"After a while you learn to ignore it," Francesca said simply like it was perfectly normal. She sucked in a deep breath as I placed the towel against her cheek, but then she relaxed.

"I should have killed him." I said to myself.

"You shouldn't have let me marry him in the first place," she said but there was no anger in her voice, just resignation.

Francesca was right, I shouldn't have let her marry him. I should never have let her go, but it had been my only choice. I couldn't marry her, doing so would only lead to more sorrow and pain.

I wasn't myself back then. I was nothing but a drunk who couldn't even recall his own name. After Arabella died, I lost myself and, in the process, lost Francesca, too. I thought I was saving her from me, from the monster I became. When I finally had the courage to fight my demons and realized that breaking up with her had been the worst mistake of my life, it was already too late—she'd married Paolo.

I wiped away the dried blood, the wound was nothing of great concern, but I applied some antiseptic and then a band-aid. She looked so breakable, like glass, and it scared me because I had the power to break her.

"I'll get you some painkillers."

"No," she grabbed my hand. "No pills."

"It might not be hurting now, but tomorrow it will."

"No pills, Cassio," her big eyes pleaded.

I nodded. I hoped from the bottom of my heart that this meant she had stopped using. I knew it would be hard, but I needed her to stop. I needed her to get better.

Because I couldn't help myself, I caressed her cheek, careful not to hurt her. Francesca breathed in deeply, closed her eyes and leaned into my touch.

"Who, Francesca? Give me a name."

19

FRANCESCA

It was a simple question. The name was on the tip of my tongue, and I had a feeling Cassio knew exactly who it was.
Yet I couldn't say it.

All I wanted was for Cassio to put a bullet through Donato's head. I didn't care what it made me, but if I told Cassio the truth, he was going to leave me. It was foolish, but I was desperate for closeness. Just the thought of him leaving me alone made my stomach twist.

"Francesca," he called me back to reality, and I opened my eyes to find him staring. There was a fire in his eyes that I hadn't noticed before. "Who did this to you?"

This time his entire hand rested against my skin. Cassio was warm, almost blazing, and like a cat, I leaned into it, seeking his comfort. Yearning for his touch. I pretended nothing had ever happened between us. Pretended it was just Cassio and me. The past was forgotten.

I didn't answer.

"One name."

"I can't," I whispered.

His hand left my face, and my make-believe moment was severed, the bubble burst, making me shiver. My body weighed a ton and all I wanted to do was wrap myself in a cocoon and sleep forever.

There was no reason to remain here in his apartment. He had come when I called, and I was thankful for that. Cassio had saved me yet again.

"Why can't you give me an answer, Francesca?" He sounded angrier now.

Both of his hands cupped my cheeks as he came to stand between my legs, his mouth inches from mine. I inhaled him—his scent was addictive, and I breathed again.

I acted before I could think. I closed the distance between us and smashed my lips against his. The kiss was shy and awkward, and I realized I was the only one kissing. Then, finally, his lips moved, and the kiss wasn't gentle anymore. His grip on my face tightened and I flinched slightly.

"Shit," he took a step back letting go of me as if I burned him. "Francesca." He shook his head.

I pulled his shirt to bring him closer and kissed him again. This time it was hungrier, he didn't hesitate. I matched his pace, kissing Cassio with my entire being. Lips, tongue, and soul. I was desperate for him. For his intoxicating taste. I bit his lip and pulled it slightly. Cassio groaned deep in his throat. One of his hands slipped to my neck and he pulled my hair, changing the angle of our kiss.

He consumed me, heat traveled through my body and settled between my legs. I had never felt this kind of pleasure before, my body had never been so out of control.

Cassio kissed my lips, then my jaw, and nibbled my ear, breathing me in. "You're playing with fire, *Principessa*," he groaned low in his throat.

"Then I'll gladly burn." I closed my eyes as he sucked on a particularly sensitive spot, leaving another mark on my skin. "Cassio," I moaned as pleasure boiled my blood.

Cassio pressed in closer and used both hands to pull me flush against him. I could sense his heartbeat. It was fast and violent—he wanted me. His hand slipped beneath my shirt and gripped my waist.

Electricity coursed through my veins, causing my skin to tighten and my nipples to pebble. My breasts grew heavy, and my core tightened.

Cassio massaged my skin and kissed me, slowly he trailed upward until his thumb caressed one of my aching nipples. I sucked in a deep breath as pleasure shot through my body. He grinned like a feral cat, but then he looked at my face and let go.

He took a step back then another, until he had put a good distance between us. Cassio shook his head and then wiped his lips like he needed to remove my taste from his mouth.

"No." He raised his finger and pointed at me. He looked at the ceiling and then at me again like he was fighting an inner battle. "I'm not doing this," he announced.

My heart skipped a beat and my jaw almost dropped to the floor. I was mortified. Ashamed. Embarrassed, but mostly I was starting to regret what I did.

"You don't want me," he said, running his fingers through his hair. "You just don't want to be alone. You're confused," Cassio stated. "I'm not a good man, but I don't take advantage of women."

"Cassio, I— "

"Don't, Francesca." He stopped me. "You can stay here tonight, I'll take you home tomorrow, or when you're ready," he said and then left me.

I lay in bed replaying the kiss. It had been as it used to be between us. I touched my lips; they were still swollen. I still ached between my legs. With Paolo, sex had never been about me. It had always been about him and what he wanted. To me, sex was an obligation, but tonight it had almost been more.

Was Cassio, right? Did I kiss him only to make him stay with me? To a small amount, yes. I was scared to be lonely, but there was another part of me that wanted him. Even after everything that happened between us, I still wanted him. Physically. This had nothing to do with feelings. I was still angry at Cassio—and I might never forgive him—but I wanted him.

I pulled the covers and walked determinedly toward his room; this time I didn't hesitate to knock on his door. I slapped the poor thing repeatedly. Cassio opened and pulled it open with force.

"France—"

"You were wrong." I side-stepped him and entered his room. "You were wrong, Cassio." I turned to face him.

"Francesca, don't," he warned me, but I was way beyond listening. I took a step toward him.

"You don't know what you're doing, Francesca." But he took a step closer, too. "You don't know what you're asking."

The space between us ended and I looked up into his eyes. "I do, Cassio. I know exactly what I want."

His arctic green eyes began to shift before me, the black of his pupils bled into his irises. His long lashes lowered as he watched me. He wanted this; I knew he did.

Cassio cupped my neck and brought me even closer until our bodies were flush together. "Francesca," he groaned out my name. "You need to get out right now."

"No." I stood my ground. "I want you, Cassio," I confessed.

He shook his head. "You want comfort and someone to hold you," he spoke against my lips. "Things I cannot give you."

Can't or won't, I wanted to ask. "I don't want that." And it was the truth. "I want you to make me feel good."

I had no doubt Cassio could. Sex with him must be stellar. Out of this world. When we dated, we had agreed to wait until our marriage —as was the custom, but we had tried a few things. Cassio had thought me what pleasure was, had given me the opportunity to feel it before I was married to Paolo. And thanks to him I knew sex could be good. Now there was no more reason to wait. I wanted a taste of the forbidden fruit, even if it sent me straight to Hell.

He smirked and used his other hand to remove the strands of my hair from my face. "Oh, *Principessa*," he mused and pulled on my lower lip. "I'm going to count till ten and if you're not gone by then…" he warned me. "One." He began.

I shook my head. "I'm not leaving."

"Two." He let go of and took a step back.

"Cassio," I called.

"Three."

"I said I'm not leaving."

"Francesca," It sounded almost pleading. "Four."

I stood my ground.

"Five. Six. Seven." His eyes twinkled with desire. "Eight. Nine." He stopped and I lifted my chin in a dare. "Ten." He enunciated with finality. He looked at me like a lion that circled its prey. "I'm going to tell you how this is going to play out," he instructed, causing my skin to pebble.

He grabbed my hair and pulled it back until I was looking at him, neck straining. My body rested against his and then I felt him pressed against me. Cassio was hard.

"I have dreamed about this for so long, Francesca. You have plagued my mind day and night." He pulled my hair and kissed my exposed neck. "I have played this out so many times…in so many ways," he mused.

All I could hear was the loud beating of my heart in my ear. My head was spinning with desire, my skin burning. "Are you going to talk all night?"

He chuckled. "I have waited too long for this, it's only fair that you suffer, too," I whined as he let go of me.

I couldn't take it any longer, my entire body was going to combust if he didn't do something. Cassio stepped away and headed toward the lights.

"No." I stopped him. "Leave them off."

"Why the fuck would I?"

I looked away. Two fingers lifted my chin. "Francesca, why would I leave them off?" I didn't answer. "Francesca?"

"Please."

"We are not doing this until you tell me why." He stood his ground.

"Because Cassio...because," I answered.

Because it's how it had always been with Paolo, how he turned off the lights because he didn't want to see my tears or the hollowness in my eyes. Or rather, he didn't want to see how young his wife was, how inexperienced and highly repulsed she was.

"It's him, isn't it?"

I nodded.

"Fuck, Francesca." He let go and turned the lights on regardless. "I'm not Paolo. He isn't here. I am. And I've waited too long not to see you." He strode toward me.

Caressing my collarbone gently he said, "You were always breathtaking, Francesca." My eyes found his. "Trust me in this, your beauty is astonishing, the kind men would go to war for. The stars and the moon, and even the sun pale in comparison to you."

I sucked in a deep breath, deeply affected by his words. Cassio always knew how to make me feel like the world belonged to me. The only problem was, he also had the power to destroy it.

I didn't want this to be about feelings. This was supposed to be carnal, just sex, and nothing else. So, I got on the tip of my toes and kissed him.

Cassio lifted me up, his large hands cradling my ass, and carried me toward his bed. He dropped me gently and prowled towards me, a smile painted his lips as he removed a strand of hair from my face.

"You have no idea how long I have waited for you, Francesca." He caressed my cheeks.

God, I knew. I knew it because I had been waiting for this, too. "I want you to kiss me," I confessed.

Cassio smirked, and leaned down to capture my lips, the kiss was slow at first and got more momentum as we lost ourselves in it. He cupped my cheeks with one hand while the other he used to caress my breast. I couldn't help the moan from escaping my lips.

"Shirt, off, now," he ordered.

I complied eagerly. He stared at my chest for a while and used one finger to outline my nipple. I shuddered in anticipation. Cassio pulled the straps of my bralette and pushed it down so that my boobs slipped out. He cupped them and massaged me gently.

"They are as perfect as I imagined them to be." He twisted one of my nipples with his calloused fingers and I cried out in pleasure.

He grinned and took his time twisting and then soothing my nipples over and over again until I couldn't help but squirm. "Cassio," I begged not knowing what I wanted but knowing I needed more.

"Yes, *Principessa*?" He seemed completely lost in my breasts.

"I...I need more," My cheeks blazed.

He leaned down and captured one nipple into his mouth. The wetness and the heat made my head go blank, and I arched my back.

Cassio looked up at me, and I could feel him smiling. He reached under me and expertly unclasped my bra and helped me out of it.

"Beautiful." He kissed my collarbone. "Exquisite." He kissed my jaw. And then he hovered over me. "I'm going to fuck you hard, and you're going to take me. I want every person in this building to hear it, do you understand?"

I nodded in a daze.

"Good girl." He kissed my lip.

Then he began kissing down my body, starting with my nipples, down my ribs, and to my belly button—wherever his lips went, his hands followed. My skin was tight and pebbled while my insides burned, making it hard to think straight.

What was he doing to me?

Cassio stopped at my navel, kissing me twice before he looked up and offered me a feral grin. I rested on my elbows and watched him, confused and transfixed.

"Cassio, what are you doing?"

"I'm going down on you," he answered like it was obvious. I must have made a face because he frowned. "Don't tell me he never did that."

"No," I emphasized, shaking my head.

"What a fucking bastard," he cursed. "Trust me, you'll like this very much."

"You're awfully sure of yourself."

He smiled. "No, I'm awfully certain." He reached for my button, but I tensed. "Trust me, *Principessa*?" he asked.

I nodded and tried to relax. He opened the button, unzipped my jeans, and removed them. That's when it hit me. I was lying practically naked in Cassio Moretti's bed, about to finally have sex with him.

Memories of the last time we were naked together in bed invaded my head and the butterflies in my stomach took flight. We hadn't had sex, because we wanted to wait, but he had showed me there was more to it than sex.

When I came back to reality, he was removing my panties. I tensed again. He didn't seem annoyed, instead, he moved back and looked at me. "Sorry." I couldn't help but apologize.

"It's okay," he assured me. "let's do something else." He prowled upwards again and began kissing me. He played with my breasts and massaged me until I was squirming. I felt one of his hands slip down and before I tensed again, he kissed me just as he fingers slipped in between my legs.

I gasped.

The sensation had me traveling back to that night five years ago, when he had touched me for the first time. Just as it had been then, the sensation was exquisite. He kept on touching my clit repeatedly through the fabric of my panties, his fingers moving from side to side adding a bit of pressure with each touch. Before I noticed, I was melting.

"There you go," he whispered against my feverish skin.

Cassio pulled my drenched panties aside and the second his fingers came in contact with my bare skin, I moaned loudly. His fingers slipped through my folds downward toward my entrance, and he slowly eased one finger inside.

"Cassio—" I gasped.

"I know, *Principessa*. I know." He watched me as he pumped his finger, in and out, in and out, the repetitive motion driving me insane.

When he added a second finger, I was so lost in the sensation that my entire body ached with the need for release. "Are you going to come all over my fingers?"

Oh God, I was.

He increased the speed, and with his thumb, he began massaging my clit. That undid me. I arched my back, bending it upward, almost breaking it. My fingers dug into the sheets as I cried out his name.

He kept on pumping his fingers even as I clenched around him, I breathed hard trying to settle down from my orgasm, but Cassio kept on working me until he slowed down and pulled his fingers from me and placed them in his mouth sucking them dry.

"Sweet like cherries," he said and came down to kiss me.

I tasted myself in the kiss and it was one of the most erotic things I had done in the last four years.

"There's more from where that came from, *Principessa,*" he said. "So much more."

Cassio moved away from me, and I groaned in frustration, ready for another round. I rose onto my elbows to watch as he began to strip. First went his shirt and then he began removing his pants. Cassio was a god sculpted from marble. His body was deliciously on display for me to watch.

"Can I…" I swallowed hard. "Can I touch you?"

Cassio offered me his hand and pulled me up onto my knees. I knelt at the edge of the bed and stared at him, not knowing where to start. He took my hand and placed it over his chest. "Just touch me anywhere you want."

So, I did.

I traced his defined shoulders—the scar on his left one. Then his chest and his pecs, my fingers hovering over his new scar. The one I had bandaged. It was raw and pink but healing. I placed a kiss over it.

"Does it still hurt?" I looked up at him.

He shook his head. "I'm used to the pain." He repeated my words from earlier.

A sudden wave of anger arose in me. I wanted to hurt the man who had hurt Cassio. The reaction hit hard, and I pushed it aside worried for what it meant.

"You shouldn't."

"It's our way," he said simply. "We give our blood and our lives to the Outfit."

I nodded because I understood him, but it didn't mean I liked it. So, I continued drawing a path on his body. Each time my fingers ghosted over his skin, he shivered goosebumps erupting all over him.

Eventually, I got close to his briefs, and lingered there watching how his eyes fluttered and enjoying how his breath hitched. I never felt so powerful in my life. To know *I* was doing that to him.

Cassio stood there patiently as I rediscovered his body, much as he had done mine. Feeling bold, I slipped my hand down and cupped him through the fabric of his boxers. He sucked air through his teeth. Cassio was large and heavy, a massive difference from Paolo. It was comical even.

In my four years of marriage, I hadn't done much, Paolo had his mistresses to do it for him. When we had sex, it was hard and fast, thankfully lasting a few minutes. Most of those times I had been drunk or drugged. "What do I do?"

"Anything, *Principessa,* anything is fine."

I kept on caressing him through his briefs and eventually curiosity and desire made me grab them and pull them down. Cassio's cock was strained against his stomach, large and imposing. He groaned loudly when I circled it with my fingers. He was soft and warm in my hand, soft like velvet. I pumped it a few times, and circled his head, enjoying the feel of him in my hands. I increased the pressure and sped up, but he placed a hand over mine, forcing me to stop.

"Later," Cassio promised.

So, I let go and returned to inspecting his body, now trailing upward toward the black ink over his heart. I traced the intricate letters, my heart aching as I read the name tattooed on his chest.

Arabella.

I wanted to ask when he had it done, but I knew talking about her would sever this moment. Cassio had tensed while I traced her name.

I looked up at him and cupped his chiseled jaw. His green lust-filled eyes met mine.

Cassio captured my mouth. This kiss was savage, like he was trying to purge his mind of dark thoughts. I couldn't blame him. He bit my lip and grabbed my waist, throwing me back onto the bed, and climbing over me.

He kissed me leisurely like we had all the time in the world, and I pretended we did. When we pulled apart, he knelt in between my legs and rubbed my thighs up and down repeatedly.

Cassio curled his fingers around my panties and looked at me, a silent request. I nodded, and he began removing my drenched panties. I was no fully naked, he kept on rubbing my legs and slowly opened them and gazed at me.

"Beautiful, so fucking beautiful." He leaned in and kissed the inside of my left thigh.

"I'm scared," I confessed.

"I'll make it good; I promise." He kissed me slowly.

In that moment, I realized I wasn't simply scared of what was about to happen, but I was scared by how my heart was starting to react, to his words and touches. To how he was cherishing my body as though I were a goddess. His goddess.

"I know." I replied.

Cassio positioned himself and I felt his tip pressing against my entrance. I could sense how large he was, and I sucked in a deep breath anticipating the pain. "It won't fit."

"Yes, it will," he assured me. "And you're going to take all of me, *Principessa*." He pushed in slowly, but he was too large. "All of me, Francesca." He held me down with his body. I dug my nails into the skin of his back, as Cassio eased himself fully into me.

"Jesus," he groaned. "You're so fucking tight around me." I watched as his chest rose and fell.

Cassio looked at me and I realized he was waiting for me. Despite his eagerness and need, he was waiting. He was stretching me and despite not being in pain, I wasn't feeling any pleasure either.

"What do you need?" His concern caused my heart to clench.

"J-just... kiss me." He did, he kissed me slowly and gently, not once moving. Slowly the pressure began to turn into pleasure. I tilted my hips upwards.

"Fuck, Francesca," he groaned.

"I need you to move," I begged.

Cassio eased out and then entered me again. He repeated the process until the pressure finally turned into pleasure. "I can't go slow."

"Then don't." I moved my hips upward as I started to feel the beginnings of an orgasm.

Cassio pushed into me repeatedly, increasing the speed with each thrust. My nails kept digging into his skin. I gripped his hair and bit his shoulder, anything to tether me to this moment because I was slowly losing all sense of myself.

I was combusting from within. Burning. "You feel so good, *Principessa*. So, fucking good."

"Don't stop," I begged.

"Couldn't, even if I fucking wanted to." He thrust in deep, hitting my G-spot.

I cried out as it hit me suddenly, so hard, I saw stars. I had never felt anything like that. Never. "Oh, God."

"God is not here, Francesca." He bit my neck. "I'm the one doing this to you."

"Cassio," I moaned his name.

"Good girl." Cassio's lips tickled my ear. "Do you think you can take more?"

I must have nodded because he flipped me over, my stomach pressed against his sheets. Cassio entered me again from behind and started pounding into me. I screamed his name into the pillow.

"No, Francesca." He stopped. "I want to hear it." He pulled the pillow from me. "Who's fucking you?" he whispered against my ear. "Who, Francesca?"

"You," I shouted. "You!" I screamed as he hit that delicious spot again.

Cassio went on and on, tirelessly, until I felt my third orgasm coming. "I c-can't." It was too much; I was too hyper-sensitive.

"Yes, you can, and you will." He reached under me and flicked my clit. "Fuck, I can feel it." He leaned down and kissed my back. His hand gripped my hips, and he flipped me again. "Open your eyes, want to watch you come all over me." He ordered.

"I...can't."

"It's an order, Francesca." He was panting harder, too, and I knew Cassio was close.

I shouted his name as my orgasm hit me, probably waking up the entire building.

He pumped a few times into me and then I heard him groaning loudly as he reached his climax, spilling into me. Cassio fell sideways, keeping himself from suffocating me. The loss of him made me feel cold, but I was so spent, I had no strength left to move. He did instead, wrapping an arm around me, and pulling me flush against him. That's how I fell into oblivion wrapped by his strong, protecting arms.

"Thank you," I mumbled.

20

CASSIO

I sat on the sofa trying to read the files on my phone. I couldn't sleep, and I knew there was not a chance in the world that I was going to get any work done. Not when there was a woman in my room, in my bed, in my private space. Not just any woman, but Francesca Manci, the girl I used to date. The one I had planned on spending the rest of my life with.

I had never brought any woman to my place; this was my sanctuary and twice already Francesca had stayed here. I didn't know how to react. The strange thing was it didn't bother me like I thought it would.

Thank you.

Her sweet words echoed in my head. Fucking her was a gift, not a task. Did she not understand how much I had wanted to? How long I had waited for this moment? A part of me had tried to stay away. Francesca was no longer mine, but thinking about her with anyone else gave me indigestion.

Thank you.

As if pleasuring her had been a hardship.

"Fuck," I cursed. I made a vow four years ago; this wasn't supposed to happen. I should have refused her, Francesca was off limits, but I couldn't. *She was fucking promised to another man...again.* But no sane man could refuse Francesca, least of all me. Apparently, I had lost all sanity because the moment she walked into my room, there was no way she was ever getting out.

This was dangerous. Francesca had lips of a witch, pouring poison into my veins. Slowly consuming every inch of me. Settling herself into my mind, owning me completely. I was bewitched. This had to stop. It was maddening, this temptation. This need to have her. She was driving me insane.

The sound of footsteps stole me from my thoughts. I turned and found Francesca heading my way, wearing my shirt, and a look of satisfaction on her face. She was so fucking beautiful, like a goddess. I wanted to worship at her feet.

"Couldn't sleep?" I asked as she came down the stairs.

"I reached for you, and you were gone. Couldn't sleep?" she asked me.

"Work," I said simply.

"Do you always work this late in the night?"

"Do you always have trouble sleeping?"

She walked shaking her hips on purpose, my shirt riding up but not enough to show me if she was totally naked underneath or not. I, on the other hand, was sitting buck-ass naked on the sofa, blood rushed down to my groin and my dick sprung back to life.

She pulled the phone from my hand and threw it beside me. Francesca straddled my lap, and I hissed as her heated core kissed my dick. She was naked underneath my shirt. *Dear heavens.* This woman was going to be the death of me.

"Will you answer my question?"

"Will you?" I tried to sound cold, to push her away. I needed to put space between us or else I was going to lose control all over again.

"What do I get in return?" She moved her hips, causing friction between us.

I placed my hands on her hips trying to stop her, but it was too good. She felt too good against me. "If you want me to fuck you again, all you have to do is ask." The words slipped out of my mouth.

Francesca leaned into me and whispered softly. "I want you to fuck me, Cassio." The way she said my name was sultry and dirty, and I fucking loved it. Apparently, she wasn't as tired as I thought.

I lifted her hips and guided myself inside her again. Francesca was warm and tight and so damned wet, gripping me so hard, I had a feeling I wasn't going to last long. She moved her hips, and I let her do whatever she wanted. Letting her discover what she liked and what she didn't. My hands rested on her waist, and I held her tight.

Her chest rose and fell as she rode me, and I couldn't take it any longer, I removed her shirt. Her pale skin shone in the light, golden and bright. Her pink nipples were tight and begging for attention, I leaned forward and captured one in my mouth and sucked on it.

Francesca increased her pace almost frantically as she chased yet another orgasm. We were on a roll tonight. I couldn't blame her, neither could I stop her. She felt too good around my cock.

She opened her mouth and let out those breathy moans that were music to my ears. I rested back against the couch and watched as she came undone clenching around me like a vise. Francesca arched her back and called out my name again, and eventually stopped moving. I was about to bend over and fuck her as I wished when something on her skin grabbed my attention.

I had seen it before, but I'd been too focused on fucking her, to stop. She had a tattoo on her chest, it depicted three birds flying. I ran my finger over it and stared at her.

"Francesca," I traced the scar–hidden by the tattoo–with my fingers. "What's this?"

"Nothing." She lied.

Well, it didn't look like nothing. It looked like someone had stabbed her. My blood boiled to the point I could erupt. This was no small thing. Someone had hurt her.

"Explain," I bit out. She tried to get up, but I stopped her again. "Stop running."

"Stop making me," she begged.

"Fine." I let go of her. "Go." I looked away.

Francesca got up and sat on the other side of the sofa, her gaze stuck on the view before us. I didn't want trouble. I already had enough of it in my life. I didn't need more of it, and here I was asking for more.

"No one hurt me," she said after a while. "I did this to myself." I found her looking at her hands. It was obvious that she wasn't proud of this, of what happened. "I lost control."

"Of what, Francesca?" I snapped. She looked up at me for a second and I saw how embarrassed she was.

"I was high, Paolo and I had fought about something, probably one of his whores and I just...I wanted to make him hurt, too." She inhaled deeply and exhaled slowly. "He'd bought this new sports car, which cost him a fortune. I didn't know it was so fast. I lost control and hit the wall."

I stared at her not knowing what to say. The hurt and the shame were written all over her face. "I wasn't wearing a seatbelt," she explained.

"What did he do?"

"He called a doctor and told him I had tried to kill myself and that I needed help. He gave me pills." The ones I had seen in her house.

"Did you ever talk to this doctor?" She shook her head. "Then how did you know the pills worked?"

Francesca looked at her hands and was silent for a long while. I thought she wasn't going to answer but then her weak voice startled me. "Because I was numb."

I sighed deeply. "Come here." I offered her my hand. Francesca took a while to come but, in the end, she straddled my hips again.

There was nothing sexual about it. I stared at her for a while and played with a golden strand of her hair, wrapping it around my fingers.

"Did you ever..." I didn't know how to say this without hurting her, so I just said it. "Think about finding help?"

Francesca laughed cynically. "I'm a mess, Cassio. I fucking know that. A month after the accident, I was using and drinking all over again. I know I have problems, that's not the fucking issue." She was trembling. "I have daddy issues, mommy issues, relationship issues. My issues have issues, Cassio."

Without realizing what I was doing, I brought Francesca into my arms and held her tight. It had been ages since I had this kind of physical contact with a woman, the kind that didn't involve my dick.

"I don't want to be broken," she whispered against my neck.

"You're not, *Principessa*," I whispered back. "You're perfect."

But deep down I knew she was, and guilt began to eat me up. Paolo wasn't the only one at fault. Bitterly, I realized that I, too, was to blame for what happened to Francesca.

She was right, I should have never let her marry another man. Now I questioned if I did the right thing, if letting her go was the right choice. I hadn't been ready to marry her, I had just lost my sister and my father. I couldn't give my life to her when I hadn't planned on living. The only thing that kept me afloat had been my need for vengeance.

How could I marry someone, love and cherish them, when I didn't want to live? If I had married Francesca then, her life would have been miserable. I would have destroyed every beautiful part of her with all my darkness. Francesca was the light that I had always fed on.

I stared down at Francesca and realized she had fallen asleep in my arms. Her chest rising and falling against mine. I ran my hand hesitantly against her hair. It was so soft. The smell was so intoxicating. So undoubtedly her.

How could she sleep in my arms knowing what kind of man I was, knowing the things I did and would keep doing? Yet here she was. Inhaling her scent one last time, I carefully lifted her in my arms and took her to my bed—where she belonged. Some part of me wanted to keep her there forever.

I woke up with a jump start. I reached out for the gun under my bed. There were noises coming from downstairs. I couldn't recall falling asleep, but now that I was fully awake and alert, I focused only on the sound. Stepping out of my bed, I looked at the clothes dropped all around my floor. Memory of last night came rushing in. Francesca, me, what we did. The best sex of my life. *She slept here.* I looked back at the bed, but it was empty. The clothes on the floor were both mine and hers. Gun in hand, I made my way toward the noise.

Once I reached the edge of the stairs, I stopped. Francesca was still wearing my shirt; she was flipping something in my pan—pretty sure I'd never even used it. Her hair was tied in a messy bun which gave me the unnatural urge to set it free. It was a pleasant sight. Having her in my bed last night affected me more than I realized.

I would make it so good she wouldn't want to leave. *Fuck.* That wasn't the point here. She was making breakfast in my kitchen. Wearing my shirt. And all I was worried about was how to fuck her in order to make her stay.

Where had things gone wrong? Why wasn't I thoroughly pissed that she was invading my personal space? If this were anyone else, they wouldn't have even reached the kitchen. Yet again, there she was, flipping the pancake with expertise and setting out breakfast on two plates.

Two.

I headed into the kitchen setting the gun on the table, right where she could see it. No hiding it, no pretenses. I wanted her to know fully who I was and what I was capable of. Francesca jumped back but something told me it wasn't the gun that made her do it.

"God, I didn't see you coming. I made breakfast. I figured you must eat, even the devil must feed on something other than souls."

I just stared at her. She wasn't unfazed, not in the least. Not by me, not by the gun sitting centimeters from her. She pulled the plate toward her and began to eat. The one I figured was for me was still in the middle of the island.

It smelled so fucking great, my stomach rumbled. She looked at me but said nothing. It was chocolate chip pancakes...my favorite. And she wasn't wrong, I did like eating something other than souls. I liked eating her. The thought brought a smile to my face. I pulled my plate toward me and began to eat as well. In silence. Ignoring the fact we were both eating together.

"When did you learn how to cook?" If memory served me well, and it usually did, she couldn't cook, not even boil water.

"I had a lot of spare time. Paolo traveled a lot, I was home most of the time, and boredom led me to learn how to cook."

"You must have been very bored."

She chuckled. "I was, I hated cooking, but then it kind of felt therapeutic. It gave me something to think about other than...well, other than whatever was in my head."

"It's good." I had to give in, it was really good. I loved breakfast food, but anything with chocolate and cherries were a given.

"I didn't know if you liked it, but I knew you liked anything with sugar so…"

"I do. I like breakfast food." I added. We got back to eating and as strange as it sounded, Francesca was the most relaxed about all of this. I was the one who was on edge. I don't think she even realized how uptight I was about this situation.

"Did you cook a lot?" I asked trying to take my mind off the dirty thoughts that kept coming back. Especially about the one where she ended up sprawled on this very island as I ate her up.

"No. Not at all. Paolo hated that I cooked. He wanted a trophy wife, not a domestic one." She bit her lip and looked at her plate. "I try cooking for my mother though, but she hates it as usual."

"I like it." I don't know why I felt the need to add that, but I did. She gave me a weak smile in response, but it was obvious she didn't believe me. Standing up, she took her plate to the sink and left it there.

"I should go." Suddenly she was awkward and blushing. It made her eyes bluer, and her hair looked even more golden as the sunlight lit her up. "I promise I won't ever call you again. I don't want to be a problem. I'm not your mess and I didn't mean to be yesterday. I can't take back what I said yesterday," she blushed even harder. "But now that you know the entire truth, I'm sure you're beyond glad that I'll be gone."

Yeah, I don't think so.

"Sit down." I simply ignored all the bullshit she just gave me.

"What?"

"Sit." She did. "Where did you think you were going?"

"Hmm?" she frowned and tilted her head, looking at me as if I was an airhead. "Home, I literally abandoned Reginald, and well, you know, I visit my mother every day."

I pushed my finished plate aside and stood up. Stretched my legs and looked at her confused expression.

"Come then, let's go."

"I'm pretty sure I didn't poison that thing, so you've probably come down with something on your own. Are you feeling well?"

Fan-fucking-tastic.

"Good to know you thought about poisoning me. I'll add that to the list of things I need to worry about. Now let's go." I urged her.

She didn't realize it yet, but Francesca wasn't going anywhere. Yes, I heard the entire truth yesterday, and all the unspoken words in between. The hidden truths about her. There was more to her, so much more and I was going to figure it all out. Goodbye, my fucking ass. Not now and not in a million years. This was where she belonged.

"Come on, Francesca," I said impatiently. "Let's get that ugly gray rat of yours and visit your mother."

"You didn't!" She looked possessed. "Don't ever talk about my baby like that."

"You have an ugly baby," I pointed out and she gasped but was fighting a smile.

"Reginald is not allowed at the hospital," she said pointedly.

"Who cares, I own the place. Now *come on.*"

She fought a smile again and finally relented, coming toward me. She stopped right in front of me, got on the tip of her toes, and when I thought, she was going to kiss me, she leaned in, grabbed my balls and whispered against my ear.

"Call my baby ugly again and poison is the least of your worries." She let go, spun around, and left me hard as a fucking rod. Did she just threaten me?

God. She was trouble.

The best kind of trouble.

21

CASSIO

"Okay, so something is wrong."

I pinched my nose, feeling the start of a migraine. "What?"

"Your mood is oddly good today. I can practically see the sun shining." Vitelli sat in the chair before me. All bright and smiley. "You're not sour, or bitter, or even gloomy."

"I get it, Vitelli. Is there a point to all of this?" He narrowed his eyes and looked at me for a while.

"How many?"

"How many what?"

"Women. There is no chance in hell that you're in a good mood because of this," he looked and waved around the office. "So, I can only assume women were involved. Or you finally killed Donato Manci."

"Fuck's sake, Vitelli. You're ruining my mood."

"So, it wasn't Donato?" He deflated.

Honestly, after everything that happened this past weekend, it was a fucking miracle that the man was still breathing. There were no *good Mafiosi*, but Donato was straight out deranged. Cruel.

There were different kinds of men in the same spectrum varying from bad to borderline satanic.

"No," I bit out. "I didn't kill him."

"So, it's women then," he pried, broad smile on his face, one I wanted to wipe off.

Woman.

Single. Not plural as he believed.

It wasn't supposed to have happened; it had caught me by surprise. I thought it would have been a one-time thing and then we would be back to ignoring each other.

One day turned into two, and two ended up turning into her staying at my place for the weekend. Sleeping in my bed—although there wasn't much sleeping involved. It was clear to me that she hated being at her place. So, I brought her back to mine again and again.

The sex was great. Mind blowing really. The best sex I had in my entire life. Watching Francesca lose herself was one of the best experiences of my life. I might not have been her first, but knowing I was the one to show her this world, the one to offer her so much pleasure...it humbled me.

"Has Romeo contacted us?" That took Vitelli by surprise. It would keep him from asking questions I didn't want to answer.

"He wasn't pleased with you leaving like that, but thankfully he understood. I'm good at persuasion. But you made me late to pick up Marie and she was pissed."

"I imagine you made it up to her." I raised one brow. "Good at persuasion, I'm guessing."

"Something like that." He smirked. Where did you drive off to?"

"Somewhere important." I waved him off.

"What could be more important than the meeting with Romeo Ferraro?"

Francesca. Simple as that. Francesca was starting to become the most important thing in my world, and that unnerved me.

"Romeo suggested we tie our alliance with a marriage." I pondered Vitelli's words. "He suggested you marry his cousin Livia, the girl—"

"I'm not marrying her," I pointed out simply.

Vitelli smiled and nodded. "I thought that would be your sentiment, so I said we could work something else out."

"Good." I agreed. Marrying was the last thing I wanted to do right now, especially to Romeo's sister. I liked the guy, but I wasn't ready to be part of his family.

"Well...I'm not marrying her either," Vitelli said with sudden determination. The thought hadn't even crossed my mind, but a smile pulled at the edge of my lips. "I'm not, Cassio," he warned me.

"And why is that?" I knew he wouldn't, and it wasn't my idea to marry him off. I just wanted to see that look on his face. Marriage had never been a reality for my brother. Not even now with his girlfriend, the poor girl would be strung along until she was old and dying. Vitelli had a fear of commitment and marriage was a big one.

"I asked Marie LeRoy to marry me," he practically blurted.

Well, that was unexpected. "Is this a joke?"

"I'm not laughing," he said seriously. "I meant to ask you after dinner, but then you disappeared, and I couldn't reach you. I wanted to ask her the week after we met, but I knew you would never approve, so I gave it some time. One thing led to another, and I asked her yesterday. No one knows, and I asked her to keep it quiet. I said I would talk to you, out of respect as my brother, but I'm marrying her," he said with determination.

"I'll always be loyal to you, that doesn't change things, that just means I'll be sharing that loyalty with her. Marie would never harm me or the Outfit, and she loves me, Cassio, she really does, she makes me happy. I can't remember a time when I was actually happy—"

"Enough, Vitelli." I didn't let him finish.

"I just meant to say that I'm happy with her and that it doesn't affect what we have here. You're my brother and my Capo. That doesn't change."

I was actually stunned, but my schooled expression didn't give away my inner turmoil. We never really talked about the past. The days following what happened to my father and to my sister were a blur. We didn't stop to think about it. For me, those days had been chaos, filled with guilt, anger, alcohol, and the need for revenge. It had consumed me so much; I couldn't even recall what happened during that first year.

I never stopped to wonder how my brother took it. Vitelli didn't have a close relationship with my father, but he was close to *Bella*. We all learned to deal with the pain and our grief differently. I had never known his still haunted him.

"Do you love her?" He tensed but without hesitation, he nodded. "Do you plan on being loyal and faithful to her?" He nodded again. "Do you plan on protecting and keeping her from harm, meaning from you as well?"

"I would never harm her," he said fiercely.

As his Capo and older brother, it was my duty to make sure my brother would never do that. I was beyond redemption, but he wasn't.

"Don't ever put out the fire in her. Promise me that, and you'll have my blessing."

He was stunned for a full minute, not caring to hide it from me. Vitelli had always been light-hearted and fun to be around. I was the dark cloud. But even I'd noticed the change. The fucker was lovestruck and he was going to be a married man.

"I promise," he said without a shadow of a doubt. "Thank you, Cassio."

"Don't thank me. Thank her for being brave enough to accept a lifetime with you."

He grinned like a schoolboy. "Fuck, I'm getting married."

Yeah, he was, my little brother was getting married, was moving on with his life. From the depths of my being, guilt exploded, and I couldn't rein it back in. It refused to remain locked up the way it had been for the past four years. It struck me violently and true, and it didn't let go.

She was pacing outside the doctor's office, her blonde hair

following her around like a golden aura. She wore a pink floral dress that hugged her body, offering me a view of those delicious curves as well as her long legs.

A sudden image flooded my brain, a memory. Her legs wide around my waist, the heels of her feet digging into my ass. Then it changed, those legs gripping my face tight as I ate her out for the first time. I could still taste her, sweet and addictive.

I stopped and she turned to face me. Her eyes widened and then she was glaring. I closed the space between us, hating how much I desired to take her into one of these offices and fuck the hell out of her.

"*Principessa.*"

"What are you doing here?" She crossed her arms, cheeks turning pink. Was she remembering our nights, too? "Wait," she paused. "How did you know I was here?"

"You know how, Francesca."

"Are you ever going to stop?"

I shook my head. "No." I would have her followed for as long as possible. Francesca needed protection, and she was mine to take care of. Mine to keep safe. My problem now.

I faced the door and then turned to look at her, she dug her nails into the palms of her hands. I knew she had been out here for the past half hour. Two days ago, Francesca had agreed to visit a psychiatrist, but somewhere along the line that had changed.

"I can't do this," she admitted and started pacing again.

"Francesca," I stopped her and grabbed her shoulders. "Breathe."

"Why are you here, Cassio?"

Good question. Why was I here? I had so much fucking work to do it had started to pile up in my office. For the first time in four years, I had taken a weekend off. Although I did work, my attention was elsewhere.

I had no other explanation for her other than I wanted to be here. Like I wanted to bring her back to my apartment. Like I wanted to keep on fucking her.

"We'll do together if that's what you want," I said instead.

Francesca stared at me like I had lost my mind and I probably had. "Unless you would rather do this alone."

She took a few seconds to answer and then she shook her head. "You've seen me naked, so I guess this won't shock you," she blushed.

I chuckled. Seeing her naked had almost shocked me into a coma. Francesca was everything I had always dreamed of and more. "*Principessa,* there's little in the world that is capable of shocking me," I reminded her.

She took a deep breath and looked at the door like it was a portal into Hell. "Our problems are the only loyal things in our life. No matter what happens, they will always be there to haunt us. So, you can either deal with them or you can spend a lifetime being chased," I told her.

Francesca's sapphire eyes were filled with fear, but she nodded in agreement. She took the first step toward the door, and I followed. She knocked and when she looked at me, she sported a tentative smile, that made my fucking day.

The doctor answered and led us toward a sitting area. Francesca sat straight, her back stiff and her shoulders tense. She was digging her nails into the palms of her hands once more. A nervous tick that was starting to annoy me. I despised watching her hurting herself. Without thinking, I grabbed one of her hands and held it in mine.

Francesca looked at me surprised but said nothing. The doctor, an old woman with gray hair and large round glasses, took her seat before us and looked at our intertwined hands.

I knew coming here wasn't a good idea, there were things Francesca needed to deal with on her own. But the honest truth was that I wanted to be here for her. Maybe it was the guilt talking, maybe it was this need to be close to her. I spent an entire weekend by her side, and I realized it wasn't enough.

I wanted to see her happy, to see her healthy.

22

FRANCESCA

"**F**uck!" I grabbed her hand.

"Frankie," Marie blushed.

"You're getting married?" I asked trying to hide my shock, but so help me God, it wasn't working. "So soon." I didn't want to sound negative or anything, but they had been dating for what? Two months? Three?

"He asked me to keep it quiet for now, but I couldn't hide it from you." Marie was glowing. "And I know it's soon, but he's the one, Frankie. He makes me so happy. I love him."

My heart couldn't take it. I was so thrilled for her. Marie had been with other guys, but I'd never seen her like this before. She was in...love. *Love.* The realization struck me hard. I knew that feeling, of what it meant to be loved by someone. How everything around you suddenly felt ten times better. The colors were more vibrant, the food tasted better. Even the very air you breathed seemed to fill you differently. I had felt that once.

"I...Marie." I stared at the massive diamond on her finger. "I can't believe it," I chuckled in happiness.

She met me on the other side of the kitchen island, and we hugged. I held on to her tightly and couldn't contain the wave of emotions that crashed into me. I held back a sob. I was beyond happy that my best friend actually managed to fulfill her dream. She found her prince; she was going to get married.

Deep down, a small part of me, one I was ashamed of, was jealous of her. I wanted to crush that part, destroy it, but it had latched on and wouldn't let go.

Marie and I talked for hours, she told me how magical the proposal had been and how she was already planning the wedding. I sat there listening to her and imagining how lucky she was to have it all, and Marie deserved it.

She headed toward the bathroom and returned holding an orange pill bottle. "Frankie?" she said sadly. "What is this?"

My cheeks turned pink. Cassio had told me not to be ashamed. He said there was nothing wrong with me. Dr. Alma, my physiatrist, had said the same, but it was hard getting over an old habit.

"I visited a psychiatrist," I confessed. "And next week I have an appointment with a therapist," I added. Marie's jaw dropped.

"Frankie, that is wonderful." She sat beside me on the sofa. "I'm so proud of you." She held my hand. "Sorry for judging." She offered me the pill bottle.

I took them from her and placed them on the table before me. I couldn't blame her for doing so. For four years, Marie watched me use all kinds of drugs and take various kinds of pills. She had remained my friend through thick and thin, so I couldn't blame her for wanting the best for me, just like I wanted the best for her.

"I'm still adapting," I told her. Taking the correct medication scared me. I didn't want to become addicted, again.

"I'm here for you."

I leaned into her. "I know." I smiled.

"Frankie."

"Yeah?"

"Why are there black boxer briefs on your couch?" Marie sounded calm, but I could hear her loud thoughts.

Mortified, I looked at her. It was a miracle that my face remained calm and composed. "Oh, I didn't know they were there." I waved at her dismissively.

"Frankie! Why is there male underwear on your couch? What happened? Are you seeing someone? Are you getting some?" She was equally horrified, confused, and excited.

Heat traveled from my neck all the way to my cheeks. Marie looked at the boxer briefs one more time before settling down. I almost reached to take them from her, but I thought it best to remain where I was.

"It's his isn't it?"

"Who's?" I played dumb. Marie raised one brow and it was all that it took for me to admit it. "I slept with Cassio."

Her jaw dropped a few inches and her dark eyes widened. "You... Francesca." She then laughed.

"Slept as in plural," I added, and Marie squealed. "I feel so guilty." I added.

Her face morphed into shock. "Why would you be? You're a twenty-three-year-old gorgeous woman, who spent the last four years of your life in an unhappy marriage."

"It wasn't all that bad." I didn't know why I still defended him.

"I hated seeing you with that man. I know you owe him a lot and that he helped you through a bad phase, but he hurt you just as much. Paolo watched you suffer, and he watched as you slowly began to fade away and did nothing to stop it. You might hate me for saying it, but Paolo is dead, and you aren't."

"Cassio was the last person I should have allowed back into my life." I argued.

She tilted her head and was silent for a while. "Is it just sex or something more?"

"Just sex," I said quickly, but when I stopped to think about it, it had turned into more than just that.

"Then you have nothing to worry about." Marie pointed out simply, as if it was that easy. She didn't understand the power of Cassio Moretti. "What are you worried about?"

Was it that obvious? "What if he hurts me again?"

Marie's face softened. "As long as you don't fall for him, then he can't hurt you."

And that was the problem, Cassio was the last person I could allow myself to be happy with. There was no way the words happiness and Cassio could be used in the same sentence. And I hated that lately all I could think about was Cassio.

How he had visited my mother with me. How he had brought me home and fucked me senseless, against the door, then the wall. How he went down on me and ate me up like he was starved. Then he took me to bed and fucked me there, too. Even the kitchen counter wasn't spared. How he had held my hand at the doctor's office.

What if I was falling for him? That couldn't happen, right? Not after he broke my heart and tore it to pieces. How could I ever forgive him? But he was everywhere. Consuming every inch of me and I couldn't allow that to happen.

I needed to get away from him because I knew Cassio was going to hurt me again, it was not if, but when. I couldn't dare hope with him because hope was dangerous.

Cassio was addictive.

Stronger than any drug I had ever used, and like any other drug, there was a moment when I would have to come down from that high. So instead of crashing into the bottom of the pit like I usually did, it was best to push him away. To go back to being strangers, it was the only way to save my heart.

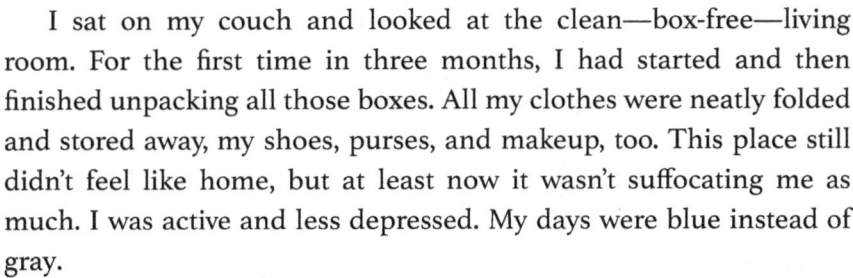

I sat on my couch and looked at the clean—box-free—living room. For the first time in three months, I had started and then finished unpacking all those boxes. All my clothes were neatly folded and stored away, my shoes, purses, and makeup, too. This place still didn't feel like home, but at least now it wasn't suffocating me as much. I was active and less depressed. My days were blue instead of gray.

My phone rang, and a shiver raced down my back. I had taken

two days off from visiting my mother. The hospital was the only place that could be calling me right now. Ever since my doctor's appointment four days ago, Cassio had vanished. And it was for the better.

"Francesca." A male voice sounded on the other side. It was hard to identify at first since all I could hear was my pulse. "Francesca?"

"Marco?" How hadn't I recognized him?

"Can you come to the hospital?"

"Marco, is everything all right?" I shot up, my hands becoming sweaty.

"Francesca, please."

Fuck. Fuck. Fuck.

I was not ready for this. My heart was beating so fast, I thought I was going to have an attack. I didn't have the courage to ask, but I knew something had gone wrong.

"Marco is Mamma..."

"Shit, I can't talk, just meet me at the cafeteria."

He hung up before I had the chance to say something, as if he knew what I was going to say.

I bolted inside the hospital, my head spinning, my stomach churning and my blood pressure lower than the pits of hell. My first instinct was to head toward my mother's room on the 9th floor, but if something was happening, I didn't want to be there to see it. I didn't care if it made me a total coward.

When I reached the wide area, I looked in all directions, searching for my brother, it took me a while to remember I wasn't looking for a kid anymore. Even so, I couldn't spot his blond hair anywhere. My hands were shaking. I walked myself over to the counter and asked for a bottle of water. I waited as the barista took my order, my nails incessantly tapping on the counter.

"Francesca." I began to turn around at the sound of my name. "Don't. Don't turn around."

"Marco?" I wanted desperately to turn around but didn't.

"Please, just pretend I'm not here." I was about to scold him till kingdom come when the barista arrived with my order.

"Can I help you with anything, sir?" she asked my brother who proceeded to ask for a bottle of water as well.

He remained there standing beside me, but neither of us looked at each other. It was as though we were just two strangers in the line. Out of curiosity, I glanced over at him, his face was hidden by his Chicago Bulls cap, and he wore a black zipper jacket and some jeans. He was so out of character that I understood now why I hadn't seen him before. I was looking for a boy in boyish clothes or someone in a tux like most Made Men wore.

"Mamma?" I asked as the barista handed him his bottle of water.

"*Va bene,*" was all he said, but those two words telling me she was okay, was all that I needed to calm down—at least as much as was possible. "Do you know where the gardens are?"

I nodded. "Yes," I added because he wasn't looking.

"Meet me there."

"Mar—"

But he was already walking away from me. I squeezed the water bottle, trying to channel all my inner rage toward the poor thing. The desperation and fear I had been feeling just a few seconds ago were completely replaced by rage. I wanted to kill my little brother for making me so freaking scared.

"Thank you," I told the barista and moved toward the side so that others could order as well.

I searched the room and instantly my eyes settled on a man dressed in jeans and a leather jacket. He was dressed casually but there was nothing casual about him. It took me only a couple seconds to realize he was one of Donato's men, keeping tabs on my brother.

The man wasn't looking my way, he was standing by the door, his head turned towards where Marco went. I understood his secrecy now, Marco didn't want them to know he was here with me. He was trying to protect me.

With shaking hands, I opened the bottle and took one hard sip. Slowly my anger dissipated, and I didn't feel the need to strangle him. I hurried toward the garden but instead of taking the same route as him, I went the other way. If he took all that trouble to remain unseen, then I wasn't going to be the one to ruin his plan.

The hospital's garden wasn't exactly a garden, it was an outside area filled with a couple of trees and flower bushes. There were a few paths and some benches scattered around them. I passed some patients as I made my way through the main path. Marco had sat on a bench on the furthest side, his head hung low, his elbows resting on his knees, but I knew for a fact he was one hundred percent ready to move if someone drew near.

The bench he had chosen was equally hidden but also placed in a good spot if he wanted to keep an eye on the passersby. That was the Outfit's doing, both with him and with me. I could easily see these things now.

I sat on the bench but kept my distance so that if others saw us, they wouldn't know we were together. We remained in silence for a moment, he no longer had his head hung low and he now leaned against the wood, he looked forward as though he were in some deep thought.

"*Ma che cazzo*, Marco." I finally lost my patience. I couldn't hold it anymore.

Marco on the other hand seemed to have all the patience in the world. He sighed deeply as he shifted on the bench, one leg folded over the other, he turned to face me completely—Marco removed his cap.

"Marco!" My hand shot toward him, to touch my little brother.

"Don't, Francesca." He stopped me.

I couldn't take my eyes away from him, or better yet, from the enormous purplish-black bruise on his face. His left eye was slightly swollen and his lips as well. There was a small tear right in the middle. My heart ached at that sight. Fire coursed through my veins, anger like I had never felt before consumed me. I shot from the bench.

"Was it him?" I practically shouted.

"Francesca." He tried to shush me, looking both ways to see if someone was looking. He moved to put his cap on once more, but I took it from him.

"Marco," I threw back. "I'm going to kill Donato." I turned around ready to murder my father.

Marco's hand encircled my wrist, causing me to look back. His face was paler now, he looked concerned, but I also saw fear in his eyes. That was what unmade me. My shoulders slumped, and I didn't fight him as he pushed me back. I stepped in front of him, and he sat there, his head held low once more.

Gently, I lifted his face, he flinched but didn't move away from me. I exhaled in relief. He looked at me now as I ran my finger slowly through his bruise, praying I wouldn't hurt him.

"I've had worse." He tried to laugh it off, but it was the wrong thing to say.

Thirteen. My brother was a teenager, and his face was all busted. He'd had it worse! How? I looked at him and all I could see was my baby brother, and I wondered what kind of a monster would do that to a kid. I scoffed inwardly; I knew exactly what kind of a monster would do that.

"It's better now. It's okay."

"It's not okay, Marco! It's not…" I sighed.

"Can you please sit?" He practically begged. He watched the garden with eagle eyes, afraid someone would spot us.

"Fine," I grumbled and sat beside him. "Did you at least get it checked?" He gave me something in between a nod and a shake of his head.

"Francesca, it's fine, really."

"Your face is busted, Marco, it's not fine," I shot back. How couldn't he see it?

"I was worried about you," he confessed. If we weren't this close, I wouldn't have heard it.

"Me?" I was taken aback by his comment. He looked at me with those dark blue eyes, twins to mine. In this moment, Marco seemed to be ten years older than I was. His beautiful face was marked with concern.

"I tried, Francesca." He shook his head. "I'm sorry, I tried to stop him, I just...he shouldn't have hit you like that."

"Marco." I took his hand. "It wasn't your fault, do you understand? What happened back there wasn't your fault and neither was it your responsibility."

"I'm your brother," he said with genuine determination, a kind of protectiveness I never heard from my older brother Savio. "I should have defended you."

"You did. You tried, and that is more than anyone has done." *Holy God.* "Is that why he hit you?"

Silence.

"Marco."

"I confronted him. After you left, I tried to go after you, he sent me to my room and right after, when I finally got out, I confronted him." Marco scoffed. "He didn't even beat me himself, he had Enzo do it."

"God," I cursed.

"Is it true? What you said about Mamma?"

"I'm sorry you had to find out that way." There was no point in lying to him. As much as I wanted to shield my brother from the horrors of our family and the world I couldn't. There was nothing I could do when he was closer to becoming a Made Man with each day that passed.

Marco only nodded, he didn't speak, and silence settled once more over us. I didn't know what to do, we were still getting to know each other again.

"I need to tell you something." He blurted after a while. "I don't know who to trust right now and—" he paused and looked around searching the premises, but no one was here with us.

"You can trust me, you know that, right?"

Marco didn't answer, instead, he removed his phone from his pocket and unlocked it, searched for something, and finally handed it to me. I took it and frowned at what I was seeing.

It was a picture of Donato in a meeting, the door was slightly ajar, and I couldn't see the others who joined him. Marco swiped to the next photo and this one was much like the first, but the only difference was that I could only see their faces.

Then he showed me a third one. I recognized the place instantly despite the years since I hadn't been there. The picture was taken in my family's lake house, it was night, and three figures sat on the pier; Donato, and two others I didn't know.

Marco zoomed in on the picture, right on one of the strangers, and zoomed in until all I could see was the man's arm.

"What is this?" I asked.

"Papa once told me that almost every mafia had its own tattoo," he explained. "This is the Bratva's."

I looked at Marco beckoning him to continue. He took the phone from my hand, and quickly locked it, and shoved it back into his jeans pocket. Again, he looked around making sure no one was nearby. I realized that even if we had power, life in the Outfit was a life of always being in a constant state of alarm.

"I think Papa is up to something," he whispered. I looked at my brother as he avoided looking at me.

I couldn't believe those words were coming from his mouth. Ever since I moved away, my greatest fear was that I would lose my brother. Savio had always been a lost cause, we were never truly siblings, but Marco was mine, as I had practically raised him. As I looked at him now, I had no shadow of a doubt that he was still the same little boy I knew.

"Why me?" I whispered as well, suddenly catching up with what he was telling me and what he was here for.

"I don't...I don't know who to trust, he's my father, and I owe him my loyalty, but Cassio is our Capo, and I know I owe him my loyalty, too. I can't just..." He sighed slouching on the bench. "I don't know if it's all in my head or if something is really going on between Father and the Russians. I can't just simply take this to either of them. This isn't exactly proof, and even if it were, how could I betray our own family? Our name." He looked at me and I saw his despair. "I want to make them proud." He practically whined.

In this moment I watched as the mask of the man he was trying to be, fell and in its place was a child who so desperately sought to prove himself.

I pulled him so that he faced me, I didn't give a damn if Donato's men saw us. "I can't offer my opinion because you know it's going to be biased. I can't tell you what to do because it's up to you to choose. You know what Donato has done and you know what kind of a man he is," I spoke. "Either way, no matter what happens or what you choose to do, I will always be here. You can always come to me. I don't care if Donato threatens to hurt me, if anything happens, you come to me. Do you understand?"

"Francesca, I can't."

"Bullshit, of course you can. Look at me, Marco, I'm already screwed, what more could happen?" *A lot.* My conscious answered, but I pushed it away. "I hope it's nothing, maybe it's just business." And I did, no matter how much I hated Donato, he was still my brother's father and Marco still cared for him. Not only that but if something happened to my father, Marco would be the one to suffer the consequences one way or the other.

"He was Russian, Francesca." He chuckled bitterly.

"It doesn't matter, what matters is that whatever you choose to do, I will be there with you. Okay?"

He seemed to ponder it for a while and then he nodded his head a couple of times. Instantly I felt as if the muscles on his shoulders relaxed.

"I have to go. Papa must be coming home." Marco stood up. I stood as well, and we were both stuck in that awkward moment, unsure of what to do. He took the first step and began to head away. Suddenly he turned and smiled under his cap.

"I like this version of you," he confessed and walked away.

I wished I knew which version he was talking about.

23

FRANCESCA

It had been days since I had seen or heard from Cassio. It seemed that our little liaison ended before I had the chance to do so. I was grateful, really, I was. Happy even. Cassio must have felt the same way I did about what we were doing. I wasn't angry at him, I really wasn't. It was all *fine*.

Great even.

Instead of wallowing in my misery or staring at my phone waiting for at least a message from him, I dressed up, picked up my keys, kissed Reggie good night, and decided to explore Chicago's nightlife.

I hit the Magnificent Mile and pretended I was a tourist seeing Chicago for the first time in my life. I stopped by some shops and took my time trying on clothes I knew I wouldn't buy but did so anyway. In the end, my resolve ended in the third store I entered, and I ended up buying some new dresses that fit me better than the ones I owned.

When I was done, I did something I hadn't done since the day of my wedding. I visited the 4th Presbyterian church which was on the neighborhood. I sat there on my own in the silence of the house of God, and for the first time in a while, I was grateful. I had incredible friends, I was seeing my brother again, and my mother was finally getting better. She was even bumped up on the transplant list, which meant she might get one soon. I was getting treatment, too. Visiting the therapist and the psychiatrist were some of the best choices I'd made this year.

My mind instantly traveled to Cassio, how, despite it all—our fights, our past, and my initial hatred of him—I was thankful for him, too. He'd helped me in more ways than I could count. Not to mention sex, which for the first time was something I enjoyed.

Sorry, God.

I looked at the cross and begged for his forgiveness, but it was better to tell the truth, right? God wouldn't want me to lie. Sex with Cassio was beyond words, something I couldn't begin to explain. He made me feel like I was special. Cherished. Like my body was the only one he wanted to worship.

When thoughts of him clouded my mind, I left the church, cheeks blazing. A priest passed me by, and I swore he could tell what sins I had committed. I rushed out of the church and headed toward Navy Pier where I enjoyed an ice cream and watched a dance group perform on the square.

As the night drew in, it was like the world decided to spin slowly, giving me one night to enjoy myself and forget about my problems. I wanted to get better; this time was different from the rest. I needed to get better, for my brother, for my mother, for my friends, but most importantly for myself. There was so much of life I hadn't yet lived.

I scooped a bit of ice cream and ate it while my eyes followed the crowd, not really paying attention to anything. That's when I caught sight of a couple taking a picture of each other. I ate the rest of my ice cream and threw the empty cup away and made my way towards them.

"Excuse me, would you like me to take a picture of you two?"

"Oh, yes!" The woman squealed and offered me her phone. "Thanks so much."

The woman stood before the Ferris wheel and her partner did so as well, when I shot the first picture, he got on his knee and removed a black velvet box from his pocket. My jaw dropped and the girl's phone almost did so as well.

"Oh God," I stared at them.

That's when the woman realized what was happening. She placed both hands to her mouth and began crying. The whole scene was very emotional, and I took it upon myself to film them. A crowd had gathered around us to watch the young couple get engaged. After the entire spectacle, she came to grab her phone, and I congratulated her with a hug and a smile that reached my ears.

I couldn't stop smiling at the look on the man's face as he knelt before the love of his life and asked her to marry him, it was so pure and filled with joy. Like he had just won the lottery. I giggled to myself and came to realize that I deserved that, too.

That kind of happiness. Why did I have to content myself with what I had, with what my father was forcing upon me? I wanted more than an arranged marriage to a man I didn't know. I wanted more than an unhappy life. I deserved more than what I was told I could have.

For the hundredth time tonight, Cassio came to mind and in that moment walking through the streets of Chicago, I realized that I didn't hate him like I thought I did. Maybe I never truly had.

I wanted Cassio and it was about time I stopped depriving myself of what I wanted most. This one year I had was about enjoying my freedom to do as I pleased.

The hairs on the back of my neck rose, and I had the feeling someone was watching me. Perhaps I was being paranoid, but I looked back either way. I didn't remember the street being so empty. My apartment was just around the corner, but this place was always packed with people.

I squinted my eyes, trying to see through the shadows. Two figures appeared walking my way. I had seen them. I recognized their jackets and their matching black Adidas; I saw them at the Navy Pier earlier tonight.

What were the chances they lived nearby? Panic settled, and I wanted to bolt but didn't. I tried to maintain my calm.

Quickening my pace, I took my keys from my pocket and searched for the one that opened my apartment. My hands shook. The faster I walked, the faster they seemed to follow me. The dim lights from the street made it hard to see them, but I wasn't interested in that now, all I wanted was to reach my apartment. *And then what?*

I ran now. The door to my building was closed, and I fumbled with the keys to open them up, the two men following me didn't stop, they kept on coming, dismissing the fact that I was entering the building. The key finally fit the lock and I opened them almost twisting my wrist. Then I was running up the stairs toward the eighth floor. I couldn't see them, but I heard the building door open.

I closed the door of my apartment and ran to the kitchen, taking a sharp knife. I sat against my refrigerator, trying to look small in case they walked in. There were sounds and I could hear men's voices. Then there was a shot.

Don't do it. Don't do it. Don't.

I picked up my phone.

"Fran—"

"They are in my building."

"Who?"

"I don't know, Cassio, I didn't stop to ask them," I snapped but my voice was already trembling.

"Stay there." He seemed strangely calm when I was freaking out to the point of having an attack.

"Where else would I go?" I cried.

God, no.

Tears ran down my cheek and I couldn't help it. This was the second time I cried with him on the phone. There was something about hearing him that made me lose it.

"Sorry," I cried again. All I heard was him cursing and then he was gone. "No. No!" I looked at the screen and my phone was off. My battery had died.

I made to stand but heard footsteps that sounded close to my door. I heard knocking in the distance and knew they were searching for me. Resting my head in between my knees, I hugged myself tight and closed my eyes praying for this to be over.

There was a loud noise, it sounded like something had been torn up—destroyed. *My door.* Hugging myself even tighter, I bit my arm, keeping myself from making any sounds. Footsteps neared me but all I could hear was the desperate beating of my heart. It was so loud it was almost deafening.

A hand touched my arm.

I cried out.

I bit my arm harder, hoping that whatever they wanted to do to me would end quickly.

"Francesca." I heard my name. "Francesca, it's me." The voice was definitely male, but I couldn't make myself look.

I waited for the pain; there was only a soft caress. "Francesca, please look at me," he said again. I shook my head, or I think I did because he called me again. "*Principessa,* please." As though I had been given a shock, I woke up from whatever nightmare I was having.

Slowly, I lifted my head from that small cocoon and looked around. Pine-green eyes were the first thing I saw, and I swore I could see fear in them.

"Are you okay?" I saw his lips moving, and I understood what he said but it was still hard to speak.

His warm hand patted me from head to toe searching for some kind of injury. He stopped at my arm and noticed the bite. He knelt and reached for the kitchen towel, then pressed it against my arm. I winced in pain.

"It's okay." He ran his thumb my cheeks, wiping away my tears with a gentleness I would never have expected from him. "You're safe," he assured.

I nodded.

"Can you stand?"

I nodded again, but the moment he helped me up, I felt dizzy and almost fell back to the floor. Almost but not quite; one moment I was falling, and in the next, I was in the air. Cassio lifted me up with ease and settled me against his chest. I could feel his heart beating fast. He began walking toward the door and panic overtook me again.

"It's okay, *Principessa*," he assured.

We exited my apartment and came into the bright-lit corridor, making me squint. Cassio stopped before a large man.

"Pick up as many clothes as you can, and take them to my place," he instructed the man and began to move. "There's no chance I'm ever letting you come back here," he spoke against my ear so only I could hear.

All I could do was nod in agreement. I didn't fight him, and I didn't complain, there was no way I wanted to stay here. Right now, I didn't want to go anywhere else, being in his arms was enough. I turned slightly as the man entered my apartment.

"Reggie," I called. Cassio stopped and looked at me, his green eyes assessing. "Reggie." I pouted.

"Fuck." He walked back toward my door which had been kicked to the floor and stopped. "Reginald!" he shouted.

My baby came trotting toward us, his little body trembling with fear, but still he came. Cassio waited until Reginald was with us and looked back to see if my baby was following as we descended the stairs.

I rested my neck against the crook of his neck, inhaling his intoxicating scent, and closed my eyes knowing there was nowhere safer than in his arms.

CASSIO

I REMOVED Francesca from the passenger seat, she must have been drained from what happened tonight because she was out cold. I pulled her back into my arms, wanting to be as close to her as I could.

When we arrived at my condo, I headed straight to my room because there was no other place she belonged than with me. I gently settled Francesca on the bed and removed her shoes before covering her up with the blankets. She stirred and opened her eyes.

"Cassio," she called.

"I'm here, *Principessa*." I crouched by the bed.

"You're leaving." She looked at me knowingly.

"I have to," I told her. "Francesca, I have—"

"I know," she said, and I knew she understood, yet the way she sounded, so weak and tired, caused my guts to twist.

"I'll be back as soon as I can." I leaned in and kissed her forehead. "Luciano is coming over while I'm gone." She opened her mouth to protest, but I stopped her before she could. "He's my enforcer and I trust him."

"Okay." She didn't seem convinced, but I couldn't trust Vince to watch her, he had allowed those men to get close to her, and right now, the only person I trusted enough to watch over her was Luciano.

"It won't take long," I said and kissed her lightly on the lips.

As I closed the door to my room, something shifted inside of me, my heart was melting all of the ice caps that had formed a protective barrier around itself. There was no denying it any longer, I wanted Francesca, I wanted her bad. Enough that I was ready to throw all reason out the window.

The two men that had followed Francesca and given her a scare hadn't been hard to find. In an attempt to save his skin, Vince had hunted them down. It helped that the cameras in Francesca's building had captured their faces.

They were already waiting for me when I arrived at the club. Both were tied to metal chairs in the center of the torture room in the basement.

Vitelli had already started with the interrogation when I walked inside the room and removed my jacket. Once he saw me, he came my way. "How is she?" The concern in his voice warmed me.

"Shaken, but she'll be all right. Luciano is with her," I told him. "What did you find out?"

"Bratva." One word was enough.

"What did they want with her?" I began rolling the sleeves of my shirt.

"That one there said it was just a little game. They were supposed to scare her and leave." Vitelli pointed toward one of the men who was missing his front teeth.

"Who sent them?" I asked as I stopped before the tray where all our toys were displayed for me. I picked the brass knuckles and fitted them on my fist.

"The order came from high up in the food chain, they don't know."

I headed toward both men and stopped before them. It didn't matter who the order came from or what their end goal was. The only thing that mattered was their sorry asses wouldn't leave this room alive. They would pay with their lives for scaring Francesca. The only reason they wouldn't suffer more than they already had was because they hadn't touched her.

"I bet you had a fucking great time scaring her," I said to the man before me, and threw the first punch. "Watching her run and hide." I punched him again and then again. I kept on punching him until I heard a loud crack of a bone giving way.

When I stepped back, the Russian had stopped breathing. I looked at his companion whose eyes were wide and overflowing with fear. I dropped the brass knuckles on the tray behind me and picked up a sharp knife. That's when to thrash and twist trying to escape, and the begging began.

"You hurt my girl," I reminded him, "You deserve nothing but pain." I shoved the knife into his guts and twisted it.

I turned around and left it there as the Russian bled to death. Vitelli, who was watching me, looked slightly surprised by my lack of control, but he did the right thing and kept quiet.

The Russian Pakhan could threaten me all he liked, steal and alter my cargo as he pleased, but he committed the worst mistake of his life. He messed with my girl and now he was going to pay for it with his blood.

When I arrived at my apartment, I headed into my room desperate to be with Francesca. She was lying on my bed, golden hair spilled over my pillowcase. Her hands were tucked under her cheeks and her lips slightly parted. My cock strained to life begging for attention. I ignored it and headed toward the bathroom, to remove all the blood and sweat.

After a quick shower, I returned to my room to find her sitting crossed legged at the edge of the bed. She wore one of my shirts and it had hiked up to her hips. I wiped my hair with a small towel and then threw it on the floor.

Francesca watched me attentively and swallowed when I let go of the towel wrapped around my waist, baring myself to her. She proceeded to take in every inch of me, but not in a sexual way.

"I'm fine," I assured her, it was strange having someone worry about me this way. I sat beside her and removed a wild strand of hair from her face. "I'm alright Francesca. See. "I patted myself and she stared at the scar on my abdomen, and her eyes darkened.

"Are they dead?" The hatred in her voice made me proud.

I nodded, wishing I could tell she was safe now, but I didn't want to lie, as long as she remained with me, by my side she would be, but if they had gotten to her once… I didn't want to think about that now.

Exhaustion pulled at me, and I knew Francesca must be as well, so I pulled her back into the bed and wrapped my arms around her tucking her tight against me. She turned around in my arms and rested a hand on my chest, she looked up with those sapphire eyes and I became hard instantly.

Slowly she pushed me back into bed and climbed and straddled my hips. "Francesca," I warned, but she didn't listen, she removed my shirt and threw it aside.

"I need you, Cassio, please." She pleaded.

I really wanted to be a better man but when she begged like that. I wrapped my arm around her waist and flipped her, so she was lying down on the bed. "You need to rest." I said as I settled in between her legs. "I'm trying really hard to do the right thing over here, to be a good man."

"Don't," she pulled me down and whispered against my lips. "Fuck me, Cassio."

Shit.

I slipped my hand in between her legs and was surprised to find her wet and ready for me. I reached into the nightstand and grabbed a condom, and quickly rolled it down my shaft.

When I entered her, Francesca moaned and dug her nails into my back just how I liked it. I knew she wanted me to fuck her hard and fast, but I didn't, I took it slow. Her moans turned into sobs and tears began to flow down her cheeks.

I stopped.

"I'm sorry," she tried to hide her face from me. "Ignore me, please just keep going."

I pulled out and threw the condom away, I picked her up into my arms, cradling her like a child. Francesca tucked her head into the crook of my neck and began to cry. My heart squeezed painfully in my chest, hearing her cry was worse than being shot.

"I've got you, *Principessa*." She held me tightly, and I kissed the crown of her head, soothing her. "I'll always be here for you," I promised.

Even when we were nothing but dust, I would come for her, I would be there to protect her, to hold her and love her.

I sucked in a deep breath as I realized the truth. I loved Francesca, probably never stopped loving her. It was the one thing that would never change. The only constant in my chaotic life.

I was learning how to love again, to lose my fears. She was teaching me how to listen. That the beating of my heart was more than a simple action and reaction. It was a language that she understood.

]Loving her was a gift, and I would do anything in my power to cherish her as she deserved. Even if she one day woke up and realized she no longer wanted me. I would still love her.

24

FRANCESCA

Okay. I was freaking out.

I searched through the pile of clothes on top of the bed and couldn't find what I was looking for, I knew I should have kept it somewhere safer. As I searched for his birthday present, my phone rang.

"Marie?" I picked up before it went to voicemail.

"Are you okay? You seem upbeat," she remarked, and I was starting to think maybe I was different.

"Where are you?" I changed the subject before she came up with any more ideas.

"Vitelli and I are going out for dinner." I heard Vitelli's voice as he was forced to greet me, and I laughed. Then it hit me.

"Just the two of you?"

"Yeah, why? You always refuse to join us." True, I did but I was quite busy myself.

"Aren't you guys celebrating Cassio's birthday?"

"What...it's your brother's birthday?" She pulled the phone away and I imagined she asked Vitelli. "Why didn't you tell me?" Marie complained. There were a few mumblings and then she was back.

"Vitelli says his brother hasn't celebrated his birthday in years and hates to do so. So, we're going to get dinner ourselves."

"Hey, Marie, I have to go, I'm kind of late."

I heard her say something, but I had already ended the call. I looked at all the clothes on my bed and on the floor and picked them up shoving them in the closet. It had been a week now since I had moved—or rather been forced—to Cassio's place. I wasn't going to lie, going back to my apartment to grab some extra clothes and basic necessities had been daunting. Thankfully, he had been by my side the entire time.

Ever since that night and my move to Cassio's, things had shifted between us. Despite having my stuff in his guest bedroom, I hadn't slept there once. Not that there was much sleeping being done in his room either.

I woke up with him every day for the past week—at an ungodly hour—and cooked him his favorite pancakes. It was beautiful to watch him savor my food and not criticize me for doing the help's work. Then he'd drive me to the hospital where I spent my day, and Vince would bring me back. I'd cook for Cassio again and we'd eat dinner together, all very mundane, natural as if we've been doing this for a lifetime.

"Damn it." I sat on the bed, fell back, and glared at the ceiling.

How could I have lost his present? The small box was right there where I had put it this morning and now it was gone. I looked at Reginald who was chewing on a toy I'd bought for him so he wouldn't chew on Cassio's shoes—yes, he did that.

Now it was too late to find another gift for him. I'd have to think about something else.

As I recalled, Cassio had never enjoyed celebrating his birthday, he disliked parties and crowded places. He preferred spending it with family. It was sad to know he hadn't done so in years. He deserved to be celebrated.

I shot up from the bed as an idea came to mind. "Come on, Reggie, we have work to do." I picked him up from the floor and headed downstairs.

It was close to nine o'clock, I had checked my phone almost a hundred times. I didn't know whether I should call him or not. Cassio was Capo and he had hundreds of things to deal with, I didn't want him dealing with my worries.

The last couple of days he had been arriving later and his problems only seemed to get worse. Something like that must have happened today. I checked my phone again. *What if something happened? What if he had plans?* I couldn't help myself, even if I was working on it now, my anxiety was still active and made me overthink things. I thought about calling Vitelli, but then he would think something was wrong, and again, I didn't want any trouble.

I clicked play on the TV and sat back on the sofa, not paying attention to what was before me. I must have taken a nap because I woke up to Reggie barking loudly. He only did that for one person. I shot up from the sofa, but then thought about it and sat again. *Act casual.* He didn't want to celebrate his birthday, I reminded myself.

The door opened and an exhausted Cassio came walking in. His golden-brown hair was mussed, his suit jacket was open and wrinkled and he had a large stain on his shirt. I shot up kneeling on the sofa.

"It's not blood," he assured me, sounding tired and annoyed. "It's just coffee."

Cassio threw his keys on the table and then his phone followed. He removed the gun from his holster and placed it on the table as well. Finally, he turned in my direction.

"Shit, did I wake you?" he asked before I could tell him happy birthday. I shook my head, but his smile told me he knew I was lying.

Cassio came and sat beside me on the sofa, leaning his head against the cushion and let out a loud sigh. I loved seeing him like this, the unfiltered version. The one that got tired and didn't have to put up a front, the man who smiled and complained about his day. *The man who wasn't the Capo.* The man who was flesh and blood. Cassio Moretti.

"Rough day?" I asked and he looked at me, then at his shirt.

"If it were only that," he confessed.

"Do you wanna talk?" I asked.

He shook his head. "There are two more hours before this day ends, and I'm hoping those two hours are better than the last sixteen."

Two hours.

Sure enough, when I looked at the clock, it was ten. "Did you eat?" I asked anxiously.

"No."

"Did you?" He still had his eyes closed.

"No," I answered, and he looked at me. "I was waiting for you," I explained. "I got us food," I added.

Standing up and taking his hand, I forced him to follow me, and guided Cassio into the kitchen. It wasn't anything fancy, in fact, it was nothing fancy at all, but I had run out of ideas and this was all I could come up with in such short notice. I hoped it would be enough for him.

"It's not much, and I know you don't like celebrating," I said nervously, not able to look at him, afraid to see his reaction. "I got your favorite breakfast foods." I looked at the boxes of takeout I had ordered.

Cassio didn't speak, he simply moved to the kitchen island and looked at the things I bought. His favorite brownie, favorite pancakes, cupcakes, and the Italian bread he had been buying from the same bakery since he was small.

I began to freak out when he didn't speak for a long time. I knew it was a bad idea and yet here I was planning something he didn't even want.

"We can leave it for tomorrow if you're tired." He nodded slightly and even though I was prepared for it, I was disappointed.

Cassio came to my side, and I thought he was heading up to the room. He stepped right behind me, and with his hands resting on my hips, he spun me around and I gasped. He cupped my cheeks forcing me to look up at him.

"I don't ever want to see that look on your face," he expressed with such finality.

"Did you like it?" I finally asked. Cassio frowned taking a step back, he looked into my eyes and a radiant smile covered his face as he ran his hands through my hair and pulled me closer. His lips were almost on mine.

"I don't like it," he whispered. "I fucking love it, Francesca." His lips met mine and I was ready for his hungry kisses, but he pulled back, earning a groan from me.

"Is it okay? I mean did you really like it?" I don't know why it meant so much to me that he did, but after seeing the way he arrived today, I didn't want him to have a bad night as well.

"It's perfect. I can't recall the last time I was so excited to celebrate. Next year we can start in the morning and eat all day." He kissed my forehead. My throat bobbed as I tried to swallow. "Thank you, *Principessa*, but right now I really need to eat." He kissed my lips quickly and headed toward the food. No wonder people said the way to conquer a man was through his stomach.

Next year?

He dug into the food like a man starved for days. Obviously, he started with his sweets; the brownie being gulped down in seconds. Cassio was a picky eater. For someone who was Italian, his eating habits could be considered as bad as mine. With the palate of a child, he loved his sugar most of all.

"Why aren't you eating?" he asked as he took another bite of the chocolate chip cookie.

I blushed lightly and put a piece of the same pancake I had been eating for more than twenty minutes, in my mouth. I was nervous; that's the truth.

"I am." I put another one in my mouth before he could see the blush deepen.

"Francesca." He looked at me, and of course, he knew something was off. His eyes beckoned me to speak, and he wasn't going to drop this.

"I got you a present," I said standing up.

"You shouldn't have." His face fell a bit, but it didn't stop me from walking toward him.

Cassio watched me with curious eyes and for someone who didn't want a birthday gift he didn't seem all too sad. I stopped at the edge of the island, forcing him to turn his stool so he could watch me. When I had his full attention, I looked him in the eyes as I reached for the sash holding my silk robe. I opened it.

The fork he was holding dropped on the table and his mouth formed a wide O. The expression on his face was everything I had hoped for and more. He looked at me like he wanted to consume me whole, and I looked at him letting him know I wanted to be consumed.

"How l-long have you been like this?" he stuttered.

"Since you arrived," I confessed with a smirk on my face.

At half-mast, his eyes traveled over my naked body that now lay bare for him to see. The fire that ran through my body and the way he looked at me made me feel... empowered.

He jumped from the stool and reached me in less than a second. It was as if he had never seen me naked before. His strong hands hesitated to touch me and so he outlined my robe, his finger tracing the soft silk all the way up to my shoulders.

"And I've been sitting here all this time when you were...like this," he whispered with disbelief.

"You were hungry," I pointed out. He shook his head.

"Definitely not as hungry as I am for this." His smile made me shiver and my skin pebbled.

"I thought you didn't want presents," I noted, chuckling nervously.

His hands pulled the fabric off my shoulders and the robe slipped away pooling at my feet. By now I was breathing hard, my heart thundering, and anticipation driving me crazy. The back of his hand grazed my nipple which instantly pebbled. I arched my back, seeking more contact. His head finally lifted as he looked at me.

"If I had known this was my present, I would've celebrated my birthday every day." His eyes were dark, clouded with desire.

"You always have me, Cassio." I breathed and took a step forward pressing myself against his chest. His hand cupped my behind and I let out a soft moan.

"If I'm not careful, you're going to ruin me," he spoke against my mouth as he kissed me hard.

25

CASSIO

I lifted Francesca into my arms holding her perfect ass, she wrapped her legs around my waist, pressing herself against my achingly hard erection. Honestly, I had been sporting this hard-on since I saw her on the sofa when I arrived. Now it was so hard, I was afraid if I didn't have her, my dick would fall off.

She kissed my mouth with the same desperation that I kissed her. I wanted to have her anywhere and everywhere. We had had sex in almost every corner of my house, but tonight, I wanted to take her to bed.

Somewhere along the way, I had lost my jacket, and she was now fumbling to open my shirt. I almost missed the step and we both laughed as she gripped me with force. I put her down slowly as she continued laughing. *Fuck, I loved that sound.*

"Bed," I groaned, and she nodded, interlacing her fingers with mine as we entered my room.

She headed to the bed, but I pulled her back flat against my chest and kissed her hard with tongue and teeth and everything I had in me. I pulled her lower lip and let it go, then began to trail kisses down her jaw and neck, sucking on her sensitive places, which I now knew by heart.

"Cassio, please," she begged.

Francesca was always eager, always wanting and there was a fire in her that nothing would ever put out. I reached for her nipple and sucked on it hard, earning a loud moan from her. Letting it go with a pop, I let my fingers run across her burning skin. Francesca giggled when I touched her sensitive areas, and that always made me smile. Sex with her was like that. It wasn't just carnal and needy; it was fun, and it was fucking exquisite.

Stepping away from her for just a few seconds, I reached for the back of my shirt and pulled it over my head, throwing it onto the floor. She looked at me as if it were the first time she had seen me shirtless. Her reactions never ceased to amaze me. Francesca moved away from me and headed for the bed, her golden blonde hair swaying as she walked. My groin throbbed. She stood by the edge of the bed looking like a fucking painting. She glanced back at me and smiled.

I headed toward my closet and opened the first drawer, removing one of my many ties. I had never been this kind of man. Kinky shit wasn't for me; I liked it raw, no bondage, or whips, or shit like that. I marched back toward her, and she eyed the tie in my hands. I knew she wanted to ask, and I knew she was burning inside to know what I was going to do with it.

"Turn around." I helped her turn. I wrapped the tie around her eyes and made sure it was secure.

Francesca stilled for a while, her shoulders tensing and her breathing speeding up—not in a good way. I breathed next to her earlobe, and she gasped as I pulled her hair to the side, enjoying the silky smoothness of it. I kissed her neck once.

"I don't want you to focus on only pleasing me." My arm snaked around her chest and ran down her flat stomach and I stopped right at her navel. She sucked in a deep breath.

"It's your birthday," she panted.

"Trust me, *Principessa*, pleasing you, over and over again, is the best gift I could wish for."

I finally touched her where she wanted me the most. I slipped my fingers in between her legs and touched her clit before sliding them down towards her entrance. She was already soaking wet. I kept my hand down there, tracing little circles, keeping to the same rhythm. No longer than a few minutes and she was already panting hard, trying to move against me. I held her neck, forcing her to lay her head against my shoulder. Francesca began to spasm as I sucked on her skin, knowing I was going to leave a mark, one I wanted everyone else to see it.

"Don't." I stopped her before she could remove the tie from her eyes. Francesca groaned but complied.

I shoved my fingers into her channel and fucked her with them until Francesca was trembling hard and calling my name repeatedly. Her legs quivered and I had to hold her before she fell to the floor. I pulled my fingers out and lifted Francesca into my arms, carrying her to the bed.

Her breasts were full and driving me fucking mad. Her skin was smooth, and I wanted to touch her all over. I planned on doing just that. I didn't want her to see me, I wanted her to focus on feeling. I began with soft kisses here and there, and whenever she tried to touch me back, I stopped. By the third time, she stopped trying. I rewarded her by sucking on one nipple and then the other, kissing the space between both breasts, and kept to the ritual, kissing, sucking, and touching her everywhere.

"Cassio!" she cried. Always impatient.

"What do you want?" I asked, caressing her breast.

"You know," she whimpered.

"I need a little more than that." I ran my fingers over her thigh.

"I want you, god damnit," she huffed.

Francesca arched her back the moment I lapped at her clit. She gripped the sheets with force, and I began working her up again. I kept on giving her light kisses and sucking her clit from time to time. Her breathing increased and as she began to moan, I knew she was close. Francesca's legs began shaking, telling me she was close once again. I inserted my finger inside her entrance and pumped a few times knowing she was about to lose it. When I felt her clenching on my fingers, I kissed her bundle of nerves, sucking hard. She broke apart, closing her legs around me and lifting her hips from the bed.

I kept on sucking until I decided she had earned her reprieve. Licking my lips, I couldn't help myself. I smiled. Francesca was completely relaxed on my bed, a big fat smile on her face.

I needed her, like really needed her, but I wanted her to enjoy her bliss. Faster than I thought possible she removed the tie, sat up, and pushed me back onto the bed. Her cheeks were pink and her hair a wild mess.

"Enough," she said, her hands pressed against my chest. "I want to see you. I want to touch you. I want you." She sat back pressing her core against me. I groaned, my hands landing on her waist.

"As you wish." I smiled.

In an instant, she sheathed me inside of her, her head lolling back, my name on her lips. Francesca began moving achingly slow, finding her rhythm. I had never felt so fucking good in my life. She was heaven and she was perfection. *She was home.*

"Fuck," I groaned and pushed up from the bed, circling her waist with my arms, and pulled her against me so we sat nose to nose.

Fuck. Fuck. Fuck.

I tried to push that thought from my head, and for now, as she rode me, it worked instantly. I didn't dare think about that again. Instead, I let her do whatever she wanted to do with me.

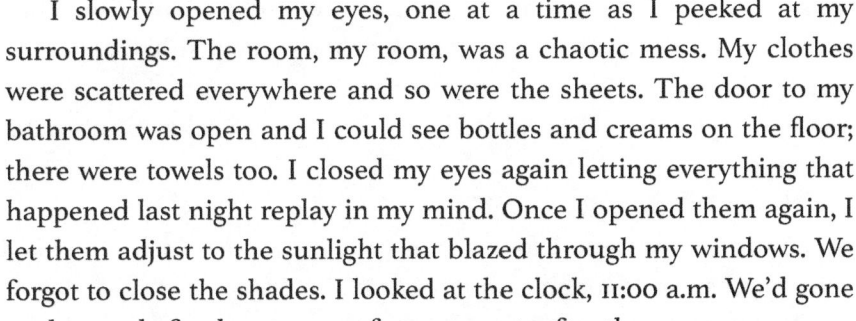

I slowly opened my eyes, one at a time as I peeked at my surroundings. The room, my room, was a chaotic mess. My clothes were scattered everywhere and so were the sheets. The door to my bathroom was open and I could see bottles and creams on the floor; there were towels too. I closed my eyes again letting everything that happened last night replay in my mind. Once I opened them again, I let them adjust to the sunlight that blazed through my windows. We forgot to close the shades. I looked at the clock, 11:00 a.m. We'd gone to sleep only five hours ago, a few moments after the sun came up.

I was feeling hot, and since my covers lay on the floor, only one thing could explain that. I looked down at Francesca who was practically scaling me. The left part of her body rested over mine, it was kind of suffocating, and yet I didn't mind. I didn't care that she was clinging to me, and I didn't care that she slept here tonight—or last night, or last week. Inhaling the sweet scent of her blonde hair, I took a while to simply...be. I couldn't recall the last time I woke up this late. It was Thursday and the last thing I wanted to do was stand up and go to my office. The last thing I wanted to think about was my phone and who the hell wanted to bother me right now. So, I didn't, I just didn't give a fuck.

As slowly and as gently as I could, I left the bed and picked up a blanket, covering her up. I headed into the bathroom and closed the door, then turned on the shower. The warm water ran down my back and my hair. I looked down at the little scar that now marked my skin. It had been a while since the stitches came off. I ran my hand through it and sighed.

That feeling I had for her hadn't changed in the four years we spent apart. I was stupid; whatever was happening between Francesca and me was dangerous. Not only for me but for her. Especially her. Francesca was already a target of the Russians, and if others found out, especially Donato, things could get messy. He wanted to marry her of...already had someone in mind. This was the past happening all over again. I was getting involved with her while she was promised to another.

Once I got back from my shower, I found Francesca sitting cross-legged on the bed, her hair falling forward, and a blanket wrapped around her. She held something in her hands, and just like yesterday, she seemed nervous. I dried my hair with the towel and threw it on the floor. I watched as she rolled her eyes, Francesca hated this habit of mine.

"What have you got there?" I asked, kind of curious.

"Your real present. I found it in your room, should have looked here first," she said making no sense at all.

"I thought you already gave it to me yesterday. Over and over again," I added. She tried hard to hide the smile on her face but failed.

I had stopped receiving gifts on my birthday five years ago, a day just like any other in my life—until her. It wasn't exactly a celebration and that was why it had been perfect. I walked toward her because I knew she had done this to make me happy.

"It's nothing…it's nothing fancy, I wanted to buy you something nice like one of your watches, but I don't feel good about using Paolo's money—it's not mine," she rambled, and I couldn't agree more. I didn't want her to use his money. Ever again.

"You don't have to, Francesca," I assured her. "And if you ever need money, you can ask me. I will call the bank today and ask them for another card. My money will look good on you."

She stood up and put a hand on my naked chest. I tensed for a while, not really knowing why but that simple touch surprised me.

"I don't want your money either, Cassio," she said with finality. "What I meant to say is that it's not much, but I hope you like it."

I took the little black bag from her hand, and she sat on the bed again. I fumbled with the knot for a while until I finally managed to open it. I emptied the contents into my hand. I looked at it for a while.

Words failed me completely. It was like my mind went blank and everything inside was paralyzed. I picked up the chain and looked at the coin that dangled from it. I imagined the chain part was also her idea. The longer I looked at it, the longer I seemed to lose myself in it.

"It's a medallion of St. Michael to keep you safe," she explained, "so you can come back to me," she whispered softly. I finally met her eyes. "Did you—"

I shut her up with a kiss so desperate and hungry that we both fell back into bed, and I had no plans of leaving it anytime soon.

26

CASSIO

"Your enthusiasm is contagious." Vitelli approached and offered me a glass of water, and in that moment, I wished I could take his tumbler of whiskey and drain it dry. "I've seen you happier at funerals."

"I'm ecstatic, brother," I said, my eyes glued on Francesca who had decided to provoke me today.

"In case you didn't know, this is supposed to be a happy day," Vitelli continued.

I gripped my glass, almost shattering it as Francesca danced with Michelangelo Martini. His hand was low on her back, and she was laughing at something he said.

"You know…" Vitelli began. "You could just go over there and ask her for a dance." I turned to face him; Vitelli rolled his eyes. "It's kind of obvious, Cassio. You haven't taken your eyes off her the entire night. Every man that touches her, you look at them with murder in your eyes."

"She's Donato's daughter," I explained.

"And?" Vitelli stepped in front of me, blocking my view of her, and I was forced to look at him. "If you want her, then do something before Micky Martini does." He tapped my shoulder, but I grabbed his hand and moved it away.

"I don't want her," I lied. I needed Francesca. Those things were different.

I had promised myself not to get involved with her, to stay away. I had tried to. I didn't need this kind of attachment in my life. There was no space for it in my heart. There was only revenge. Murder. Anger. Hatred. Francesca didn't belong in there with those things, she deserved so much more.

I turned my attention to the glass in my hand.

"You know," Vitelli spoke after a while. "I think you just don't want to accept that you *do* want her," he said, scratching his cheek. "I reacted the same way with Marie, it was... weird."

"Love is a weapon, Vitelli," I recited the words our father would always say.

It was love that broke our family apart. Love that turned me into a cold bastard. Grigori and his men might have killed my sister, but it was love that led me on this quest for revenge. It was my love for Francesca that broke us apart. I feared losing her as I had Arabella. There's wasn't a world where I could live without Francesca, I'd rather spend an eternity in hell.

Francesca was my everything. So, I couldn't allow that kind of power to be wielded against me. But that was the problem, what if it was too late? I knew there was something growing between us. When I killed my feelings for her all those years ago, I might not have buried them deep enough.

"Yes," he agreed and looked at his fiancée. "But I'd rather experience it than never know it at all."

I tried my best, but I couldn't stop looking at her. Francesca was a queen. A goddess and I wanted to worship at her feet. A temple I wanted to visit every day. But I couldn't, not until I knew Grigori was dead. I couldn't allow myself to want or need her. Revenge always came first.

"You sound like a sappy romantic," I teased.

"And you're a bastard," he said naturally. "You might be older but not wiser." Vitelli took a sip of his Scotch. "This need for revenge is going to consume you and everything that's still good in you."

My face fell, my nostrils flared, and my jaw clenched. "You forget her so easily." I was happy for my brother, I really was, but a part of me hated him for being able to move on.

His eyes widened and he shook his head. "You're a fucking asshole, you know that, right?" he snapped. "I will never forget, but I know she wouldn't want us to live in misery."

I fisted my hand. "They would have wanted revenge."

"That is what *you* want, Cassio, do not assume it was what they wanted. Arabella would never have asked this of you. Especially knowing how much it has consumed you."

With that he left me standing there on my own, thinking about his words. Of course, my father and sister would have wanted revenge.

As I looked at Francesca dancing with Michelangelo, my thoughts scattered, making it hard to remember what I had been thinking. Was Vitelli, right? I didn't know anymore, and honestly, with Michelangelo's hand close to Francesca's ass, I couldn't really care for revenge right now.

"Mind your hands," I snapped at the man who was dancing with Francesca. I stood directly behind him and when he was about to move, he bumped into me.

"Hey, man, mind your—" He shut his mouth when he saw me. "Sorry, Boss." He bowed his head in apology.

"Go find something else to do," I instructed him, eyes cold and commanding. Michelangelo offered Francesca an apologetic smile and quickly scurried away like a rat. I took his place, taking her hand in mine and placing another one at the small of her back.

Francesca tried to contain her smile but failed. "You can't do that," she complained.

I shrugged. When it came to her, I became a possessive beast and any man who dared touch her would lose his hand. This was the way things were going to be now. Francesca was untouchable.

"Jealousy looks good on you," she teased.

"I'm not jealous," I argued, pulling my shoulders back.

She grinned. "You looked like you were having indigestion every time I danced with someone else."

How perceptive my little princess was. "You look ridiculously beautiful tonight, Francesca. Everyone else pales in comparison with your beauty." The words slipped from my lips, yet they were the truth.

Francesca's eyes widened and her cheeks blazed. "Keep saying things like that and I'll swoon."

"And I'll be here to catch you." I took a step closer and brought her chest to mine.

"Cassio," she warned. "People are looking."

I wanted them to look. For once, I wanted everything to be different. I wanted to be someone else so that I could have Francesca all to myself, and not pretend we were nothing but two acquaintances.

I took a step back, controlling myself. "Say something else," she requested.

"Greedy, are we?"

She smiled. "It's not every day I get to listen to these inspiring words."

I made a mental note, right there and then, to make sure to always tell her how beautiful and incredible she was. Buying her flowers every day wouldn't cut it, I needed to up my game.

"By the end of tonight, I'll have to cut out the eyes of every man at this party," I said.

Francesca's head fell back as she laughed. "How romantic."

I couldn't help the tight and timid smile that graced my face. "It's true, Francesca. Your beauty is for my eyes only."

"You already have me, Cassio."

I don't think she realized what she said or if she even meant it, but my chest tightened. I swallowed hard.

"Leave these poor men alone."

"I'll concede mercy this time," I teased.

"Say something else." The music slowed and so did our movements. We had to be careful, this was the second song we had danced to together.

"I wish I could rip your dress off and fuck you right here and now."

She gulped and looked around checking if anyone had heard me. Francesca's eyes twinkled with mischief and her answer surprised the fuck out of me. "I'm naked underneath."

That was the worst thing she could possibly say; if my suit jacket didn't hide my pants, everyone at Vitelli and Marie's engagement party would know I was sporting a massive hard-on.

I let my hand slip just so it rested over the swell of her ass. Two could play this game. "I would start by removing your dress and sucking on those pink little nipples of yours." Her cheeks warmed.

"Cassio—"

"Then, I would eat you up like an ice cream cone on a summer's day. Licking your pussy dry." Her eyes widened, but I could see that her nipples were beginning to appear through the fabric of her dress. She was just as turned on as I was. "Then, only after you begged me for it, I would bend you over and fuck you hard and fast. You'd take me, all of me."

"Cassio," she panted.

I shrugged. "That's just a thought." I leaned and whispered in her ear. "Or maybe a preview of what I'll do to you tonight."

With that, I left her and headed somewhere where the air wasn't tainted with her scent, and I could breathe. Two could play this game, but it seemed that even though I was the one talking, it was Francesca who won. All I had to do was imagine the things I would do to her, and I was a goner. Now I couldn't get those images out of my head.

FRANCESCA

Why him, dear heart? I asked. *When there are so many others out there, why Cassio Moretti?* I removed the wet towel from my neck and stared at myself in the mirror, completely lost. I was still trying to get over the things he'd said in the ballroom. It had taken me a few minutes to compose myself again.

We had danced together; bodies pressed together. My heartbeat to the rhythm of the song his was playing. In that moment, we had been just Cassio and Francesca, two people who were learning what it was like to love again.

Why him?

Taking a deep breath, I dropped the used towel in the hamper and tried to compose myself so that no one would notice how crazed I looked. All it had taken was a couple of dances with Cassio and I was already drenched.

I wished our lives were different, not so complicated. That we were just two people dancing together, that there was no Donato to ruin my life or a future husband I didn't want. I wished it was just Cassio and I dancing freely because we wanted to, and we could.

I pushed the bathroom door open and was about to return to the party when someone appeared from behind the shadows. My breath froze in my lungs and my heart stopped. Donato approached me while I stood there unable to move.

"*Cara mia,*" he greeted. "There's nowhere for you to run," he chuckled.

I crossed my arms and stared him down. I wouldn't dare show him how scared I was. How much I wanted to bolt in another direction. "What do you want?"

"You are giving me quite a headache."

"Do you expect me to care?"

"Do you think he will keep his guards around when it's over?" Donato chuckled. "I want to see just how brave you are then."

I frowned, fear coursing through my veins.

"Why do you think, *Cara mia,* that I haven't dragged you back home? He keeps his men around you all the time."

"Who does?" I feigned confusion.

"Don't play dumb, Francesca, I watched you dancing with him." He stepped closer. "Actually, that's exactly what you are. How long do you think it will be before he grows tired of you?"

I shook my head pretending I had no idea what he was talking about.

"Cassio will never love you, he's not capable of that. When he marries, he will do so for an alliance. Why would he need you when he already has my support? You're just a temporary distraction. Stop this now and come back home before you ruin yourself once and for all."

"Ruin?" I laughed "You made sure I was ruined. Why would I go back to that place when all you want to do is sell me as a broodmare?"

"So you can do what you are supposed to!" he shouted, taking another step towards me. "You're my daughter and you'll do what I tell you to."

Daughter. Now he remembered I was his daughter.

"You mean spread my legs and bear children? Well, father, I'm already doing the first, maybe I'll end up accomplishing the second."

For someone so fat and old, he moved incredibly quick; before I could even blink, his hands were around my neck. I grabbed his hands with my own, trying to fight him in case he decided to squeeze."

"Open your eyes, Francesca." He shoved me back, making me stumble on my dress and hit the wall with force. "Cassio only wants one thing and that's not you. He has given me permission to marry you off as soon as I wish to."

"W-what?"

"I told you, *cara mia*," he chuckled. "Cassio is a man of business. So am I, when the time is right, I'll marry you off to a boss' son."

He let go of me. Instantly, my legs gave out, and I fell to the floor with a crunching bang. I didn't feel the impact, there was nothing inside me. In that moment, everything came crashing back. The pictures Marco showed me, Donato's meeting with the Russians.

"That's...that's betrayal," I looked up.

He lifted my chin and held it with force. "If you open that mouth of yours, dear daughter, I will make sure everyone you care for is punished for your sins. I won't be so inclined to be nice. That little friend of yours, what a lovely woman. It would be a pity if she was killed." He let me go, the threat lingering in the air. "Oh, and before I forget." He pulled something from his pocket, and I froze.

I felt something hit me and then fall to the floor. I picked it up and looked at it, the Ziplock was filled with a whitish powder. Not just any powder, I knew it just by looking. Coke.

"Who says I'm not a caring father?" He left me there and left.

I reached the parking lot on trembling legs. My entire body shook, and I couldn't seem to control it. Everyone who passed me by looked like blurry figures; I couldn't make out a single face. The doorman opened the door for me, and I finally reached outside, breathing in the chilly night air. I leaned against the stone rail and took one minute to focus.

"Francesca!" I looked back.

Oh God.

"Francesca," Gianluca called out to me as he quickened his pace to reach me.

Looking back at the parking lot before me, I didn't see anyone else and I didn't really have a way to leave, so I couldn't just run from him. I had seen Gianluca earlier at the party and he even came to talk to me as though nothing had happened. Like he hadn't forced himself on me.

"You're leaving?"

"That was the plan." I looked at the cars again.

"You okay? You seem off."

"Couldn't be better." I looked back and smiled again, trying not to force it.

He shrugged. "Wanna go clubbing?"

My jaw dropped slightly, and I scoffed. Was he that delusional? A shiver raced down my back. I didn't want to be alone with him, but returning to the party wasn't an option either. "Thanks, but I'm leaving."

"Come on, it'll be fun."

"Gianluca," I warned. "Just leave me alone."

"I heard you used to be fun," he said in disdain.

"I used to be high most of the time." I snapped wishing he would leave.

"I can see you still are." He looked at my hand.

I instantly put it back behind my back. Fuck. How long had I been holding it like this for everyone to see? I looked around, but again, there was no one but us out here. Gianluca laughed out loud as if he were having the time of his life.

"No need for innocence now." He went to touch me, but I moved away. "How long are you going to pretend, Francesca?"

"Pretend? I'm not pretending anything," I snapped at him.

I picked up my clutch and opened it, and because my hands were still shaking, I let the Ziplock fall on the ground. Before I could pick it up, Gianluca did, and when I thought he was going to give it back to me, he pulled it away.

"I know you want me, Francesca, that night at Vitelli's, I knew you wanted me."

"Wake up, Gianluca." I tried to get it back from him.

"Stop being a bitch, Francesca," he snapped, pulling me toward him.

My hand connected with his face.

My reaction was so fast that both of us were surprised. My jaw dropped, and he stepped back putting his hand over his cheek. I was horrified by my reaction, but I didn't regret it. Gianluca, on the other hand, was fuming. His eyes blazed with anger.

"Your father was right, you're nothing but a cheap whore." He moved to hit me. I flinched. But the impact never came.

I opened my eyes to find Gianluca's hand inches from my face. Cassio held onto Gianluca's hand holding it tight. I followed the extent of his arm up to his eyes to find them burning. Cassio vibrated with anger.

"You were lucky your hand didn't touch her," Cassio spoke, his tone laced with the promise of pain and death.

Calmly, Cassio pulled him away from me, but I didn't dare move. He hadn't yet looked at me, but I didn't need to know what would happen if he did.

"Do you remember what I told you the last time we met?" Gianluca, who was usually so high up on his horse, swallowed hard. "Answer me." Cassio was acting scarily calm.

"Y-you'd kill me."

"Correct," Cassio deadpanned. "Apologize to her."

"Sorry," Gianluca mumbled.

"She didn't hear it."

"Cassio," I pleaded, scared of what his intentions were.

"I'm sorry," Gianluca said with more enthusiasm. When it seemed Cassio would let go of Gianluca's hand, he did.

Crack.

Gianluca screamed, and I jumped back holding a hand to my mouth, keeping me from crying out. *Holy fuck.* The sickening sound of bone cracking echoed in my ear. The movement was so fast that I didn't have time to process it, and neither did Gianluca. Cassio's head snapped in my direction.

"Go wait in my car." He offered me his car keys and turned his attention to Gianluca. "Go," he roared.

I did.

27

CASSIO

The loud engine of my car vibrated as it came to life. I remained there in the parking lot unsure what to do. I gripped the steering wheel with enough force to make my busted knuckles ache again. I had almost killed Gianluca...almost. I had wanted to, but if it weren't for Vitelli putting some sense into my head, he would have been dead.

"Fuck." I hit the stirring wheel.

Francesca, who sat beside me on the passenger seat flinched but remained looking out her window as if her life depended on it. That was the only reaction I got from her. She refused to acknowledge my presence. She kept on bobbing her legs and her nails dug into the palm of her hands. Her sapphire eyes were wide and wild, reflected on the glass window. I had seen her like this before.

"Did you kill him?" Her voice was low enough that I almost didn't hear.

I laughed dryly. "Are you worried I killed your supplier?"

Her head snapped to the side, and she looked at me. "You saw it?"

"How long, Francesca? How long have you been using? Did you ever stop?" I laughed again. "Were you always high? Fuck, should I worry about things going missing in my house?" By the end of it, I was laughing, but at myself.

All of this time she had been high, and I didn't even notice, she was good at hiding, though, just like she was with all the rest. No wonder she was always in a fucking bliss. And...

"You fucking brought drugs to my house?!" I reached that realization and looked back at her. She was looking fixedly at her hands which shook slightly. "Is that why you wanted to come? So that you could buy from Gianluca?" That name! It was giving me an ulcer. "Was it your father who beat you that day? Gianluca seemed like a good candidate to do that as well."

She gasped again and looked back at me.

Her eyes were glassy, and I didn't know if she was holding herself from crying or if she was too high. Still, she didn't answer and still, I wanted to hit something. The fire running through my veins was too much.

"Can we fucking go now?" she snapped, and it honestly surprised me. She wasn't going to answer me now, but she would as soon as we arrived, it was about time we finally talked.

"Of course." Putting the shift gear into drive, I pressed the pedal hard.

When we arrived at my place she entered my apartment like a whirlwind, pushing the door so hard it banged against the wall. Francesca was already going up the stairs when I closed the door.

"Stop following me," she shouted once I followed her up the stairs.

"I'm heading up," I pointed out.

"Well, leave me alone!" Francesca snapped.

"It's my fucking house, Francesca!" I shouted back.

She laughed sardonically, and it riled me up. She nodded. "Yeah, it is."

With that, she entered the guest room and shut the door with enough force to break it. Not even a minute later, she opened the door and marched by me, a bag in her hand.

"Where are you going?" I shouted marching after her.

"You said it, it's your fucking house," she snapped, running down the stairs.

Until now, I had been calm, but there was a threshold, and she was really close to making me cross it. Francesca knew what and who I was. Knew that there was a darkness in me. But until tonight, she had never really seen it.

"Don't you dare leave, Francesca, do you hear me?" I stopped at the bottom of the stairs, Francesca's hand on the door.

"Why?" she asked, her voice so low that I almost didn't catch it. She didn't turn around to face me and it was annoying.

"Just stop running!" I shouted and it felt like an order, and in the end, it was, I was done seeing her run from everything.

She laughed out loud. "You're kidding me." She turned the handle and opened the door. "We're not together, Cassio. Leave me the fuck alone."

Francesca left through my door and something I hadn't felt in a long while took over me. It wasn't rage or the same iciness that made me numb, it was pure panic. I imagined her going back to her apartment—which wasn't safe—and I imagined worse. Donato putting his hands on her, branding her like he had the last time. I had no doubt that he had been the one to beat her.

Shit. She was using again, and I didn't see it.

She wasn't able to reach the elevator before my hands wrapped around her waist. "Let go of me!" she screamed.

I didn't.

Because she was twisting and turning, making it hard to grasp her, I turned Francesca around and grabbed her, throwing her over my shoulder, her bag falling to the floor. Her fists connected with my ass as she still tried to make me let go. I wasn't going to; I meant it, she needed to stop running.

Kicking the door to my apartment shut so she wouldn't go, I set her in the middle of the living room. Instantly she began to turn away, this time toward the kitchen. I wouldn't be surprised if she reached for a knife, Francesca seemed to have taken a liking to them.

"Francesca!" I roared.

"You can't hold me here by force," she screamed.

"I'm not letting you out of that door while you're still high." She gave me that same sardonic laugh.

"Why? I'm not your problem, Cassio. We're not together, remember?" she threw at me. "I'm not your mess, and I'm not yours." She was screaming still.

Francesca reached inside her purse that had been crossed over her chest, she opened it and took something from within. Instantly I recognized it to be the little Ziplock of coke Gianluca gave her. Francesca didn't even look at it as she threw it at me. Since I was too far away, it landed on the floor, right in between us.

"Not that you would care, but it isn't mine. I didn't buy it and I didn't use it. Yes, Cassio, I crave it almost every day, but for once in a long time, I want to change, to stop being that girl, the one who can barely remember the last four years of her life." She wasn't shouting anymore and as she spoke her voice began to tremble. I didn't dare move from where I stood. "I am trying, Cassio, I really am."

She exhaled deeply and looked at the window, the view of the bay and the shimmering city stretching before us. Every word she spoke was like a knife piercing my body, one more painful than the other.

I was ashamed of myself. "I know," I confessed.

I'd seen her take her meds—the correct ones—every day. She tried to stick to a healthy routine and when she wasn't with her mother at the hospital, she was working on herself. Francesca was truly trying to change, and guilt washed over me at my lack of trust. She had trusted me countless times, and here I was, doing the exact opposite.

I didn't say it often, actually, I couldn't recall the last time I said it, but I did so now with everything in me. "I'm sorry for thinking the worst, *Principessa*."

When Francesca said nothing, I walked toward her and cupped her cheeks. She wouldn't meet my eyes. I wanted to kiss those full lips of hers, to chase away the pain in her eyes. The pain I had inflicted on her.

"I'm sorry," I said again, caressing her cheek.

"What are we doing, Cassio?" she whispered. I frowned, not following her line of thought. Francesca stepped away from me and crossed her arms.

"What do you mean, *Principessa*?" I grabbed her arms. I needed to feel the contact between us because I sensed she was slipping away.

"This, us. What are we doing? How long will it last?"

Where was this coming from? Francesca stepped away from me again and headed toward the kitchen, putting even more distance between us.

"Maybe it's best if I leave, Cassio," she remarked.

"Don't." I didn't hesitate to say so.

"My father is going to marry me off again, and he has already chosen my next husband," she said. When I didn't say a word, she swallowed hard and scoffed. "So, you did know." She shook her head in disbelief. "He was right."

"He?"

She waved my question away. "You knew I was to be married."

"Yes." I didn't want to lie to her. She nodded tersely.

"How long will we keep playing this game then?"

"It's not a game, Francesca, nothing about this is a game."

"Is it not?" she snapped. "You're using me just like everyone else, the only difference is that it took me longer to see."

That struck a chord. "Using you?" I scoffed. "That's rich, given I've been at your beck and call like a fucking idiot."

Her eyes widened. I sighed, not wanting to fight with her. I had so many plans for tonight, all of them involved ravaging her body and pleasuring her in the way she deserved, and this was not how it was supposed to have ended.

"What happened, Francesca, and don't dare lie to me?"

"I opened my eyes," she said.

"No," I argued. "Someone said something—was it Gianluca? Your father?" Someone had put all that shit into her head. Francesca didn't deny it, which was even worse; she'd rather believe Donato than me. "Good to know his words mean more than mine do."

She threw her hands in the air. "What was I supposed to do?" she shouted.

"Trusted me for starters," I threw back.

"How can I when I don't even know what *this* is between us?" She waved at us. "What are we, Cassio? How long till you grow tired of me and throw me away like you did last time?"

I opened my mouth, shocked by her words, but then she wasn't so wrong, was she? I had been an asshole and left her when she needed me the most. I might have been dealing with my own shit, but I should never have abandoned Francesca.

I ran my thumb under my lower lip, growing frustrated. I wanted her, God only knew I did, and for the second time in our lives, we stood at an impasse. Francesca was promised to someone else, and I couldn't have her, not until I killed Grigori Petrovich and settled the promise I'd made to my sister. I couldn't move forward until she was avenged.

"I don't want you to go," I confessed.

"For how long?"

"Does it matter? I want you and you want me, why can't we just be for now?"

"Because it will end," she pointed out simply. "Just like it did last time." With our hearts broken and Francesca marrying another man. I couldn't let that happen.

Again, I headed toward her and placed my hands on her waist, the smooth fabric of her dress a pale comparison to her silky skin. She didn't seem happy with my proximity, but I needed her to understand that this wasn't a game for me, that if I could, I would hold her forever and never let go. Even if the world fought to tear us apart, I'd hold onto Francesca. She was my lifeline.

"I'll talk to your father," the words slipped from my mouth. "I'll convince him to dissolve this marriage arrangement." I couldn't believe my ears, but I knew at that moment I'd do anything to end it.

Not because I wanted her for myself, but because I wanted her to have her freedom. The ability to choose and to be with whom she wanted. Her sapphire eyes lit up, and in that moment, I was the luckiest man in the world to behold such a sight.

"You would?"

"For you, I would do anything, haven't you figured that out yet?" Francesca smiled shyly and stared at me through her lashes. I wanted to kiss her so badly. "He won't agree to it."

"I don't care if I have to threaten him, I will," I promised. "You deserve to have a choice, *Principessa*. To be happy with whom you choose."

She was silent for a while and then her shy smile turned into a grin. "I'm happy here," she admitted, and I swore my heart skipped a beat. It was none of that cheesy shit, it was the truth, I felt it. I swear.

"Then trust me," I asked of her. "This won't end like last time, I promise."

"I trust you." She did not hesitate.

I caressed her waist and took a step forward pushing her back, one of my hands cupped her neck and I brought her forward. "Good." I pulled her closer. "Now," I said, pulling at her hair so that her neck was exposed for me to feast on, "you'll suffer your punishment for ever thinking I'd let you go." I sucked on that particular spot beneath her ear which she loved.

"Cassio," Francesca breathed.

I sucked until I left a mark, enjoying the sight of it on her. I then trailed down her neck and kissed her collar bone nibbling on it, pulled the strap of her dress, and kissed her shoulder. I did it to the other one and then kissed the swell of her breast. Francesca's chest rose as she sucked in a deep breath. Her fingers gripped my hair as I tugged on her skin-tight dress. The fabric bunched at her waist, exposing eager pink nipples.

I pinched one just as I sucked the other into my mouth. She moaned softly, and it traveled all the way to my dick, which stirred to life. When I let them go and stood back up she was panting hard.

"Oh, *Principessa*," I tugged on her bottom lip. "You're in so much trouble."

"Shut up and kiss me," she ordered.

I laughed and leaned down, my lips inches from hers, enough that I could almost taste them. Francesca wouldn't get away so easily for scaring the shit out of me. I watched as she licked her lips in anticipation. My dick strained against my pants, but I ignored it.

"Good night, *Principessa*." I smirked, turned around, and left her standing there in my kitchen.

I left my bathroom, drying myself and dropping the towel on the floor. Francesca lay on my bed, her golden hair spilled over the pillow, her long legs exposed, and her silhouette outlined by my shirt that she wore to sleep.

When I lay down beside her, I stopped to stare at her beauty. At the soft lines, full lips, slightly darker brows. Angelic features. She was so undeniably beautiful it hurt to look at her. A man like me shouldn't be privy to such a sight. It almost felt like a sin to have her here.

It took everything in me not to wake her up and fuck her like I had wanted to do all night long. It had been a testament to my strength to walk away from her, but I wanted—needed—her to know that whatever this was between us, it wasn't about sex. It was much more than that.

With her back to me, I lay down and wrapped my arms around her like a protective barrier. I was a light sleeper but holding her always made me sleep better. She instantly melted into me and let out a soft sigh. At that moment, I couldn't have been more fulfilled.

Francesca meant the world to me, but I *needed* my revenge, without it I had no idea who I was supposed to be. But I knew one thing...one thousand four hundred and six days and I still wasn't over her.

She was mine and I was hers, simple as that. There was no fighting anymore. I couldn't do this. I was so God damned tired. I couldn't help falling in love with her, it was as easy as breathing.

"I love you, *Principessa*," I whispered against her hair and held on tight, afraid that I would lose her for a second time in my life.

Loving her was dangerous. Loving her could break me, but I couldn't stop myself from doing so. For four years I had tried to deny it, to forget her, but there was no forgetting Francesca Manci. There was only bracing for the wave and hoping it didn't drown me. So, I held on tight.

I was in love with Francesca. Deeply and madly in love with her. With all her perfect imperfections. Every part of her was made to be loved by me. I only prayed she allowed me to love her like she deserved.

28

FRANCESCA

"You look sour," Mamma said. I looked at her as she opened one eye to stare at me. "I was just thinking."

"What about?" Mamma tried adjusting herself on the bed, but she had grown weaker these last few days. Her skin had turned paler, her lips bluer and her appetite had diminished so much she barely ate.

"How could you ever forgive him?" I didn't want to strain her but that had been on my mind for a long time now.

"Honestly, Francesca, this again?"

"I don't want to argue, I just...I wanted to understand."

"Did you know your father and I lived separate lives for a year?"

That pricked my curiosity. "A year?"

"It was right after you were born, it was also when I learned he had a mistress," Mamma said, but there was no scorn in her voice. "I left and went to my parents' house and refused to leave."

I knew that there was a time when Paolo and I barely saw each other. He traveled most of the time and spent his nights in hotels. When he was back in Indianapolis, he would visit his mistress instead of me.

"Did he come after you?"

"He did." She smiled weakly. "He asked me to come home. I told him to get rid of his bitch and he did...for a while, and we made peace."

"Why did you?" The thought that I could have grown up without Donato was staggering. I couldn't imagine how healthy my childhood could have been.

"That was the worst year of my life," she confessed. "I was angry, and hurt, but living without him was worse than living with him. Forgiveness is a powerful weapon, *Cara Mia*. You can either be absolved or become its prisoner."

I sat there speechless and unsure of what to say. Silence remained between us two until Mamma reached for my hand and I took hers. "We must remember that forgiving someone is not only for them but for us, too. Letting go of that rage and hatred can be more freeing than you imagine."

"You still forgive him?"

"Yes. It doesn't mean I'm miraculously healed of all the pain he caused. But I didn't do it for him, I did it for me. Perhaps one day you will be lucky enough to understand what it means to love someone so deeply you are willing to go through all that pain just so you can live a few moments of pure happiness."

I sat there looking at my Mamma, my head spinning. I had known that kind of love. The love that could take you to heaven but also to Hell. It terrified me that I had never forgotten what that love was like because, with each day that passed, I was slowly falling for Cassio all over again.

"He hurt me, Mamma," I confessed trying my hardest not to cry.

"I know." She squeezed my hand with all the strength she had left. Her confession surprised me. "I'm not blind, Francesca, do you think I never noticed?"

"You never said anything."

"What could I say, Francesca? I couldn't lie to you and tell you it would be all right. I couldn't fight when I knew the decision would never be mine to make. In our world, love is a curse."

I nodded in understanding but at the same time, it hurt to know my mother had known it all along.

"I hope one day you'll be able to forgive me." My mother's weak voice followed me as I exited her room wanting to get away from here.

I found Cassio standing by the nurse's desk and when he saw me, I swore his eyes lit up. He said something to one of the nurses and then came my way.

When we were inches apart, he produced from behind his back a lovely bouquet of white tulips. "They were out of purple ones."

I took the flowers from his hands and shoved my nose into them. "They are lovely." And they were. "What are you doing here?"

"Can't I come see my girl?" he said casually. The flowers almost slipped from my fingers. *What did he just say?*

"I...I" I had no words. "Cassio..."

"Did you know," he said as though he hadn't just made my day, "Martha here says that the average time it takes for someone to bleed out is about five minutes." Cassio looked at Martha, and she nodded.

Yeah, I was sure he must already know that. Did she know he figured this out by doing very, very bad things to people? I bet she didn't even know who stood before her. And I bet she would run away crying if she did.

"I didn't know that." I responded dumbfoundedly.

"Come on, I have a surprise for you," he said and took one of my free hands.

What was going on?

Had someone dropped me in an alternate reality, and I was just coming to terms right now? Still speechless and replaying his words over and over in my head, I followed him all the way to his car.

"Is everything all right with your mother?"

I nodded and observed Cassio suspiciously. Had he hit his head? Had something happened? That was the only explanation.

Eventually, he parked his car before what used to be a restaurant. "*Peppe's Pizza?*" Cassio nodded, left the car, and came to open the door for me. "Cassio, this place was closed like, two years ago."

"Yeah, it was."

He grabbed my hand and led me toward the door, knocked twice, and then when I thought he was losing his mind, someone opened the door for us. "Peppe?" I gasped.

Cassio grinned at my reaction. I greeted Peppe, who I hadn't seen since I left four years ago, and he led us into his old restaurant. A single table was placed at the center, and everything else was left bare.

"What is this?" I looked at Cassio in confusion.

"I realized we never went on an actual date," he explained. "Peppe's was the first time I met you."

I remembered it like it was yesterday. Arabella had invited me to have dinner with her family. I was fifteen, a child still, but when I saw Cassio Moretti, I knew that he was going to be my everything. One sight and I was already a goner.

Tears prickled the back of my eyes and a lump formed in my throat, so large it was hard to swallow. I gulped a few times hoping I wouldn't break down right now.

We sat and ate lunch together, something we had done plenty of times in the past, but we had always been surrounded by others. Cassio and I had never been able to be alone, just the two of us, enjoying each other's company. Even if I was living with him, this was different.

After we devoured our pizzas, Cassio leaned forward and grabbed my hand, turned it around, and ran his fingers across my palm. The act was so mundane like he'd done it a hundred times before.

"You still hurt yourself," he pointed out as he traced the marks my nails left.

"You still make me nervous," I confessed.

"Why?" He sounded...worried like he might not like the answer.

The truth was, I was nervous because I was falling for him and today, everything had been more than perfect. Cassio made me nervous because he was and always had been my everything, and now I couldn't escape him, no matter how hard I tried.

He caressed my skin again. "I have one more surprise for you," he confessed and stood offering his hand for me to take it.

We left the restaurant; my belly was full and so was my heart. As Cassio drove, I kept on replaying our lunch in my head, afraid this was a dream.

My girl.

Was it true? Did he really want me to be his? Could Donato be wrong? He placed his hand on my thigh, and we drove through Chicago. Cassio parked his car inside Willis Tower, and we headed toward the sky deck. I noticed it was empty. This place was never empty, not with the number of tourists coming in every day.

"It's ours for the afternoon," Cassio explained.

"You closed the deck?" I gasped.

"Of course, I did." He drew nearer. "Or else I would have to kill every man that looked at your naked skin."

"Naked?"

"Yes," he nibbled on my neck and inhaled deeply. "You're so damned sweet, Francesca." Air got stuck in my lungs. "I think I'll have my dessert now."

"You're so confident I'll give it to you," I teased as anticipation coursed through my veins, and wetness pooled between my legs, my panties sticking to my skin.

Cassio nibbled on my jaw and then kissed me; it was fast, and yet it still left me breathless. "A man can only dream."

"I'm yours, Cassio," I confessed. He could do whatever he pleased with me, and I wouldn't care. I was too far gone. I wanted him too much to think better of it.

He had me naked in record time, my clothes scattered over the floor. I truly hoped no one was watching us through the camera feed, but I didn't care about that either. Not when he picked me up and walked all the way toward the glass wall.

"Cassio," I squealed as my back touched the cold glass. I looked down and saw the city beneath me. I was never one for heights, my heart started hammering against my chest. "Cassio," I repeated again, this time it was laced with fear.

"It's safe, Francesca," he assured me. I breathed in deeply. "I won't ever let anything happen to you," he said with determination. "Do you trust me?"

I nodded, of course, I did.

He picked up my hand and settled it over his heart, it was beating fast, too. "You're nervous," I noted surprised.

"I'm always nervous when I'm around you," he confessed with a shy smile.

"Around *me*?" Was this a joke? Cassio was nervous around me?

"Look at you, *Principessa*." He did so with wonder in his eyes. "You're so perfect."

"I'm a mess, Cassio," I pointed out with a dry laugh. "I'm full of thorns."

He shook his head. "No, you're perfect just the way you are, Francesca. Don't ever think otherwise. I don't fear pain, my skin is thicker than that." He tucked a strand of hair from my face and placed it behind my ear. "You are perfect for me."

My heart swelled. It was impossible not to love a man like him. I leaned in and kissed him; it was soft and devoid of our usual hunger. We took our time, letting our mouths dance to their own rhythm. There was no need to rush.

Cassio tasted like the dreams I once dreamt, and it was so sublime. So...pure. I wanted to live in this kiss forever.

I could feel his heart accelerating, picking up speed like mine was, both erratic. Suddenly, the kiss grew desperate. Cassio lifted me up and I instantly wrapped my legs around his powerful body. He held me like I weighed less than a feather. I wrapped my arms around his neck and kissed him harder.

"I'm going to fuck you before my city. I'm going to own you completely."

I chuckled at the shift in his voice. "Then please do, Cassio Moretti."

Cassio pushed my soaked panties aside and pushed into me in one powerful thrust. My head fell back against the window as I cried out his name.

"You." He thrust in hard. "Are." He pulled out. "Mine." He thrust back deep inside me. "Say it."

"I'm...yours." I panted hard.

"And I'm yours, *Principessa*."

29

FRANCESCA

I woke up to Cassio on the phone, his voice gruff and serious. I fought to adjust to the morning light and realized it wasn't morning yet. The sun was still asleep—like we should be.

Light poured from the bathroom, and I watched as Cassio paced back and forth. I sat up, pulled the sheets with me, and crossed my legs waiting for him to return. When he did, I noticed his expression was grave. He sat beside me and ran his fingers through his golden-brown wavy hair. His large hand came to rest on my thigh, and he took a deep breath readying himself to speak.

"Your mother... she had a relapse this night," he began. I shot from the bed. He quickly added. "She's okay, but the doctors..."

"No." I shook my head.

"Francesca." He came to stand beside me. "I'm sorry, but they think it won't be long now."

"Bullshit," I snapped. "I saw her today."

I saw her. I saw her and...Mamma was not okay. She was weak, tired, and in pain. My heart dropped as I realized my mother might not beat this cancer and that she might not survive it.

Despite the fear, I stood straight. "Does Donato know?"

He shook his head. "I told them to call me."

"Thank you." I was slightly relieved. "Shit." I ran my hand through my hair. "Marco, I need to call my brother." My voice cracked.

I needed to tell my little brother who had lost so much that he was about to lose more. How could I be strong for him when even I couldn't be strong right now?

"I...I should be the one to tell him that—" tell him what? That Mamma was dying?

"I will call him, go get dressed. I'll make sure he gets there. Okay?" I nodded because a lump had formed in my throat, and I couldn't swallow it. "Remember what your doctor said. One step at a time."

I did just do what he told me, I focused on the small things and gave them my full attention.

We arrived at the hospital a half hour later, the nurses led me to her room and before I could go in, I froze. Cassio placed a hand on the small of my back and stood there with me, waiting.

"I can stay out here if you wish," he said, but I shook my head. He must have seen the plea in my eyes because he leaned in and kissed my forehead. "I'm here with you, *Principessa*,"

I inhaled deeply and took the final steps towards my mother's room. I stared at the machines, specifically the one showing her heartbeat. They were weaker than ever.

"Mamma, *noi siamo qui*." I reached for my mother's hand.

Mamma looked at us and for a second, she looked lost but then smiled. "What took you so long?" I choked on something that sounded like a laugh or a sob.

"We were..."

"I mean him." She looked at Cassio. "My daughter has a good heart, Cassio Moretti, one you broke and threw away, yet still she found it in her to let you in once again. If you ever break her heart again, I promise I will come back from my grave and I will haunt you till your dying days." Mamma stopped to cough, and I immediately went to her side.

"I won't—"

"I'm not done," she interrupted. "Unfortunately, the asshole I fell in love with, who happens to be her father, does not see or appreciate the woman she has become. I ask you to promise me something, Cassio," she appealed to him, and he nodded instantly. "Promise me that whatever happens between the two of you, you will make sure she is safe and cared for, that no man will ever touch her without her permission, and that she's allowed to make her own destiny."

"You don't have to ask me that. Francesca is safe and taken care of, she always will be. The man who dares touch her will lose his hand—if she wishes for it. She has been a free woman since the day she came back into my city, and she will remain that way," he assured her.

"Even from you?" she asked. "She will be safe and protected from you?"

"Yes."

"Promise me, boy."

"*Prometto,*" he promised.

"Good, now let me speak to my daughter."

Cassio said his goodbyes and left the room. I stood there with my Mamma, holding her hand, and wishing I could save her.

"*Mamma.*" I came closer to her, but she stopped me.

"I don't know how much longer I have, Francesca, and I need to ask something of you as well."

"Yes," I said without a doubt.

"Don't be afraid to live, don't be afraid that your past will repeat itself. You are young, you are smart, and you are beautiful. Don't let others decide for you, be better than I was, be stronger than I was, and fight for what you want."

"I will," I promised.

"I was a bad mother, Francesca and—"

"Mamma," I interrupted her I didn't want to hear those words; I didn't want to think of this as a goodbye, but I let her continue either way.

"I loved you from the moment I held you in my arms, but I also knew in that moment, you would never be mine. That I would raise you for someone else. That my little girl would be sold to the highest bidder like I had been. I know it is too late now, but I regret being a coward. I regret not getting to know you, and I regret never being there for you when you needed me." The longer she spoke, the more tears fell down my face.

"Mamma, I forgive you." I felt the need to speak. The moment I watched that single tear fell from her eye, I could no longer contain myself.

"If you have grown to be this loving and strong woman whose first instinct is to help others and not yourself, then that's all on you, Francesca. Despite everything you went through, I couldn't be prouder of the woman you have become. I'm sorry for not loving you enough or not standing up for you."

"Don't," I cried, holding her hands. "I don't blame you, Mamma." And I didn't, not anymore. She squeezed my hand with the remaining force she had.

"Don't suffer my death."

"Don't ask me that," I sobbed.

"Don't, Francesca—don't stop living when I die. I want you to live, I want you to be happy, to find someone who values you and cherishes you the way you deserve. Find someone who will give you wonderful children like the ones I was blessed with. I know I never said it enough, but I love you, Francesca, and you were my blessing. You were the only reason I lived this long. I'm sorry, *cara mia*."

"I love you, Mamma."

I don't know how long I remained there crying and telling her how much I loved her and that I forgave her. Eventually, Cassio was the one who escorted me out. I didn't say goodbye because I knew there was no need for it. She had lived this long; she would live longer.

Cassio wrapped his arm around me. I don't know whether he was keeping me up or if he was trying to shield me. When we both exited the room, I stopped. Donato stood right next to the nurses' counter. Marco stood behind him but not close.

I made to step away from Cassio, but he pulled me closer tucking me into him. He straightened himself and walked toward my father. He didn't greet him and neither did I. Donato only looked at us, his jaw slightly dropped. Cassio stopped directly in front of Marco who looked at us now, at how Cassio held me.

"Thank you for coming," he said to my brother.

"You don't have to thank me." He tried to hide his emotions, but his voice gave him away.

"If you need someone to talk to, you can call me," Cassio said, surprising us both.

Marco nodded and despite my father being here, he hugged me quickly and whispered. "I'm happy for you," he said before he let me go.

30

FRANCESCA

Marie and Vitelli's wedding would be held at the old Moretti mansion. Being back brought memories of a time much simpler than this. As I walked through the house, I remembered Arabella, her easy smile, and her heart of gold. I remembered our days out here, bright and filled with excitement. It was so...uncomplicated.

Being here also reminded me of Cassio, how we'd sneak out into the garden and lose ourselves in each other. Those moments of escape were the few ones we got to be together. They had been our everything.

"You look stunning, *ma chérie*." Antoine took my hand and placed it in the crook of his arm and helped me down the stairs, bringing me back to reality.

"You don't look bad yourself." I followed as he led us toward the garden where Marie and Vitelli's pre-wedding dinner would be held.

I looked around, cheeks blazing as old memories of Cassio and I filled my mind. I tried to push them aside for now, but it was hard since he was starting to become my everything.

The garden was packed with guests mingling around, but my eyes were focused on one man and one man only. Cassio wore a perfectly tailored navy suit that offered me a view of his sculpted body. His hair was finger-combed back, and I could practically smell him from all over here.

I noticed I wasn't the only woman looking at him tonight. But when his eyes met mine, I felt like the only woman he had eyes for. He stared like he was slowly consuming me. Like he saw something inside that called to him.

"*Mon Dieu.* I can feel the heat from all over here."

I smiled. "Shut up."

"Seriously, Frankie, he's fucking you with his eyes." I looked at Cassio again and felt naked. "You minx," he laughed. "You're liking it."

I snorted but smiled. I shamefully was.

"Just tell me one thing, is it any good, with him?" Antoine knew about Cassio and me, we had dissected this hundreds of times. For once, Antoine's question didn't have a sexual connotation.

"Yes," I confessed as he led me towards our table. "It's paradise."

Antoine chuckled. "You deserve it, Frankie." When he let go, he gave me a quick kiss on the cheek and looked at Cassio offering him an apologetic look.

Cassio's nod was almost imperceptible, but then he met my eyes, and I forgot about the rest of the world.

We sat at the same table but barely spoke, we exchanged in total two words, but we couldn't risk it. At least I couldn't, one slip, and everyone out here would know I was having sex with Cassio Moretti.

We needed to keep it a secret until Cassio found a way to dissolve my arranged marriage. So, I sat there talking to Marie, Vitelli, and Antoine for the rest of the night. Yet my eyes kept turning toward Cassio. That man had no right looking like that. It should be a crime. It could lead to accidents.

After dinner was served and the dancing began, I watched as he stood and headed toward the gardens. "You should go after him," Vitelli said as he sat beside me. "Being here has been hard on him. On all of us."

"So why have the wedding here?"

"Because it was Bella's favorite place in the world, and I don't want to taint it with bad memories. So, I decided to make new ones."

"Bella would be so proud of you." I swallowed a lump in my throat.

"Sometimes I wonder if they would have approved of Marie…"

"She would. One hundred percent. Bella would have loved her, and so would your father."

He pulled on my hair teasingly. "Thanks, *Frankie*." I stood up and pushed my chair in. "Be careful with him," Vitelli pleaded. "Cassio thinks he must carry the weight of the world on his shoulders."

"If he lets me, I'll help him carry it," I stated truthfully. For him I'd do anything.

Vitelli smiled. "I always knew you were the right one for him." Those words followed me as I searched for Cassio.

I found him in Arabella's room, he sat at the edge of her perfectly made bed. Everything was in order as they were waiting for her to come back. It was just like I remembered, not a single item was out of place.

Cassio froze when the floor creaked, but when he saw it was me, he relaxed again. Tentatively, I sat beside him and stared at the pictures attached to the vanity mirror before us.

I placed a hand over his thigh, and he put his over mine, interlacing our fingers, and rested my head on his shoulder, inhaling his scent. Citrus and Sandalwood and home.

Bella's murder had happened four years ago, and the thought that the Russians had tried to kill Cassio as well… haunted me.

"She would've been twenty-four by now," he blurted.

"I forgot how she looked when she smiled." I looked at the pictures on her vanity.

"I still blame myself," he whispered.

"Cassio, don't." I cupped his cheek, but he stood up and moved away.

"Bella was my little sister, mine to protect, and look what happened."

"You couldn't have stopped it," I tried to argue. "How could you have known they would attack your home?"

"Grigori is a maniac, he'd tried to have us killed before, I should have known he would try again."

"Cassio," I said softly. "There was nothing you could have done." Couldn't he see that?

He looked away, so I stood up and forced him to face me. I placed my hand over his heart right where his tattoo was. He inhaled sharply and stared at me.

"What happened to Arabella was a tragedy. I miss her every single day and still hate facing it, but there was nothing we could've done. That you could've done."

"Ara—she was my responsibility."

I smiled weakly. "Arabella, say it, Cassio. It's not just guilt you feel, its grief. You never had a proper moment to mourn her. With your father gone, you needed to be strong, and I understand that, but there is nothing wrong in admitting it."

"I don't." Cassio stepped away.

"This need to live for the Outfit, to be distant from others and to push people away, it's fear, Cassio. Fear that you'll be hurt again."

He was silent for a long while, his attention on the pictures attached to the vanity. I walked toward him once again and took his hand in mine, interlacing our fingers. Reminding him that he was not alone, that I was always going to be here for him, if he accepted me.

"This need for vengeance is corrupting what good is left in your heart. I know it hurts, and I know you want them dead, but you need to move on, Cassio. Let go of that rage."

"I can't." He fisted his hands. "I won't, Francesca."

"Then you'll lose me, Cassio. Because if you continue down this path, I refuse to watch you self-destruct." I would not watch him die! It was either me or them, he couldn't have both.

He frowned. "What does that have to do with us, Francesca?"

I took a deep breath and exhaled slowly. "Either you forgive yourself and let it go, or you'll live a lonely miserable life."

"Maybe that is what I want," he shouted. I didn't flinch, but he saw the pain in my eyes. I could see he regretted those words the moment he said them.

"Francesca." He ran his fingers through his hair. "I didn't mean it."

"You did," I argued. "You think having feelings makes you weak? They don't, Cassio, this need for vengeance is making you weak. It's keeping you from living."

"I miss her," he said softly, and I almost didn't catch it.

"I hate them, too, Cassio, but that rage is consuming everything that is good in you." I closed the space between us and placed a hand over his beating heart. "The love you felt for Bella will never be replaced by the love you feel for others. Each person is loved in a different way." My eyes found his. "I will not lose you to them, Cassio," I said with finality. I refused to do so.

"You won't," he said with conviction.

"Then promise me you'll let go of this rage."

"I can't."

"Then let go of me," I said as tears filled my eyes. I couldn't watch Cassio wither away because of this rage. He might have hidden it from me, but I knew what lay within.

He stepped closer to me and cupped my cheeks. "Never, *Principessa,* I'll never let you go."

"Why?"

"Because, I am a selfish man, and I love you too much to let you go." he confessed.

My eyes widened and my heart inflated. Those were not the words I was expecting but they were everything I needed. Pure, unfiltered, happiness cursed through my veins like a drug offering me a new kind of high. The only kind I wanted to experience from now on.

Tears streamed down my cheeks. "Well, that was not the reaction I was expecting." The concern in his voice caused me to chuckle.

I wrapped my arms around his neck and brought him down for a kiss. When we pulled apart, I confessed what had been in my heart forever, something I had been refusing to listen to.

"I love you, too," I admitted.

He sighed deeply and kissed my nose. "You have no idea how beautiful those words are, *Principessa*."

So, I said them again. "I love you."

He cupped my cheek, pine-green eyes staring into mine. They were warm and welcoming. "I love you beyond what is physically possible. I love you enough it hurts, yet still I will brave the pain because for you I'll do anything, Francesca. *Anything*."

I rested my head on his chest and listened to his heartbeat. We stood there like that for ages, simply enjoying this newfound love, or rather a love that had always been there to begin with.

I left Arabella's room shortly after Cassio. I needed some time to collect myself after such an emotional moment. I was on cloud nine.

"*Cara mia.*" I heard the monster's voice coming from behind. I turned and there he was.

My nightmares wrapped up all in one. Donato approached me looking all smug like he had just won the lottery and was on his way to rub it in people's noses.

"You didn't heed my advice, did you?" He chuckled. "No worries, you silly fools are not going to stand in the way of my plans."

"Plans." I crossed my arms. "Who cares about your plans, Father?"

"How invincible it must feel to have Cassio Moretti by your side." He shook his head. "In a few months, you'll be mine to do with as I wish."

I shivered, but at the same time, my body became warm, I was burning from within. "I'm not marrying anyone." Cassio had made me a promise, and I believed in him.

"Oh, but you are, and he's eager to meet you."

Oh, but I wasn't. "I'll tell Cassio about your meeting with Grigori," I threatened. I had no idea if the man in the picture my brother had shown me weeks ago was in fact Grigori, but I seemed to have been correct because he blanched.

"What did you say?"

"You heard me all right."

He took a step toward me, and I took one back and raised my hand stopping him. "Touch me and he'll know that, too."

"So confident of your power over him."

It wasn't power, it was love. Cassio loved me and that made me feel invincible, even against Donato.

"You committed treason," I said. The only reason I hadn't told Cassio was because Donato had threatened to hurt the people I loved. I hated my father, but I trusted his promise to me. I wasn't going to risk it, not for the world. I couldn't live with myself if something happened to them because of me. They were the only family I had.

Donato smiled. "There is nothing you can do about it, Francesca. Not if you want to see your friend walk down that aisle tomorrow. Or if you want your beloved to keep breathing."

"You wouldn't dare harm them."

"Oh no, *I* would never, but I have some friends that would be glad to. After all, in the throes of war, who knows what might happen."

"You're a monster," I snapped.

He laughed. "Tick-tock, Francesca, your time is almost over. One of these days Cassio is going to slip, and I'll be there to catch you."

31

FRANCESCA

After the vows were exchanged, we all moved to the wedding reception to watch their first dance together. I watched with teary eyes, I couldn't recall the last time I was this happy, a kind of happy that made me want to cry.

After the toasts, the newlyweds headed to the dance floor and after their first dance the guests followed. Antoine was my first partner, then Vitelli, and on and on the men came wanting a dance. I could feel Cassio's eyes burning through my skull, but he kept his distance.

It was equally frustrating and annoying. All I wanted was to be with him now that I knew how he felt. Maybe I had always known, but having heard the words come out of his mouth was a relief.

I reached my seat, tired from all the dancing, and out of habit, I reached for my phone, I knew no one was going to call me, but I checked it either way. I dropped the phone on the table when I saw the three missed calls. Everything happened as though I was on autopilot. My fingers swiped the name on the screen, and I pressed it to my ear. Slowly, I turned to the dance floor where everyone else was smiling and enjoying the party. The phone rang twice before it was answered.

"Francesca? Thank God. I tried to reach you before," came his voice.

"Dr... Dr. Conrad?" My voice croaked.

Silence stretched between us.

"Francesca? Are you there."

No. "Mhmm," I hummed, unable to speak.

"I'm sorry, we tried but—"

The phone slipped through my hand and in that moment, I felt the entire floor give way and it was like I was the one slipping away. My vision blanked, not before I saw Cassio watching me, I turned away and used the table to keep me standing.

"Francesca?" came his voice but it was muffled by the sound of my beating heart, which felt a lot like it was going to explode. "Francesca?"

I closed my eyes hoping that the dizziness would stop. Hoping that when I opened them up, this was just a nightmare, and I was still in Cassio's arms as he said I love you.

"Shit!" he cursed.

He must have left me. I couldn't tell what was happening around me, but seconds later, I heard Marie's voice calling me. I felt her arm around mine and she escorted me somewhere into the house, or was it the house? I couldn't tell.

"Don't let her out of your sight," Cassio shouted. "I need a fucking car right now," he shouted some more.

"What's going on?" Marie asked me and Cassio, I think. My eyes were open, but I couldn't process the things happening around me.

"*Principessa*, look at me." He placed his hands on my checks and forced me to look at him. "Stay with me, okay?"

I think I nodded; I don't know but he let go of me. There were people around me, I heard their voices, but nothing made sense. Only when I felt myself being lifted up, being pressed against a hard chest, my head tucked in the crook of his neck, smelling his comforting scent, it was then that I broke apart.

The day after I ruined Marie's wedding, I stood beside my brother. Donato stood closest to the coffin. Slowly it was lowered into the ground. I didn't know who had moved first, but I now held Marco's hand and he held mine. Over the past twenty-four hours, he was the only thing I could think of. The only thing I worried about. Without my mother, he was alone in that house with the monster.

The priest said a couple more words, and like the rest of his sermon, it vanished in the air. I hadn't been able to make sense of them, the only thing anchoring me to the world right now was my brother. I needed to be strong for him, at least I could do this... I hoped.

Once the dirt was finally placed over the coffin, I felt the first tear escape and trail down my face. The thick black glasses and the large hat would thankfully hide them. As was customary, I waited there as people came to talk to us. They went on and on, and I couldn't seem to see their faces, all of them joined in a blur. It felt a lot like a drug haze except this was reality. I don't know how many people offered me their condolences, or how many offered their sympathies. I didn't want them; I just wanted the pain to go away.

Two figures stopped in front of me, and I was given a comforting hug I could never forget.

"Frankie, I am so sorry," Marie hugged me.

"I'm sorry for ruining your wedding." My voice sounded robotic.

"Don't." She held my hand with force. "We are here for you, okay? Both of us." She hugged me again and waited for Vitelli, who, like her, hugged me as though I was family.

They stopped a few paces from me and stood there waiting for something. I didn't know what. Nothing was making sense today. Their faces diminished, and one by one they disappeared.

"Time to go, Marco." Donato practically ripped him away from me and he protested. "Stop embarrassing me like you have been doing all this time," Donato whispered wrathfully.

Marco wiped his eyes quickly; he looked at me but followed my father. I watched as they both entered the car and left. My mother hadn't even been buried for an hour and he was already anxious to get away. I stood there on my own as a few others remained to give me their condolences.

The world around me began to close in. It became harder and harder to breathe and I could feel my lungs constricting. No matter how much I tried to pull in air, it didn't come.

"Excuse me," I said to no one in particular and walked away from the gravesite.

The longer I tried to distance myself, the quicker the trees began to close in on me until I couldn't hold it anymore.

I stopped.

Placing a hand against the tree trunk, I tried to breathe but I just couldn't. Desperation settled over me, and I tried to fight against the current that was pulling me back under. I was tired. So, fucking tired of fighting.

"I'm going to die." I realized as I tried inhaling.

"Francesca." I felt someone put a hand on my shoulder.

"I'm drowning, Cassio, I've been drowning for a long time." I sobbed, fighting the tears. "I can't breathe. I'm dying," I repeated, complete desperation taking over me.

He spun me around and grabbed onto my cheeks.

"Look at me," he ordered, and somehow, I managed to do so. "You're not dying, Francesca. I'm never going to let that happen. Do you hear me?" He spoke with conviction. "Hold on to me. Let me fight the current for you."

I broke down, tears that had been painfully pressing against my eyes now fell freely, they blurred my eyes and wet my cheeks. He kissed my forehead and brought my head toward his strong chest where I buried my face. I grabbed onto him as if he were my lifeboat.

"Let me help you," he spoke against my hair as his hand caressed my back in soothing circles. "Let me save you."

I couldn't breathe. I wrapped my arms tightly around him, afraid that at any moment he would let me go and I would drown in the darkness. *Please*, I begged with each cry. *Please*.

"Breathe, Francesca. Breathe for me," he soothed me. "Please breathe, *Principessa*." The words caused me to become still.

One word and my fears abated, the tidal wave was drawn back, and I was once more left on the beach. Simply. Just like that, I was breathing. Air filled my lungs as I inhaled and exhaled following the rising and falling of his chest pressed against me.

When I finally looked up, the summer sun was shining through the trees, lighting him up as if drawn to him. The person who stared down at me was the same person I fell in love with all those years ago. The same considerate, compassionate, loyal, protective, and perhaps a bit possessive person, was looking at me through bright green eyes. *The person I am in love with*. Always was, always would be. Even when I hated him, that hatred was fueled by love.

I felt drained, the events of the past few days finally took hold of me, and with the addition of my panic attack, my energy was depleted. The words left my mouth, but I was too tired to take them back.

"Don't let me go." It was a desperate plea which held so many meanings.

"Never again." He held me tighter. "Never. Again." He repeated. A promise. An oath. "Let's go home, *Principessa*."

32

CASSIO

It pained me to leave Francesca so soon after her mother's death. A week wasn't nearly enough. Francesca had been doing well. She had been taking her meds and visiting her therapist and now, I feared she was going to spiral again.

"I heard you refused my proposal," Romeo Ferraro stated. He meant the arranged marriage between his cousin and me.

"I'm afraid I'm taken," I said simply.

Romeo looked at me with those disconcerting blue eyes, as though he was trying to get a read on me. "Good, Livia refused you as well."

I couldn't help myself, I chuckled. "Probably a wise choice."

"That's what I said," he deadpanned. I was a stone-cold bastard, but Romeo Ferraro was something else.

"I believe a marriage is not needed for our alliance," I pointed out. "I'd say our friendship would be enough." I extended my hand.

Romeo stared at it for a while and took it, shaking it hard. "To our alliance," he remarked. "To new friends." He said the word as though it was bitter. He looked like a man of few friends if he even had any. In that aspect we weren't so different. Maybe that was why this alliance between the Outfit and the Cosa Nostra would work out.

My phone rang and I sighed in frustration. Although our meeting was at an end, I disliked being interrupted. I picked up my phone because it might be Francesca, but when I saw my brother's number on the screen, I cursed.

I ended it without picking it up. Vitelli and Apollo were outside since Romeo, and I had decided to meet Capo-to-Capo. A few moments later, Apollo Ferraro came into the room, my brother pushing him aside.

"I need to talk to you." He tried to mask his emotions, but I saw concern shimmering in his eyes.

"Can't this wait?" I glared at him despite the hairs on the back of my neck rising. He shook his head.

I excused myself and headed outside with him. We were in a small restaurant in Little Italy, New York. Once I stepped out, the scent of trash, pollution, and piss hit my nose. I couldn't wait to go back.

"Vitelli, I swear to God," I warned him.

"The cargo from Mexico was stolen just now," he said. "Luciano just called, said he was going to move the product as you ordered them to do, but the Russians intercepted us before we could make the move."

My chest inflated and I tried to breathe out slowly, but the air didn't come out. I turned around and stared at the brick wall of the alley. "How many dead?"

"Three," Vitelli said angrily. I began to pace, worrying at the pavement. "That's the cargo you told Donato about." Vitelli reminded me. "The one you used as bait—"

"I know," I interrupted him.

"Cassio, this means..."

"I know, Vitelli," I snapped. "I fucking know it."

A few months ago, I had given my underbosses a time and place where our cargo would be taken from and transported to a new location to be distributed and sold. Each of them received unique information. As time had passed and no cargo had been stolen, I almost forgot about it, but now...now I had my answer. Now I knew who the spy was, who the conniving little fox was. I had a gut feeling and it never left me hanging, but even if I had suspected it, a betrayal was a betrayal, and I felt the blade in my back being twisted.

"What now?" Vitelli inquired.

"We'll use the fox to catch Grigori." I answered simply.

"And how are you going to do that, Cassio?" He threw his hands in the air.

I was thinking about it. "We'll have to tread carefully," I said. "Donato Manci cannot suspect we are on to him."

"He fucking betrayed us," Vitelli said in disbelief. "All those years serving Father and then you, and he betrayed us."

"He's going to pay for what he's done," I said, my vision turning red.

This was all I needed to make him pay. All I needed was a reason to put him six feet under. "Call Marie, I want her and Francesca out of Chicago as soon as possible."

When I entered the restaurant again, I mustn't have hidden my emotions because Romeo said, "Trouble?"

"One of my men betrayed me," I confessed. If we were to be friends, and if this alliance was going to work, then I needed to learn to trust others.

Romeo's blue eyes turned dark. "You can have as many of my men you need."

"I appreciate it, but I'd rather deal with him on my own."

A terrifying smile ghosted the Capo's face. "Then I bid you good hunting," Romeo said extending his hand. "I'll have you escorted to your jet."

"Thank you," I said and meant it.

"That's what friends do," he said and although there was no emotion in his voice, I could tell he meant it.

Three hours later when I arrived at my apartment, Francesca was lying in bed, her hands tucked underneath her cheeks. She was so goddamned beautiful it hurt.

Gently, I tucked a few strands of hair from her face. "*Principessa*." I tried to wake her up. "Love." I kissed her cheek.

Francesca stirred and looked at me, her eyes were red-rimmed. She had been crying. I understood what it was to lose someone you loved, and I wished I could take that pain away.

"You have to wake up." I smiled when she shook her head.

"I want to sleep."

"*Principessa*, this is important," I said trying to keep my anxiety at bay. I needed her out of this city as fast as possible.

If I was going to act against Donato, I needed to be sure Francesca was okay. That she was safe.

"What is it? Has something happened?" She sat up, her back against the headboard.

I took a deep breath. "Actually, yes," I admitted. Her blue eyes went wide. "Your father betrayed us."

She was in shock for a few seconds and said nothing, I wondered what was going on in her head. "Cassio," she blanched. "A few weeks ago, Marco came to me with a few pictures of Donato and some men. I think they were Russians."

I sat back. "Why are you only telling me now?" I snapped.

"Because Donato threatened you and everyone I care about. He said he was going to kill you all."

"Francesca." I shook my head. "You should have told me either way."

"I'm sorry." She came to sit on her haunches. "I couldn't risk it." She threw her hands in the air. "If something happened and it was my fault...Cassio, I couldn't."

I understood her fear, her father was a powerful and cruel man who had hurt her countless times. He had given Francesca reason to believe him. I couldn't blame her for trying to protect those she loved. For protecting me.

"What is going to happen now? What about my brother?"

"What about him?" I questioned.

"He's my father's son."

Yes, but he was also Francesca's brother and a victim of the same man who had given her so much pain. "Marco will be safe," I assured her. "Now get ready and pack a small bag," I told her. "You and Marie are leaving for the lake house."

"What about you?" She stood and came toward me. "Cassio, what about you?"

"I'll meet you later, right now I have to clean this up."

"Are you going to kill him?" I nodded.

Without any remorse, she said, "Good, make sure he suffers for what he has done."

I stood there impatiently as Francesca quickly packed a bag, shoving in everything she could in such a short period of time. When she was done, I held her by her shoulders.

"Vince is going to take you to Marie and Vitelli's place and from there you two are going to the lake house. No detours, no stops, do you understand?"

She nodded, eyes overflowing with fear. I took her hand and we both headed down toward the parking lot. Once there, I stared at my car and the one that was going to take her away from me.

"I don't want to leave you," she said as she held Reggie in her arms.

"You have to, *Principessa*."

"Promise me you'll come back."

I hesitated, but for her, I would fight till the very end. Until there was nothing left but the dust of my bones. I would come back for her, even if the world ceased to exist.

"Promise." And with that, I brought her in for a kiss, and not just any kiss—like the ones we had shared over these months—there were a million words I wished to say to her but didn't have the time to express them all. It was all my love for her.

"I'll be waiting for you," she said.

My heart constricted in the oddest of manners, like it was being torn out of my chest, but made whole at the same time.

"This isn't goodbye," I promised.

"I love you," she touched my heart. "Never forget that." Then she turned around and got into the car, leaving me behind with that nagging feeling in the back of my mind that I was doing the wrong thing in sending her away.

The hairs on the back of my neck rose when my car left the garage, taking Francesca away from me. I tried to shut up the voices, but they wouldn't let me be.

I had to; Francesca is safer this way.

33

FRANCESCA

A thick silence settled over us, there were no words that could be said in a moment like this. Marie sat beside me, her hands tucked into her legs, while mine shook freely.

I had been scared before, but this was something else entirely. It wasn't about me, this fear—it belonged to the man who owned my heart. Cassio had said he'd come back, that he'd be alright, and I believed him. The only problem was that I didn't trust Donato.

"We are ready to go." Vince came into the room together with Marie's guard Matteo.

I jumped to my feet. We had been waiting for an hour, and I was starting to lose my mind, my body vibrating with anxiety. My palms were sore from having dug my nails in too hard.

"What about Vitelli and Cassio?" Marie asked coming to her feet slowly.

Vince shook his head. "The boss has given orders."

I swallowed hard. We hadn't heard from Cassio or Vitelli in that hour, but that didn't mean he was in danger. Cassio had told me he had a plan to take down Donato and the Bratva's Pakhan, Grigori.

"Alright," I agreed because I didn't want to make Cassio worry more than he already was. If going to the lake house was what he wanted, then I would go there.

Marie looked at me for guidance, as if I had ever been in a situation like this, but right now, I tried to be strong for the both of us.

"We'll go separately," Vince said. "Marie, you'll ride with Matteo, and we'll leave a few minutes later," he said to me.

Marie grabbed my hand and when I looked at her, she was seconds from crying. "It's going to be alright," I lied because it was all I could give her now.

Picking Reggie up from the floor I handed him to her. "For moral support."

She hugged him tight against her. "Are you sure?"

No, I wasn't. Nothing about today was going as planned. If it had been up to me, I would have spent my day in bed, mourning my mother, but even that Donato had stolen from me. "You need him."

Marie smiled weakly. "I do." She agreed.

We hugged each other, and I watched as my best friend walked out of the door and that's when the pressure behind my eyes began to grow. Cassio had it under control. I knew he did.

Thirty minutes slipped through my fingers and when the clock struck four, Vince came into Marie's living room. "It's time."

I nodded and followed him, a shiver raced down my back, and I looked around, trying to identify what was holding me back. It was an odd feeling, something strange, it had settled in my bones and wouldn't let go. I had a bad sensation about this.

"Where is Cassio?" I asked Vince as he led me toward the car.

Vince didn't answer.

"Please, I need to know he's alright." I stopped by the backseat door and refused to enter.

Vince shook his head. "I don't know," he confessed. "But don't worry, the Boss knows what he's doing."

I got into the car and as we drove toward Cassio's Lake house cabin, all I could think about was that I loved him and that I wanted to get to say that again, and again, for the rest of my life.

It happened so quickly that I didn't have time to react. Vince swerved our car trying to avoid the other one that ended up crashing into us. I hit my head against the seat and cried out in pain.

"Get down!" Vince ordered as shots were fired against the glass.

I scooted low and placed my hands over my ears trying to cover myself. The windows were bulletproof, but the shots wouldn't stop.

"Fuck," Vince shouted just as the front window shattered, and I heard the sickening sound of a bullet hitting flesh.

That's when I screamed. It did me no good as my door was yanked open and I was dragged outside. Instinct kicked in and I fought my assailants with everything I had in me. I couldn't see their faces; they all wore black balaclavas.

I screamed, hoping someone would stop and help, but no one came. "Shut her up." It was all I heard before someone hit me with the butt of a gun and I blacked out.

"There she is. Welcome back, *cara mia*." That voice...

I blinked a few times trying to see, and when my eyes adjusted, I caught sight of Donato.

"W-what..." I looked around and saw armed men, there were at least five of them. I tried to move, but I was tied to a chair, my hands bound with tape. "Where am I?" I fought against my bounds.

Donato remained silent as two other men walked into the room. Both large and stocky, with hairy arms and thick bushy brows. They looked feral, like grizzly bears. The tallest between them looked older, his hair peppered with white. While the youngest wore a matching Adidas hoodie and pants and stared at me like I was his next victim.

Through my fear-induced haze, it hit me; I'd seen them before in the pictures my brother had shown me. The hairs at the back of my neck stood up, and my chest grew heavy as pressure increased within. They were Russian. Not just any Russians, but one of them—I judged the eldest—was Grigori. Cassio's enemy.

"Is this her?" the youngest asked, his accent thick.

"You have my daughter, Grigori, my end of the bargain has been met."

Grigori came to stand before me and the younger version of him came, too. He made to touch me, but I looked away.

He laughed. "Fierce." His grimy, meaty hand landed on my cheek and as he caressed me, bile rose to my throat, and I forced it down. "I'll take her."

What?

"Of course, you will, we had a deal," Donato said.

"She could be ugly," the youngest said. "Bad teeth and small tits."

"Does it really matter?" Donato asked.

The man shrugged and looked at Grigori. He exchanged a few words with him, and he nodded.

"My son will marry her," Grigori said, and it hit me now.

I began to tremble. Hard. "*P-papa.*" I hated that word but maybe, just maybe I could make him change his mind. "*Per favore,*" I begged.

"Shut up, Francesca," he snapped.

"Please," I begged again. I knew he was going to marry me off; I just never expected it would be to a Russian. But he'd said it, hadn't he. I would marry a Boss' son. *Grigori's son.*

"I won't marry you." I glared at Grigori's son. "I won't go willingly."

It was the wrong thing to do, to grab his attention. He walked back toward me and grabbed my face with his meaty hands. "Oh, you will." His yellowish teeth flashed. "You will be mine, little bird. I will break your wings if I must."

His grip hurt and I whimpered, but he didn't let go, not until tears trailed down my cheeks. "You will have to kill me," I said because there was no way I would marry the enemy. No way I would do this to Cassio—

Cassio, of course. That was it. I looked into the man's dirty brown eyes and smiled through the fear and the pain. "Cassio will kill you."

The man threw his head back and laughed. "I don't see him here, little bird."

"He will come," I said with all the faith in the world. He must know about what happened by now. Someone must have warned him.

Giorgi's son leaned in close, enough that I could smell his putrid breath. "Oh, I am counting on it." He grinned and pulled on my bottom lip. "It will be so fun breaking you," he mused in excitement.

He stood, took his phone out of his pants, and snapped a photo of me. "W-what are y-you doing?"

"Making sure your beloved comes to rescue you."

Oh God. No.

And that's when I realized this was all a trap. Not only for me, but for Cassio as well. So, I prayed with every fiber in my body that he wouldn't come. That he refused to rescue me.

"Why?" I looked at my father. "You owe me at least that much," I pleaded.

He made his way toward me, took a cigar from his breast pocket and watched it with interest, not giving me his full attention, he spoke. "It's not personal, Francesca."

Well, it felt like it was.

Still, I kept my mouth shut because I needed to know, it wouldn't change a thing. It was not like I could escape, I wasn't stupid, but I needed the truth.

"Grigori needed to solidify our alliance, he has a son and I have a daughter, you refused to come willingly, so I took you."

My nostrils flared. "Why?" my voice came out weak. He understood what I asked.

"Because Cassio Moretti has no idea what's he's doing. He's a boy playing at being Boss. The Outfit needs a man, someone who knows how to rule."

"And that's you," I said with distaste. He smiled, put his cigar in his mouth and left me there. "You already have me," I shouted. "Leave Cassio alone."

Donato paused, turned around, took his cigar from his mouth, and shook his head. "And where's all the fun in that?" His face morphed into anger. "Send the picture, we don't have all day. It's about time Cassio Moretti paid for his sins."

34

CASSIO

I sat at the table with some of my underbosses, some whom I knew I could trust and who had been loyal to me and my father. Those I knew hated Donato just as I did. As much as I wanted to head to his house and shoot the man, I couldn't. I needed to do it through the right channels.

The Outfit was a well-oiled machine, and even if I ruled it, there were still processes, laws, and codes I had to follow. Donato was one of the highest-ranking members, and I needed the vote of at least half of my underbosses to sanction his death. Betrayal was a crime that no Made Man would stand to accept.

Which didn't surprise me when everyone in the room voted in favor of his death. "My men will stand with you, Cassio," Fabrizio said.

"We should attack his house while he's still there," Eduardo Rocha, another one of my underbosses, pointed out. "If he's working with the Russians, who knows what else he's been doing?"

I agreed, but I couldn't rush this. As much as I wanted Donato, I needed Grigori as well. Killing Donato would satisfy me immensely, but it was the Russian Pakhan who held the strings. Donato was just a puppet in his game.

"We are," I answered. "But we need to make sure Grigori steps out of his fort. We are going to kill two birds with the same bullet."

My phone rang and I checked the caller, Vitelli was at one of our warehouses, checking on our weapons and what we might need for this operation. I excused myself from the table and answered on the last rings.

"Cassio," he sounded breathless. "I need to talk to you."

"Can't this wait, Vitelli, I'm in the middle—"

"I'm in your office." He ended the call.

I swear to God, sometimes he drove me to the brink of exasperation. Since Vitelli knew how important this meeting was, and had called anyway, I left the room and headed towards my office.

"You might want to sit down."

"Vitelli," I opened my mouth to scold him, but when I saw the look on his face, I knew... I just knew something had gone terribly wrong.

I didn't sit though, I remained standing, head held high and ready to solve whatever was coming my way.

"Francesca has gone missing."

My knees almost gave out. The floor opened beneath my feet. I reacted so fast I didn't have time to think. I grabbed Vitelli's collar and pushed him against the wall.

"What the fuck did you just say?"

"Cassio." He tried to sound calm. "Let go." I did once I realized what I was doing.

My hands shook.

"Marie called saying she arrived at the lake house, but Francesca hasn't."

"That doesn't mean—"

Vitelli raised his hand stopping me. "It's been three hours since she arrived and when she called Francesca, her phone was dead and so was Vince's."

I picked up my phone and called Francesca. She didn't answer, and when I called Vince, he didn't answer either. Vince always answered my calls. "There is more, Cassio," Vitelli said solemnly.

"Speak, for fucks sake."

"The police found your car. Someone crashed into it and there were bullet holes all over it. The front seat was stained with blood."

"Fuck." I grabbed my hair. That probably meant Vince was dead, and someone had taken my *principessa*.

I arrived at Vitelli's house minutes later. I could smell Francesca's cherry scent, which still lingered in the air. I tried my best to act cool, to remain unfazed, and to deal with this as I would have done a few years ago. But I was afraid, terrified that I would lose her like I had lost my sister. I knew Grigori was the one responsible for this; it had his name written all over it.

There was no way I'd survive this. No way I'd want to. If Francesca was harmed in any way, I don't know what I would be capable of, what kind of monster would arise and take control of my body. A part of me wanted that monster to surface. At least I wouldn't have to deal with the fear.

"Where is he?" I asked one of my soldiers who shot from the sofa the second we walked in.

"In the living room." I nodded.

"He doesn't know anything, Boss," he said.

I stopped and looked at my *Soldati*. Anger dripped from my voice when I answered. "I'll be the judge of that."

I entered the room to find Marco sitting at the head of the table, four of my men guarding him—not that he posed such a threat.

I walked over toward him and leaned closer, crowding his space. "Where is your sister?"

His eyes were wide with fear but clear. "I-I don't know," he croaked.

"Marco, you have one chance to save her—where is your sister?"

He shook his head and the first tear fell. "I don't know."

I would never harm a child in my life, but if Marco didn't speak, I would be forced to do something I would probably regret for the rest of my life. "Marco, your sister was taken, she's probably hurt. If you love her, then you need to help me."

He nodded and a tear ran down his cheek. "My phone," he said. I looked in confusion, but he asked for his phone, and I had one of the guards hand it to him.

Marco searched for something until he showed me a picture of his father and two other men I instantly recognized. Grigori and Mikail Petrovich.

"What is this, Marco?" I tried to keep my composure when all I wanted to do was hit someone.

"*Papa* met them a few months ago, and at the lake house. I didn't know who they were—"

"Russians, Marco, they are Russians," I snapped. "Our enemies."

I knew that already, Francesca had told me about what Marco found out, but seeing the pictures for the first time was like being stabbed in the back all over again. I already knew Donato was working with the enemy, but it still made me feel like a fool for ever believing in him.

He looked down. "Please, don't kill me," he begged and suddenly my heart shattered for an entirely different reason.

He was Francesca's little brother. Her family. If I intended on spending the rest of my life with her, then he was going to be my responsibility, too. He was my family now.

"Do you have any idea where they might be?" I asked trying to sound softer.

Marco shook his head. "Papa left to visit his mistress this morning and didn't come back home."

"Get him something to eat and drink," I ordered my men.

"Will you find her?" Marco called as I left.

"Yes," I vowed.

Vitelli was waiting for me in the living room, I shook my head before he could ask me his question.

I was about to...do something, anything when my phone chimed.

I clicked on the message and froze. My phone almost slipped to the floor. My eyes took a second to adjust as my hands trembled with both rage and... terror. Something I hadn't felt since the day my sister was killed.

It was a picture of Francesca tied to a chair, blood trailing down her forehead and her eyes wide with fear. Under the picture were two other messages. One was an address and the other said to come alone or she'd die.

"What is it?" Vitelli was by my side in seconds, he must have seen the picture because he swore. "I'll call some of our soldiers. Prepare them for—"

"You will do nothing," I told him.

"You can't be serious." Vitelli threw his hands in the air.

"I will not risk her life," I said fiercely. "I will not risk her, Vitelli."

"It's a trap, Cassio. You know that. They will kill you; they are using her as bait."

I knew that. Of course, I did, but nothing mattered. Francesca needed me, and I was going to save her even if it cost me my life. I wasn't going to lose her. *Not her. Never her.*

"Cassio, please," Vitelli begged.

"I love her," I confessed. "I will die for her if I need to." But most importantly I would kill for her.

Vitelli went silent.

"Do you understand, brother. I will *die* if it means she gets to live." He understood what this kind of love did to you. It made me invincible. "As of now, you are Capo," I announced. "If I die, please make sure Francesca is all right, that she is taken care of." I made a promise to her mother, and I was going to keep it.

Vitelli nodded; he was about to argue when I pulled him into a hug. "I love you, brother."

He hugged me tighter and we broke apart. I took one look in the dining room and caught sight of Marco. He was looking at me, and I nodded at him, a silent promise that I would get his sister back without harm.

I didn't look back as I made my way toward the elevator. If this was the end of the line for me, then I would go gladly. I'd do anything for Francesca. *Anything.* Dying was a small price to pay if it meant she got to live instead. At least I was going to die knowing what it was to be loved by her.

35

FRANCESCA

The room I was in smelled of mildew, and I could hear the night wind howling outside. A man who had been in the shadows approached me and I tensed. He had been there all along, but now that Grigori, his son, and Donato had left, he walked my way.

When he came into the white light, my heartbeat oddly, like it wanted to accelerate but lacked the strength. Umberto, my old guard was here. The man I had considered a father was here. Was he a part of this?

Two of the other armed men in the room started to stop him. "I'm checking her wound," he explained. "Your boss won't like it if it becomes infected."

Whether they believed him or not, Umberto kept coming my way. Once he reached me, I glared daggers at him. He crouched beside me and tried to touch my forehead where I was hit.

"Don't touch me." I couldn't help but cry out.

"Francesca," he whispered, with a gentle hand he checked my wound. It made me cry harder.

"Why?" I wanted to know why he would betray me.

Umberto crouched lower and we were face to face. "Look away, pretend you're angry."

"I am," I snapped.

"Good, keep that attitude."

Was he deranged. "Cassio is coming for you," he announced.

"No."

"Quiet," he pleaded as he checked my bindings, and I noticed he had a small switchblade concealed in his jacket which he began cutting the tape with.

"He's coming with his men, don't worry. It will be alright." He cut one than the other, still using his body to hide us from the other guards.

"Why is he doing this?"

He looked at me his black eyes filled with sorrow. "Power. Your father always wanted to be Capo—"

"Enough," one of the guards snapped. "Boss will deal with her later."

Umberto kneeled closer and whispered quickly. "Don't do anything stupid. Wait for Cassio." He snapped the last of the tape.

Looking from above, it was still attached to my skin, but it was no longer holding me. If I desired, I could move. Not that I would, I wasn't stupid, I was seriously at a disadvantage. Even if Umberto was on my side, it was two against many. Or rather one since I had no idea how to shoot.

A commotion took me by surprise and Grigori, his son, and Donato came rushing into the room. They didn't look concerned or scared, in fact, they looked happy. Eager almost. Like they had accomplished what they wanted. Fear began to take hold once more.

The guards in the room, all five of them, turned their guns toward the door—which I had my back turned to. Slowly, the temperature in the air shifted and a figure surged in my line of sight. I knew it was Cassio even before I saw him. There was this pull, this energy between us that made me aware of his presence when he was near.

Cassio walked into the room like he owned the place, his face stoic and cold. He didn't look at me, he didn't even acknowledge my presence. One guard followed him, a gun aimed at his head, but Cassio didn't even seem to care.

My heart hammered against my chest. He was alone. He walked toward the center of the room and stopped, facing all three men who had plotted against him.

"I am here, let her go."

Grigori laughed. "Always so entitled." He shook his head. "I always despised you, boy. So sure of yourself. So arrogant."

"Are you done complimenting me, Grigori?" He ran his thumb under his lip.

Grigori's smile fell. "Get on your knees." He pointed a gun at Cassio.

"I kneel for no one," he said coldly.

Slowly the gun shifted, and the barrel was facing me. "What about her?"

Cassio looked at me for the first time and for a flicker of a second, I watched his eyes change from murderous to terrified. Slowly, I watched as the most powerful man I knew got down on his knees.

"Tell me, Donato," he turned toward my father. "When was it that you woke up and decided this is the day I'm going to betray all I have ever stood for?"

"You are a boy!" he snapped. "You have no idea what you are doing," Donato shouted. "This war, it was consuming us."

Cassio scoffed. "So, you decided to ally yourself with them."

"It had to stop."

"So, you decided to sell your daughter to the enemy in exchange for what? Peace? Come on, Donato, we both know you're not a man who enjoys peace. It's bad for business."

Donato smiled. "I've waited four years for this, *boy*. Four years to take everything from you like you did from me. I was supposed to have been Capo when your father died. *Me.* Not a drunk child who barely knew what to do."

Cassio went silent for a while, and I watched as the wheels in his head began to work. "So, you killed Paolo Biancini because you needed his money to fund the attacks on our cargo, and Francesca free to be married again." He pointed, speaking to himself.

He paused, looked at me, and smiled. "Except she refused to come home and with my protection, you couldn't touch her."

"You had to put your nose where it didn't belong."

"So, you had Grigori's men try to take her by force, but it didn't work," Cassio said pensively.

"Can we get this over with already?" Grigori's son complained. "Now that all plans were unmasked, can I fucking marry the girl now?"

"Touch her and you die, Mikail," Cassio warned, his tone frosty and murderous. A promise of death.

Mikail laughed. "Or what? You're surrounded. No one is going to stop me."

Mikail walked my way and Cassio moved, but Mikail pointed his gun at me so fast, even I gasped in shock. "Move and I'll kill her." Cassio sat back on his haunches.

"Good boy," Mikail taunted.

He stepped behind me, placed his gun against my head and leaned in to kiss my cheek. I hated the tears that fell from my eyes. I wanted to be strong for Cassio, but I was so afraid. "I'm going to love making you mine. Maybe I'll do it right here in front of him."

"Are you going to let him do this to your daughter? Shame your name like that?" Cassio pleaded with Donato.

"She has already shamed my family," he said, but then added. "We had a deal, Grigori, your son would wed her first, and I would kill Cassio."

Neither Cassio nor I breathed. "Fine, fine," Mikail complained. "You can have him if you wish."

I watched as Donato raised his gun and pointed it at Cassio. He was about to shoot when something in me snapped. I jumped from the chair, the tape pulling at my skin. I fell before Cassio and used my body as a shield to protect him.

FRANCESCA

"Don't shoot!"

Panic like I had never felt in my entire life took hold of me and pulled me under. One moment she was tied up, and in the next, she was kneeling before me. Her beautiful face was shrouded in fear.

I watched as Francesca fought the vise-like grip Mikail had on her. Francesca twisted and turned but he was pulling her by her hair until he managed to snake an arm over her chest. I moved instinctively, but when I did, Donato had his gun trained on me. *Son of a bitch*. Mikail was hurting his daughter, and he didn't even care.

"Let her go!" I shouted.

"I don't think I will." His grip tightened around her enough to make her cry out.

"I will fucking kill you," I warned him. God, I didn't even know what I would do to him if he harmed a single hair on her body.

Mikail's laughter echoed in the room. The fucker thought I was joking.

With the gun trained on me, I didn't want to do anything stupid. My priority right now was to get Francesca out of here in one piece. Francesca surprised me and Mikail as well when she bit him hard on his forearm, and when he let her go, she head-butted him.

"You fucking bitch." He held his bleeding nose.

Francesca wasn't fast enough to escape him; he gripped her by her arm and spun her, hitting her with the back of his hand. She fell to the floor with a loud thud.

"I wouldn't." The barrel of the gun connected with my head when I tried to move.

"She's your fucking daughter," I roared, almost begging him to see it.

"That's enough," Donato ordered.

Mikail stopped moving toward Francesca who was slowly sitting up. "She's my wife," he said simply.

"Not yet." Donato pointed out.

Francesca finally sat up and wiped her bleeding nose. I never thought I would be this angry in my life. There had been moments when I lost it, but now looking at her large, scared eyes, and the blood running down her nose and forehead, I knew right then I was going to skin him alive, slowly, so that he felt each agonizing press of my blade to his skin.

Her eyes found mine and then followed them to where the gun was pressed to my head. She turned so white that I thought she was going to faint. I shook my head urging her to look away. She did, but what came later, scared me even more.

She slowly crawled toward me and kneeled before her father, tears already trailing down her face. "Don't kill him," she begged. "Please, please let him go, and I will do anything you ask."

"Francesca." I tried to stop her, but she wasn't having it, she didn't listen to me, she kept on going.

"Please. I promise I'll behave, that I will... that I'll marry you." She turned to Mikail. "I'll marry you and I'll be an exemplary wife. I'll do what you ask of me, and I will never speak up, I will never try to run or disobey you."

What is she doing?

"I'll marry you right now. There... are witnesses and—just please," she cried. Still on her knees, begging.

I had been hurt before, I had broken bones, been cut by knives, and then stitched up, I had been shot and watched as they used tweezers to remove the bullet from my flesh, but nothing, and I mean nothing, prepared me for what I saw before me.

"Now?" Mikail seemed interested.

"Yes. Yes!" she cried. "Just let him go. Exile him, send him far, far away." She turned toward me and, in her eyes, I saw all that despair. "Do whatever you want with me but just let him go."

"No," I roared. I tried to move but the end of Donato's gun hit my head and I felt dizzy.

"Don't!" I heard her scream. "Please. Just take me, and I'll come willingly. Hurt me however you want but just let him go."

"Why?" I heard Mikail's voice but couldn't see him, my vision was still blurry.

There was a pregnant pause, then I heard her voice loud and clear. "Because I love him. Because I would rather suffer and know he's alive than live in a world where he's not in it."

My heart broke.

"This has grown boring. I think I'll have you and kill him." I opened my eyes.

Everything happened in slow motion, I watched as Mikail lifted his gun and trained it on me. I saw his finger pressed against the trigger and then the shot echoed in the room.

36

CASSIO

I twisted my body as fast as I could trying to shield her with my body. But the sound that tore through the room was deafening and the cry that followed shattered my heart.

Not again. Please, God, not again. I can't lose her, too.

When I moved away from Francesca, she was on the floor, face twisted with pain. A red stain began to appear on the sleeve of her floral dress. I pressed the wound and she screamed. Someone pulled me back, but I used all my force and elbowed them in the face. A grunt followed and then a second person came at me, and I acted faster this time twisting and grabbing his gun, shooting the man dead in the chest. Then turned around pointing the gun.

All five guards plus Mikail and Grigori had theirs trained on me. Slowly, the fifth guard came into the light and moved toward Mikail where he raised his gun and pressed it to his head.

"Put it down or I'll shoot," Umberto said.

I had been acting on pure instinct. My heart hammering against my chest. When I realized it was Umberto, I took a deep sigh. He had been Francesca's old guard, had worked for Donato a lifetime, but it was clear to whom his loyalty belonged.

All I wanted to do was go to Francesca to know if she was alive... but I wouldn't dare move now.

Suddenly, I caught movement in the back door, I looked at Umberto and gave a slight nod.

In seconds the room turned into a war zone; shots were fired from all directions but mostly from the back. Umberto killed Mikail with a shot to the head, and I emptied my magazine into Grigori, who barely had time to shoot me. I wished I had more time to torture him, a quick death was not something he deserved. But I'd rather have him dead than walk this earth a second longer.

Before I noticed, the room was filled with my men. Luciano, my enforcer, and all my other loyal soldiers. Vitelli lifted his gun and me and fired, I turned back to find Donato had been ready to kill me.

Vitelli bypassed me and reached Donato who had been grunting and crying on the floor. The bullet had hit his kneecap. He tried to crawl away, but my brother shot him again, and then again. He looked at me asking for permission. I nodded. Right now, I didn't care how he died, I just cared that he did.

When we secured our surroundings and all the Russians were killed, I dropped to the floor and turned toward Francesca. She was bleeding a lot. The bullet had hit her shoulder, and her face was turning paler by the second.

"Shit," Vitelli came to stand beside me. He removed his jacket and offered it to me.

I pressed it to her shoulder and looked around the room. "I told you not to come," I snapped, adrenaline and fear coursing through my veins.

"You're welcome," he snapped back. "You made me Capo; the decision was mine to make."

I wanted to hug him and kill him at the same time, but right now I had something more pressing to deal with. I lifted Francesca in my arms, she cried out.

"I'm so sorry, *Principessa*," I begged her forgiveness, as I carried her out of the warehouse.

Her eyes were open, but she was in shock, not responding to me when I spoke.

There were dead men all the way to where I parked my car. I stopped and turned toward Vitelli. "I'll take care of this. You go take care of her," he said.

I drove like my life depended on it because it just might. "Open your eyes for me, *Principessa*," I ordered.

She did but it was clear she was being pulled under. "It hurts." Her voice was weak. "I feel so cold."

"It's going to be all right, *Principessa*." I grabbed her hand and kept my thumb on her pulse, it was becoming fainter by the second. "If you die on me, I swear to God, I'll never forgive you."

A tear ran down her cheeks. "I'm sorry." Her eyes fluttered.

"*Principessa*," I warned. "If you die, I die." Simple as that.

She closed her eyes and wouldn't open them again.

I sat by her bedside and looked at all the flowers that I had bought over the last three days. Because when she woke up, I wanted Francesca to be surrounded by her beloved tulips.

My brother and his wife were in the waiting room, where they had made camp since I brought Francesca here. They had barely left my, or her side.

I hadn't left either, not being able to be separated from her. Parting with Francesca was physically painful. Watching her being taken to the OR had been a test of my patience and self-control. As much as I knew these people were here to help, knowing I wasn't there to make sure they didn't screw up was terrifying.

"You should get something to eat," Marie said as she walked into the room and sat by my side.

In these past three days, I have learned to appreciate her. She had been here every moment, leaving only when Vitelli forced her to.

"I need to be here if she wakes up," I said and quickly corrected myself. "When."

Marie placed a hand over Francesca's forehead and looked at her friend. "Vitelli wants me to go home for a bit, I'll be here tonight." I nodded. "He said Luciano is here in case…"

I nodded again not knowing what else to say.

I just wanted my *principessa* to wake up. I'd give anything to have her with me again. Everything!

When it was only the two of us again, I did something I hadn't done since I was a boy. I got on my knees and prayed. I promised God that if she woke up, I would make Francesca mine forever and would never give her reason to doubt that I loved her.

I broke up with her once, to protect her. When Bella and my father died, I wanted to follow them. I closed myself off to the world and to all notions of love. I thought I was doing the right thing, but the truth was, I had been afraid. Afraid to love. Afraid to lose. Afraid to feel. So, I pushed Francesca away because she had been the most precious thing in my life. Letting her go was my biggest mistake. I thought it was the right thing but, in the end, it hurt us both.

So, I prayed that I could keep her forever. If God gave her back to me, I would never let her go.

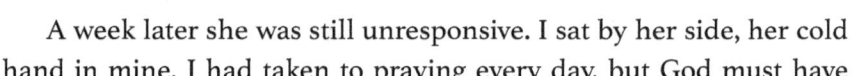

A week later she was still unresponsive. I sat by her side, her cold hand in mine. I had taken to praying every day, but God must have forgotten me.

I stared at her lying on the hospital bed and pulled at my hair. I couldn't do this. I couldn't lose her. Despair was eating me away in large quantities. I needed Francesca to wake up. I needed her here beside me, and I didn't care if I was selfish for needing her so much.

"Please, *Principessa*, please wake up."

I had just entered the room bringing her a new bouquet of purple tulips; I was placing them on the vase like Francesca liked, two weeks had gone by, slipping through my fingers. That's when I heard my name.

It came in a soft whisper, and it was the most beautiful sound I ever heard in my life. I turned around and saw Francesca's big sapphire eyes watching me.

She tried to sit up and I raced toward her. "Hey, slowly." I helped her. When she was slightly raised up, I watched as she regarded her surroundings. All I wanted to do was kiss her senseless, but I let her adjust first.

"What happened?" I went still.

"What do you remember?"

Francesca frowned and then looked at her shoulder. "They were going to shoot at you."

After everything happened, I was furious at her, a part of me would always be, but how could I blame her for wanting to save me when I would have done the same to save her?

"Don't ever do that, Francesca, do you understand?" I took her hand in mine, enjoying the warmth—she had been so cold before. "I know why you did it, but if you had died, I would have followed, so your heroics would have been for shit."

She smiled weakly. "I can't live without you." A single tear fell. "I was so scared."

God. My heart was breaking. I wiped that tear away and sat closer to her. "It's all right, *Principessa*." I wiped another tear. "We killed Grigori and his operations here in Chicago. The Bratva won't dare return so soon. You're safe now."

I had made sure of it. After that night, I had Vitelli and all my men hunt down the Russians and gave them a choice, either leave my territory or die. I hated not being able to fight beside my men, but Francesca was more important now. She was my family and family always came first—even before the Outfit.

"What about Donato?"

I shook my head. "Dead," I confessed, and she sighed, visibly relieved.

Francesca looked at her wounded shoulder and then at me. "Will

Marco pay for my father's mistakes?"

I had thought about that. He had known about Donato's meetings with the Bratva and hadn't warned me, but he was just a kid and in this I was biased. He was Francesca's brother.

I shook my head.

Francesca sighed. "Thank you."

"He's your brother, I would never harm him," I confessed. I kissed her nose and she grinned. It was the sweetest sight in the world.

I closed in and kissed her lightly. She tried to deepen the kiss, but I moved back, eliciting a frustrated groan from her which made me chuckle.

"I love you," I proclaimed. "I want, no, I need you to be mine, forever."

Her eyes shot wide. "Is this a proposal?"

Fuck that's not how I planned this, but almost losing her had opened my mind and made me see that everything I needed and wanted had always been right in front of me.

I removed the box from my back pocket and opened it for her. "Four years ago, I broke your heart, and in the process, I lost you. It was the biggest mistake of my life, and I will regret it forever. I know I don't deserve this, or you, but I am literally begging you. I have lived these past four years in darkness and misery. I am only alive when I am next to you. You make me want to live. You are the very air I breathe, Francesca. Without you I am nothing."

"Cassio–"

"Wait," I stopped her. "I need you to know that I always loved you even when I broke things off. I never stopped, and I never will. You are it for me, Francesca. Seeing you in this bed unresponsive, made me realize that if I can't have you then I don't want to live anymore."

"Don't say that." Tears snaked down her cheeks.

"It's the truth, my heart beats only for you." I confessed.

She reached for my hand, and I offered it to her. "I love you, Cassio, and I forgive you. I have for a while now."

Those words hit me hard like a baseball bat to the stomach. I had never expected how much they would affect me and how much I needed to hear them.

"I love you." I stood up "Will you marry me?"

She beamed bright as the sun. "Yes, yes!"

"Thank fuck," I placed the ring on her finger and kissed her.

"Love you, too," she mumbled through kisses.

I lay beside her in bed and watched as she inspected the ring, a fat, satisfied smile on her face. The doctor had come earlier and checked on her. Marie and Vitelli were on their way, which meant we had a couple of minutes to ourselves. Francesca lifted her head from my shoulder and looked me in the eye.

"Why are you crying, *Principessa?*"

"I'm happy, Cassio. I never thought I was going to have this," she confessed.

"What?" I asked.

Just then Vitelli, Marie and Marco stepped into the room. When they saw her awake and smiling, they entered and began to fuss over her. When Marie saw the ring, she gasped and the two wouldn't stop smiling. Vitelli came next and he hugged her, too, like a brother would. I saw then in his eyes a promise that he would always protect her. Marco came last, and we all let the two of them talk for a while.

"Congratulations, man." Vitelli tapped my shoulder. I grinned. "So, marriage...who would have thought."

I smiled at him. "Not me," I confessed. "I need to tell you something," I confessed. "I learned it a few days ago," I explained.

Vitelli eyed me suspiciously, but I couldn't stop grinning. "You're making me nervous," he teased.

"Francesca is pregnant," I said happily.

"No fucking shit." His jaw dropped.

I nodded. The doctor had told me when she came out of surgery two weeks ago. Imagine my surprise when I learned she was with child. My child. Fear had gripped me harder than before, but the doctors assured me the child would be okay, both of them would.

I wanted to desperately tell Francesca.

"Cassio," Vitelli shook his head. "How, I mean... you, a father, you didn't even want to marry." I knew where he was coming from.

"I love her, Vitelli. I want everything *with her*."

He chuckled and slapped me on the back. "Well, congratulations then."

When Marco and Francesca ended their private conversation, we entered the room again, and I sat beside Francesca while she leaned into me, and I held her close.

"I never thought I was going to have this," she repeated the words from earlier, and as I looked around, I understood.

A family...her own family, one that would love her no matter what.

Vitelli must have heard it because one look from me and he understood what I was silently asking. He escorted everyone out promising they'd be here early tomorrow.

When it was just the two of us, Francesca grabbed my hand. "You're nervous," she said, reading me easily.

"I have something to tell you," I said.

I hadn't planned on doing this. It was usually the other way around; I didn't know how to break the news to her. Why was this so nerve wrecking? It was good news, yet I was terrified.

"What is it, Cassio?" She sat up slowly. There was fear in her eyes and that was the last thing I wanted.

I took a deep breath and exhaled. "You're pregnant."

Silence.

"I'm sorry, what?"

"You're with child, *Principessa*, my child. Our child." I couldn't help smiling at the thought that she was pregnant with my kid. *Mine*.

"H-how?"

"Francesca," I chuckled. "I think the amount of unprotected sex we had is explanation enough."

"Oh God." She dropped her head into her hands.

Why wasn't she happy?

"*Principessa*." I lifted her head, so she was looking at me. "What's wrong?"

"I'm pregnant, Cassio," she said simply.

"Yes." I agreed.

"I'm not cut out to be a mother," she pointed out, then her eyes widened. "Cassio, I was shot." They widened so much I thought her eyeballs would fall from their sockets. "I take heavy medication. I used drugs. GOD."

"Francesca," I cupped her cheeks. "Calm down. Our daughter is fine, she's healthy and safe."

"D-daughter?"

"Yes. She's going to be as perfect and as beautiful as you are." I couldn't help but smile.

"You're not angry with me?"

My smile faltered. "Why would I be?"

"We never discussed this."

I chuckled. "I want it all, Francesca. You, children, a house with a white picket fence. Even that gray rat of yours, as long as you're by my side."

She placed a hand over her still flat belly. "I'm pregnant." She smiled for the first time since I broke the news and then...she cried.

I held her while she did, and I knew those were tears of joy because Francesca wouldn't stop telling me how her dream had come true, and how happy she was.

Francesca never had a proper family, one that loved her unconditionally. But us, we would always be here for her to love and cherish her as she deserved.

"Your heart is my favorite place to be," I confessed. "So, take care of it. I love you with all that I have in me."

"I love you, too, Cassio Moretti, with every fiber in my body. I love you beyond what's possible."

That night, I lay beside her with her tucked in my arms while laying a hand on her belly where my daughter was growing. I never wanted or even dreamed of this, but now I couldn't see my life without them. Suddenly they became everything, and I would protect and love Francesca and my daughter for as long as I lived.

Francesca was always my maddest temptation. The one girl I could never stay away from and could never forget. And now... now she would be forever mine. Forever Mrs. Moretti.

THE END

37

BEFORE YOU GO

Did you know? Readers reviews are very important to an indie author's success? They validate our work and help others find our stories. If you enjoyed Maddest Temptation, please leave a review filled with stars, on Amazon.

ACKNOWLEDGMENTS

First of all, I want to thank my sister for being there with me through thick and thin. Through every laugh, through every tear and through every accomplishment. Thank you for being there when I was scared of following my dream and thank you for giving me the push I needed. You were the first person I entrusted with my stories.

To my parents, I thank you both for supporting my dream, for being there when I was lost and for believing in me even when I didn't. When I doubted myself neither of you doubted me for any second. Thank you for being the best.

To my family who was my safety net when I needed it. Writing a book is not an easy task and all of you were there for me.

To my friends who have been there with me from the start and became my fans too. To the friends I met along the way, and the ones I hope to make.

To my coach Joe Gilbert, thank you immensely for guiding me into this world, for being there when I needed you and for answering my hundreds of questions.

To Sherry my lovely editor, your help will always be so appreciated. You've helped me perfect this book in so many ways. Thank you for everything.

To my readers, there are no words to express what I feel right now. I thank you all for believing in my story and loving it as much as I do. Publishing a debut novel is no easy task, and it's beyond scary. I am profoundly grateful for your love, support and kindness. I hoped you fell in love with Francesca and Cassio the way I did. So much more is coming your way.

And lastly, to Francesca and Cassio, thank you for letting me write your story.

ABOUT THE AUTHOR

Fernanda Graziano (also known as Fe) is a twenty something Brazilian, romance author, addicted to happy endings. She's slowly emerging in the publishing world with the release of her debut novel, Maddest Temptation.

Fe has always had her head up in the clouds, lost in her imagination. She started her writing journey in her teenage years. Avid reader of romance and fantasy, she can often be found cozied up on her favorite sofa, or typing frantically on her laptop.

Her passion for books and incredible stories was what inspired her to become an author. When she's not reading or writing she's stuck in her head creating new swoon-worth characters and stories.

Find Fe, on her socials for news and updates on her upcoming releases.

- instagram.com/fegraziano.author
- amazon.com/stores/Fernanda-Graziano/author/B0CZBWMX8J?ref=ap_rdr&isDramIntegrated=true&shoppingPortalEnabled=true
- tiktok.com/@fernandagraziano.author

www.ingramcontent.com/pod-product-compliance
Lightning Source LLC
LaVergne TN
LVHW011910080426
835508LV00007BA/319